RENEGADE RHYMES

RENEGADE RHYMES

Rap Music, Narrative, and Knowledge in Taiwan

MEREDITH SCHWEIG

The University of Chicago Press   CHICAGO AND LONDON

The University of Chicago Press, Chicago 60637
The University of Chicago Press, Ltd., London
© 2022 by The University of Chicago
Published 2022

31 30 29 28 27 26 25 24 23 22   1 2 3 4 5

ISBN-13: 978-0-226-82059-0 (cloth)
ISBN-13: 978-0-226-81958-7 (paper)
ISBN-13: 978-0-226-82058-3 (e-book)
DOI: https://doi.org/10.7208/chicago/9780226820583.001.0001

Library of Congress Cataloging-in-Publication Data

Names: Schweig, Meredith, author.
Title: Renegade rhymes : rap music, narrative, and knowledge in
Taiwan / Meredith Schweig.
Other titles: Chicago studies in ethnomusicology.
Description: Chicago : University of Chicago Press, 2022. |
Series: Chicago studies in ethnomusicology | Includes bibliographical
references and index.
Identifiers: LCCN 2022008944 | ISBN 9780226820590 (cloth) |
ISBN 9780226819587 (paperback) | ISBN 9780226820583 (ebook)
Subjects: LCSH: Rap (Music)—Taiwan—History and criticism. |
Rap (Music)—Social aspects—Taiwan | Rap (Music)–Political aspects—
Taiwan | Popular music—Taiwan—History and criticism.
Classification: LCC ML3531 .S39 2022 | DDC 782.421649/0951249—dc23
LC record available at https://lccn.loc.gov/2022008944

IN MEMORY OF MY PARENTS

CONTENTS

ABBREVIATIONS

DPP: Democratic Progressive Party
HHCRS: Hip-Hop Culture Research Society
KMT: Kuomintang, or Chinese Nationalist Party
NTU: National Taiwan University
PRC: People's Republic of China
PTT: Professional Technology Temple
ROC: Republic of China

NOTES ON ROMANIZATION
AND TRANSLATION

Romanization is not standardized in Taiwan. If one travels the island, one will observe multiple systems in use to render into the Latin alphabet the sounds of Mandarin, Hoklo, Hakka, and Indigenous Austronesian languages. This is the case for a variety of reasons, some of which are historical and some of which are political.

In light of this complexity, *Renegade Rhymes* adopts a pragmatic approach to romanization. As a general rule, romanization is provided only (1) when having some sense of the sound of language would benefit those unfamiliar with Sinitic characters, or (2) when context favors the use of a romanized term over a translation. In addition to streamlining the reading experience, this approach invites those who are fluent in Mandarin, Hoklo, and/or Hakka to read characters in the language that makes the most sense to them. Where romanization is provided, Mandarin is rendered according to the Hanyu Pinyin system and Hoklo according to the Tâi-lô system, except in cases where the term, title, or name in question is widely known by an alternative spelling (e.g., "Chiang Kai-shek" rather than "Jiang Jieshi," "Taipei" rather than "Taibei").

For authors with Sinitic names whose English-language works are cited in the text, preferred personal name spellings are provided without characters. The names of those whose Sinitic-language works are cited are romanized according to their preference, if known. In some cases, I provide English titles selected by artists that may differ in meaning from the title in the original language. This is intended to assist English-speaking readers who might want to locate the source material in question. For performers who follow the convention of having different English- and Sinitic-language names, both names are provided. In some cases, individuals known in their lifetimes by their Hoklo or Hakka names are instead referred to using Mandarin romanization (e.g., "Zhou Tianwang" rather than "Chiu Thiam-ōng"), concordant with the majority of references to these individuals in non-Sinitic-language literature today. Characters are given for Sinitic-language names the first time they appear in the text; thereafter, only romanization is provided.

Unless otherwise noted, all translations are the author's own. Translations of song lyrics do not attempt to preserve the rhythm or rhyme of the original-language texts but are intended to provide a sense of meaning, tone, and emphasis. In most cases, Sinitic-language lyrics are formatted according to the way they appear in album liner notes or on widely read or artist-authored Internet sites. Rap songs are rarely transcribed with punctuation marks—question words indicate questions; small gaps in the text appear in place of commas, colons, and periods; and diction, rather than exclamation points, often communicates emphasis. Punctuation is therefore provided in English translations only where it is necessary or useful for comprehension.

FIGURES AND MUSICAL EXAMPLES

Figures

Musical Examples

PROLOGUE

First, the Rain

My flight to Taiwan in mid-August 2009 touches down just days after Typhoon Morakot makes landfall, triggering the worst flooding and most severe mudslides in half a century. The north of the island, where I am to live with my in-laws in Taipei, mostly escapes destruction, but the south is hit hard. The remote village of Siaolin emerges in the weeks following the storm as a symbol of its power: there, a massive landslide buries more than four hundred residents alive, the majority of them members of the Taivoan Indigenous community. As late summer fades into fall, Morakot remains a central focus of public discourse amid an endless succession of memorials, charity events, and volunteer drives. Television news channels settle into a macabre rhythm, looping the same grainy video footage of the six-story Jinshuai Hot Springs Hotel collapsing into the churning Zhiben River, and rebroadcasting the same haunting photographs of Siaolin, now reduced to an expanse of mud. The aftershocks reverberate throughout the government as families of victims allege that those living in remote areas were stranded for days before rescue teams made any effort to reach them (Jacobs 2009). Outrage mounts at a disaster response perceived as woefully inadequate, compelling the resignation of the premier and entire cabinet, and threatening even President Ma Ying-jeou's (馬英九) seat (Bo 2009).

The island seems alternately numb with grief and apoplectic with rage. Hoping to channel righteous anger into productive action, prominent southern Taiwanese rapper Dwagie (大支) sets about organizing the 921.87 Rap Benefit Concert (921.87 饒舌慈善義演) in his home city of Tainan. The event's name kindles memories of past trauma: "87," or August 7, refers to the day that Morakot made landfall in Taiwan; "921" alludes to a massive earthquake that struck the island on September 21, 1999, killing 2,500 and leaving 100,000 homeless.[1] The reference serves as a potent reminder to those who attend, not only of previous natural disasters, but also of previous controversy surrounding the government's response to the crises. Critiques leveled at public officials following Morakot bear striking resemblances to those that followed 921, as victims accuse authorities of lacking the skills and resources necessary to mount successful search-and-rescue missions. In a conversation we have the following year, Dwagie explains to me that his primary goal in organizing the concert was simply to encourage people to remember the storm. Moreover, by linking Morakot to the 921 Earthquake, he hoped to underscore for an easily distracted public that "these things must not be forgotten; next time, when it happens again, we can't forget what came before" (interview, September 26, 2010).

I travel to Tainan, fifty-six miles west of Siaolin, to attend the all-day event. I hear the concert before I see it, and follow the booming loudspeakers down an alleyway into an open lot, where a crowd of several hundred people has gathered shoulder to shoulder (see fig. P.1). Even from some distance away, my sternum pounds so hard that it seems like the force of the sound alone could move my blood. On the graffitied walls around us, old political advertisements wilt and peel away in the humidity. Customers exit the convenience store nearby clutching cold drinks, and open-front eateries serve curry rice, dumplings, and bubble tea alongside auto parts retailers and clothing shops. At temporary kiosks, vendors hawk CDs, handicrafts, and vinyl toys in the likeness of Taiwanese folk heroes and earth gods (土地公). It surprises me that no one living or working here complains about the noise, which is substantial. And the show isn't merely loud—it is a riot of chaotic timbres and textures, distinct from the urban white noise that permeates Taiwan's cities, arresting and designed to draw rather than disperse attention. The lot resounds with an irregular, sometimes halting mix of speech and song; Mandarin, Hoklo, Hakka, and English languages; floor-thumping and fist-bumping low-end beats; and samples from stylistically varied recordings, from Hakka folk songs to Marvin Gaye to Blackstreet to Yao Su Rong (姚蘇蓉).

I turn to a young woman on my left and ask her what brought her here. In response, she gestures absently to her flimsy pink-and-white-striped plastic bag of vegetables and says that she is just passing by, on her way from the market. She is one of a very small number of women I perceive in the crowd—as I push through the throng to approach the stage, I am surrounded almost entirely by young men, arms uplifted, bodies pulsing. Many record the spectacle using cell phones and digital cameras more sophisticated than the one I purchased for fieldwork. They appear to be typical urban Taiwanese university students and young professionals, distinguished perhaps by their penchant for locally coveted streetwear

FIG. P.1. View from the back of the lot at the 921.87 Rap Benefit Concert, September 27, 2009. The image projected on the screen is of a Buddhist monk in prayer and the text reads "Go Taiwan" (台灣加油, lit. "Taiwan add oil"). Photograph by Chen Wen-Chi (陳文祺).

brands like Nong-Li (農麗), Tribal, and Joker. A small group to the right of the stage sports a rebellious look: shaved heads, heavy chain necklaces, and ornate Japanese-style tattoos. A young man positioned to my left wears a white T-shirt inscribed with the English word "RENEGADE" in black lettering, all caps. For me, the term immediately conjures the "renegade province" terminology famously favored by the global English-language media to describe views of Taiwan's political status from the perspective of the People's Republic of China (PRC). Because that phrase is seldom invoked on the island, however, I read it instead as a declaration of its bearer's self-perceived nonconformism.[2]

The atmosphere is simultaneously somber and high-spirited. Nearly fifty artists and groups take the stage over the course of the day, performing for ten or twenty minutes at a time. Some present upbeat, danceable fare with joyful lyrics about partying and romance in the hopes of cheering the crowd. Others play more solemn songs addressing Taiwan's political status, environmental degradation, and the systematic erosion of local languages and lifeways. Their lyrics are dense and complex, but surprisingly intelligible in performance. I never take for granted that popular music in Taiwan will be aurally comprehensible without the aid of a printed text, not because I lack the necessary language proficiency, but because the Sinitic languages widely spoken on the island are tonal and changes in articulation give rise to changes in semantic meaning.[3] In particular, the singing voice in contemporary popular music almost always suppresses tonemic contours in the service of melody, increasing the listener's reliance on context or the printed word to extract meaning. Rap, with its declamatory style of vocalization, facilitates articulation of tone for performers intent on clear communication. It is difficult to tell where music ends and linguistic signification begins: when uttered aloud, lyrics have contours defined by the four tones of Mandarin, the six or seven tones of Hakka, and the seven tones of Hoklo.[4] On one level, I can perceive how the pitched pronunciation of tonal language might contribute to the musical interest of a rap performance. Beyond their aesthetic qualities, however, these contours are themselves constitutive of meaning.[5]

Making meaning—of and through sound and text—is the distinct objective of events such as this one. "When the horrors of catastrophe do not overwhelm the human capacity to describe what has happened, the writing of memory can function as a means of restoring what was in danger of being lost for good: in particular, a sense both of agency and of continuity with the past" (Gray and Oliver 2004, 3). Acts of remembrance endow victims and witnesses alike with the power to interpret and make sense of trauma, intervene momentarily in the production of historical narrative, and determine whether what has happened constitutes convergence with or divergence from what has come before. The 921.87 Rap Benefit Concert provides an opportunity for rap artists and fans to engage in such remembrance, reflect on current hardships, and contemplate their relationships to prior catastrophes. In speech and song, performers make deliberate attempts throughout the day to embed Morakot not just in a history of natural disaster in Taiwan, but also in broader sociopolitical narratives characterized by intense, often combative relationships with authorities. The impulse to weave the typhoon into a larger musical narrative of discontent seems a strategic and ultimately affirming one. In the potent moments after rupture, artists call attention to an array of possible futures—some anarchic, some conciliatory—moving forward.

Taipei-based quintet Kou Chou Ching (拷秋勤) takes the stage after nightfall to present their 2007 track "Civil Revolt, Part 1" (官逼民反, Part 1). Backed by DJ JChen (陳威仲), the group's two lead MCs, Fan Chiang (范姜) and Fish Lin (林家鴻), enter from opposite sides of the stage and ask the audience to raise their hands, imploring them, in both Mandarin and English: "Fight for your rights!" The song's multilingual lyrics argue that "the government pushed the people into chaos, giving rise to a time of unrest" following the Qing Dynasty's annexation of Taiwan during the late seventeenth century. It begins with the blaring of a siren and the hypnotic repetition of the recorded Hoklo phrase "civil revolt, civil revolt…" chanted by a female vocalist who traces a pentatonic melodic figure reminiscent of the characteristic opening and closing measures of the "River and Lake" tune (江湖調) frequently performed as part of traditional vocal musics, including Taiwanese opera (歌仔戲). Taken together, the sounds of the siren and the repeated urging toward rebellion create a sense of imminent emergency, while the citation of local opera roots the crisis firmly in Taiwanese soil. As Fish Lin and Fan Chiang deliver the lines of the opening chorus in the Hoklo language—"The government fucks with the people, the people get pissed off! Overthrow corruption, Taiwanese people rebel!"—audience members respond by pumping their fists on the off-beats and shouting an affirmative "Yes! Yes!" in powerful unison.

The lyrics to "Civil Revolt, Part 1" do not address natural disaster, but disaster that is human-made—specifically, the interethnic feuds among Indigenous, Hoklo, and Hakka communities that roiled Taiwan throughout the period of Qing rule, which the central government sought alternately to curb and to exploit. Kou Chou Ching invites listeners to reflect on how the fractured twenty-first-century political landscape of Taiwan might be an extension of these events, which took place hundreds of years ago. By performing the song in the context of the Morakot benefit, they recast a story about Qing mismanagement as an allegory for the failure of the ruling Kuomintang (國民黨, Chinese Nationalist Party, or KMT), to protect its citizens from harm following the storm. Jenny Edkins has written that "what we call trauma takes place when the very powers that we are convinced will protect us and give us security become our tormentors" (2003, 4). Kou Chou Ching's performance at the 921.87 Rap Benefit Concert suggests that Taiwan's past and present tribulations are the result of repeated iterations of the same betrayal.[6] And yet "Civil Revolt, Part 1" also envisages a future, one in which Taiwan's peoples—regardless of their ethnic, linguistic, or political affiliations—practice self-determination and seize control of a collective destiny.

Kou Chou Ching proffers a counter-hegemonic narrative, but the group's imagination of life post-Morakot is characterized by community solidarity. In contrast, Taipei-based rapper Chang Jui-chuan's (張睿銓) cover of American hip-hop group N.W.A.'s 1988 track "Fuck tha Police" augurs a more dystopian future.[7] Chang recontextualizes the song—which decries racial profiling, police brutality, and other forms of state violence inflicted on predominantly Black communities in the United States—by introducing it with the dedication: "This is for our government." Backed by Taipei-based DJ Point (點), his performance summons the gravitas of N.W.A.'s original recording, the contours and intensity of his vocal inflections closely matching Ice Cube's. As he launches into the chorus, several young men thrust their hands up and begin to thrash along with the beat; a group around me, clearly familiar with the song, begins to mouth the words. Although Chang hews closely to N.W.A.'s lyrics throughout, he alters the concluding lines, in English, "And when I'm finished, it's gonna be a bloodbath, of cops, dyin' in LA" to "of cops, dyin' in Taipei."

The song's racial and geographic provenance are elided as the details of N.W.A.'s revenge fantasy recede behind the anger expressed through insistent repetition of the phrase "fuck tha police." Later, Chang tells me that he envisioned his version as a protest anthem, harkening back to episodes of colonial and authoritarian violence in Taiwan, especially under martial law (戒嚴令), from 1949 to 1987 (interview, December 3, 2009). His performance was intended to recall a historical period during which the Taiwan Garrison Command (台灣警備總司令部) actively suppressed initiatives that might have undermined KMT rule, including pro-Communism, pro-democracy, and pro-independence activism. Moreover, it implied a particular recommendation for the future—namely, that Taiwan's peoples reject such treatment and strike out against authority figures who fail to protect them in the wake of catastrophes like Morakot.

Tainan-based Brotherhood gestures more directly to Morakot with their song "LUV," written in 2008 to protest environmental degradation (see fig. P.2). In the context of the benefit, the song's lyrics highlight human responsibility for the mudslides that regularly strike rural parts of the island and attained new levels of deadliness with Morakot: "So they blindly cut down trees, and without the retention of water or earth, the landslides accelerated…." Theirs is a slow, contemplative piece, one that does not corral the furious energy of "Civil Revolt, Part 1" or "Fuck tha Police," but instead paints a series of grim pictures—of skies growing dark, of people moving slowly off the streets, and finally of a massive mudslide washing away the dreams of children playing in the rain.

The three MCs who make up Brotherhood rap in Hoklo at a deliberate pace over a plaintive, wordless melody, sped up and looped repeatedly in the fashion of Wu-Tang Clan's "Snakes." The sound of lead MC Dadi's (大帝) voice is soft and mellow as he utters, barely above a whisper, wishes for a better tomorrow: "Taiwan has suffered, you and I know, but with just a little bit of love our motherland will heal." And yet Brotherhood also suggests that "love," when rendered in the form of aid, is a limited resource in a part of the world so frequently afflicted by natural disasters. At the end of the second verse, Dadi raps: "I will not send my love out to Sichuan, but will keep my love in Taiwan." His words reflect a critical view of the financial support that the Taiwan government and individual Taiwan-based donors sent to the PRC following the Sichuan earthquake

FIG. P.2. Brotherhood performs at the 921.87 Rap Benefit Concert, September 27, 2009. Photograph by Chen Wen-Chi.

of 2008. This skepticism has a powerful visual correlate in the T-shirts worn by the MCs to the left and right of Dadi, which bear anti-PRC slogans. In a performance scarcely four minutes long, several concentric narratives ripple out all at once: the central story of "LUV," about a mudslide caused by soil erosion from irresponsible land-development activities; the story of Morakot—and perhaps more specifically Siaolin, summoned by the song's reference to a deluge, subsequent damage to rural areas, and human suffering; and a larger story questioning the government's responses to natural disasters, including those that affect the PRC, with which Taiwan has a fraught relationship.

Toward the event's conclusion, rapper and Tainan-native RPG (張活寧), who acts as master of ceremonies, welcomes Dwagie to the stage, and the two engage in some patter. Dwagie is a celebrity here in Tainan and also an active, affable member of the community. Earlier, he and many of today's performers lit incense and made offerings of pineapples, papayas, and ghost money to the local gods. Now he receives a visit from Su Tseng-Chang (蘇貞昌), a prominent member of the Democratic Progressive Party and a locally popular political figure. It is clear from the crowd's applause and cheering that Dwagie is a hometown hero, widely admired, perhaps even beloved. He announces the debut of a new song written expressly for the 921.87 Rap Benefit Concert with local R&B singer and producer J. Wu, which they call "Unforgettable Pain" (勿忘傷痛). Although I

FIG. P.3. Audience members at the 921.87 Rap Benefit Concert light candles on the ground in the shape of Taiwan, September 27, 2009. Photograph by author.

know him primarily as a performer of Hoklo-language hip-hop, Dwagie's desire for communicative expediency here favors the use of Mandarin, Taiwan's official "national language" (國語) since the KMT's arrival in 1945. The rapper's voice is hoarse as he delivers his bars in the verse, but J. Wu leans into smooth soulfulness on a sung chorus in which he vows to soothe victims:

山河大地被風雨撕裂
哭喊的我的兄弟姊妹
我讓你依慰 讓你依慰
記不記得一起祈禱的那一夜
擦肩而過的志工你是哪一位
那一天
看見 不一樣的美麗新世界

the mountains and rivers were torn apart by the wind and rain
the crying of my brothers and sisters
I will comfort you, will comfort you
do you remember the night we prayed together
among the volunteers rubbing shoulders, which one were you
on that day
I saw a new and different beautiful world

Although the chorus begins with a description of the storm's violence, it swiftly shifts focus to the ways in which Morakot has brought out the best in people, especially those who have volunteered to help out in hard-hit areas. Accompaniment to Dwagie's and J. Wu's voices is sparse, a simple drum kick and short piano riff consisting of a descending five-note figure. This is layered on top of a chopped-up and repeated sample of a vocalist performing a nonspecific Austronesian melody, a sonic mnemonic that reminds listeners that many of those affected hail from Indigenous communities.[8] The intermingling sentiments of hope and loss, poetry and pain, link the song to so many others performed throughout the day. It feels like a summation.

As Dwagie wraps his set, I head for an exit and pass a dozen young men painstakingly lighting hundreds of tealights on the pavement, arranged in the shape of Taiwan (see fig. P.3). Several weeks after Morakot, the weather is still erratic, and gusts of wind blow out the candles again and again. But the candle-lighters persist in rekindling each extinguished flame, such that the borders of the island constantly recede and reappear, always vulnerable, but ultimately intact.

INTRODUCTION

Tales of Taiwan

This book is about the community represented by the artists and audience members at the 921.87 Rap Benefit Concert and about their engagements with rap music as a trenchant form of narrative discourse in Taiwan following nearly four decades of martial law (1949–87). Building on and moving beyond debates about how global forms of hip-hop proffer resistance to hegemonic ideologies or complicity with neoliberal ones, I position rap songs in Taiwan as synergetic efforts to imagine new forms of post-authoritarian sociality. I argue that rappers' performance practices and pedagogical ambitions—their desires to teach with and through their musical activities—configure post-authoritarianism as a creative political intervention, whose ultimate object is the reordering of epistemic hierarchies, power structures, and gender relations.[1] The narrative ethos of rap is instrumental to its efficacy in this regard, shaping indelibly the processes by which rappers grapple with ontological questions about the nature of Taiwaneseness and coax revelatory musical effects from the idiosyncrasies of local languages. Drawing out the threads between their practices of masculine self-fashioning and claims to authority within the rap community, I reveal their art as a key site of knowledge production in a time of ongoing and profound transformation, a space in which to reflect, unmake, and remake their worlds.

I did not set out in 2009 to write a book about rap music or hip-hop culture. My initial interest in the scene emerged, rather, from my long-term ethnomusicological research focus on local forms of musical narrative performance and my awareness that some artists and audiences on the island posit rap as an extension of older genres. There was, I had found, no single gloss for the English term "rap." Many Internet sites and some performers used traditional musical narrative genre designations—such as the Hoklo *liām-kua* (唸歌, "songs with narration") and, more rarely, the all-encompassing Mandarin *shuochang* (說唱, lit. "speaking-singing")—to describe Taiwan rap's sound and storytelling ethos.[2] I did not know how widespread this conception of the music was, or whether the island's MCs understood their art as, first and foremost, articulated to US and global hip-hop cultural practices. Attuned to the critical importance of "globalization" and "localization" discourses in conversations about the perils of neoliberalization and the cultural and political legitimacy of Taiwanese identity, respectively, the question seemed to me an important one.

The viscerally compelling performances at the 921.87 Rap Benefit Concert offered evidence of little consensus, as some, like Kou Chou Ching, gestured decisively to traditional musical narrative forms while others, like Chang Jui-chuan, more clearly invoked the globally ubiquitous sounds and visual codes of hip-hop. Whether they heard it as something fundamentally local or as something localized, however, all artists gathered that day marshalled the sonic resources of rap to unfold tenaciously complex and contextual narratives that imagined different through lines between past, present, and future. Multiple, often contentious stories and histories interwove within and between songs, sometimes echoing, sometimes amplifying, sometimes ricocheting off one another. In addition to active listening, their successful decoding demanded of the predominantly young, male, middle-class audience in Tainan—representative of rap's broader "interpretive community" (Fish 1976)—a substantial base of heterogeneous knowledge. Songs were written in multiple tongues, heavy with idiom and rife with indexical reference. Even if feeling their affective charge did not require of listeners any specific preparation, assimilating the full totality of their meanings unquestionably did.

That rap music tells stories, and that these stories are especially meaningful to local audiences, is not by itself a revelation. Almost anywhere in the world that rap sounds in its multifaceted guise as "hip-hop music," it profits from analysis as narrative. Although insistently technological and distinguished from earlier Black musics in its mediation by sampling and sequencing (Walser 1995, 197), rap's sonic and semantic strategies have antecedents (if not necessarily roots) in an array of African and Afro-diasporic oral narrative traditions, including but not limited to the African American verbal games known as the dozens, Jamaican toasts, and West African griot. These connections and others underscore the music's identity in the United States and elsewhere as a form for telling tales, as Imani Perry declares in her pathbreaking scholarship on hip-hop's poetics and politics: "The narrative in hip hop is a kind of storytelling, a late-twentieth-century and early-twenty-first-century extension of traditional African American folktales, the MC replacing Dolemite or Brer Rabbit" (2004, 78).[3] Storytelling is also ubiquitous in the discourse *about* rap, which has, in the United States, often been credited with surfacing the stories of the Black and Latinx communities that originated rap.[4] Underscoring this point and extrapolating out geographically, Jay-Z writes in the concluding pages to his 2010 memoir: "That's my story. But the story of the larger culture is a story of a million MCs all over the world who are looking out their windows or standing on street corners or riding in their cars through their cities or suburbs or small towns and inside of them the words are coming, too, the words they need to make sense of the world they see around them" (208).

Many of hip-hop's most notorious narratives center the challenges of life in the streets, but the million MCs of Jay-Z's description exceed this subject matter to represent in their work an extraordinarily broad range of themes and affective registers. What connects their many and various rap stories—whether about politics, parties, or personal relationships—is a professed commitment to "keeping it real." Realness is axiomatic of hip-hop culture in its diverse global configurations, and its performance characteristics disclose locally specified conceptions of authenticity. As hip-hop scholar Alastair Pennycook reminds us, what passes for "real" may differ from place to place. Moreover, authenticity is not primarily the domain of individuals but represents, rather, "a dialogical engagement with community" (2007, 103). Keeping it real obligates artists to seek and convey truths—even through fiction—about and in conversation with the worlds that produced them. In order for their stories to pass muster, rappers wear their dedication to realness as a mantle, rejecting euphemism and calling out falsehoods and misrepresentations wherever they lie.

The artists at the 921.87 Rap Benefit Concert wore this mantle conspicuously, and each subsequent performance deepened my awareness of this contract between performers and their public—those for whom they performed, and from whom they emerged. With the speed of an epiphany, I shifted my research focus to the rap community and my rapidly proliferating questions about its membership's epistemic, ethical, and political commitments—its conceptions of the "real." I was captivated not just by performers' aesthetic sensibilities and technical expertise, but by the ways they expressed hope that their stories about mudslides and seventeenth-century civil uprisings would catalyze civic engagement in the present moment of radical upheaval. I also perceived what would become the crux of my readings of rap community discourse, rituals, and performances in this book: the rich interplay between craft and context, how the forms and aesthetic sensibilities of rap arm its practitioners with formidable hermeneutic tools.

Cultural theorists and philosophers have long pondered both the ontology of narrative and the innumerable means by which storytelling enables individuals to interpret or—as Jay-Z puts it—"make sense of the world they see around them."[5] Through creating narrative, which Roland Barthes observes is a transhistorical as well as transcultural practice (1975, 237), storytellers claim senses of agency and control over personal and community circumstances. Sylvia Wynter's conception of *homo narrans* posits the human species itself as constituted by and through its storytelling capabilities (Wynter and McKittrick 2015, 25). Such ruminations on narrative percolate through ethnography. In his work exploring violence and redemption in storytelling practices in Sierra Leone, Australia, New Zealand, and South Africa, for example, anthropologist Michael D. Jackson (2002) is inspired by Hannah Arendt's deployment of storytelling as both a tool for theorizing about politics and making "critical understanding from experience" (Disch 1993, 666). Storytelling, as Jackson describes it, constitutes us as active authors rather than passive observers of our experiences because there "is no denying that storytelling gives us a sense that though we do not exactly determine the course of our lives we at least have a hand in defining their meaning" (2002, 16).

Rappers in Taiwan certainly attend to such interpretation in the face of difficult-to-interpret events, but this book's analysis extends beyond their hermeneutic capabilities, also encompassing their aspirations to conscious intervention. My discussion of their work accepts, per literary theorist Richard Waswo, that "poetry, in the large, archaic sense of any fiction . . . can make a great deal happen" (1988, 541). From their perspectives as young men on the island, deep sociocultural rifts, neoliberal economics, and distortions and lacunae of history in the educational system all represent sites of disorientation and illogic, upon which they bring their talents to bear not just as commentators but also as agents of material change. They form clubs and creative collectives in which to nurture associational bonds and rehearse rituals of democratic citizenship. They tinker with compounds of words and musics that index the global and the local to limn out the contours of a "Taiwanese" rap sound. They hone identities as students and teachers in the hopes of acquiring the gravitas necessary to shape broader community norms and attitudes. They work not just to make sense of their world, but also to *compel their world to make sense*.

Situating Rap in History

The cohort of senior performers who organized and performed at the 921.87 Rap Benefit Concert in 2009—and who are the central focus of my ethnography—perhaps owe their sense of a world in need of remaking to their generational station. Born between the late 1970s and the mid-1980s, they were among the last to begin life under martial law, and most undertook the earliest years of their careers as Taiwan underwent its transition to full electoral democracy in the early 2000s. They spent their young adulthood riding the highs and lows between boom times and economic stagnation, all the while negotiating existential precarity engendered by the island's contested political status and isolation from structures of international diplomacy. The contexts of post-authoritarianism, democratization, and neoliberal capitalism are critical to my analysis of their activities, but understanding the stakes of their work requires further recourse to transformative events that transpired in Taiwan at the end of the Second World War, as well as the demographic shifts and tectonic transitions of law and governance that prefigured them.

Prior to the arrival of Han settlers from China, Indigenous Austronesian language-speaking peoples—now known as "original inhabitants" (原住民)—comprised Taiwan's majority population. Divided among more than two dozen distinct groups, they spoke at least twenty-four unique languages and kept discrete cultural traditions (Zeitoun, Yu, and Weng 2003, 218), although they also intermarried and traded with one another (Teng 2004, 104).[6] Indigenous peoples were overtaken in numbers by Han peoples beginning in the latter half of the seventeenth century.[7] Encouraged by Dutch colonists who hoped their labor would power colonial trade, most Han came to Taiwan from Fujian or Guangdong Provinces (Andrade 2007, chap. 6, para. 3); census surveys from the early twentieth century suggest that 82% were Hoklo (河洛人, 福佬人) and 16% were Hakka (客家人) (Lamley 1981, 291). Although they shared some cultural practices and maintained similar patterns of social organization, the Hoklo and Hakka spoke mutually unintelligible languages and differed in key cultural and religious traditions (284).[8]

Over the last four centuries, a succession of colonial and settler-colonial regimes set out to control the island. Between 1624 and 1662, Dutch forces battled for dominance with the Spanish, who occupied settlements in the north from 1626 to 1642. The Dutch were eventually driven out by Koxinga (鄭成功), a Ming loyalist and military commander who sought to establish Taiwan as a base of resistance against the Manchu-controlled Qing Dynasty. In 1683 the Qing defeated the Ming loyalist forces and made Taiwan a prefecture of Fujian Province. The island was promoted to full province in 1885 following clashes with the British, French, and Americans during and between the Opium Wars and the Sino-French War. Taiwan's provincial standing was short-lived, however: upon the defeat of the Qing in the First Sino-Japanese War, it was ceded as a condition of the Treaty of Shimonoseki and became a dependency of the Empire of Japan from 1895 to 1945, when Chinese forces overcame Japan at the end of the Second

World War. At this point, the island fell under the control of the KMT, then embroiled in a protracted civil war against Chinese Communist forces.

By most accounts, the KMT encountered a population on Taiwan that initially welcomed their displacement of Japanese colonial authorities. Feelings of goodwill, however, dissipated in the wake of rampant government and military corruption, massive inflation, and widespread unemployment. Tensions erupted in 1947 when agents of the government, which held a monopoly on sales of tobacco and alcohol, attempted to confiscate black-market cigarettes from a middle-aged widow named Lin Chiang-mai (林江邁) peddling her wares in a Taipei park. When she resisted, an agent hit her in the head with a pistol, setting off a confrontation with a crowd of bystanders that ultimately led to the death of a civilian. Word of these events spread quickly, and by the next morning thousands had taken to the streets to protest, leading to a bloody confrontation between authorities and civilians. The conflict spread throughout the island, prompting a violent government crackdown that ultimately claimed the lives of at least ten thousand civilians (Fell 2018, 14).[9] This event, known as the 2-28—or February 28th—Incident (二二八事件), led to the first imposition of martial law on the island. It demonstrated the KMT's willingness to employ draconian methods of social control and remains a flashpoint in Taiwan's political discourse to this day.

Following defeat by the Communists in 1949, Generalissimo Chiang Kai-shek (蔣介石) and approximately 1.2 million refugees (T. Lin 2009, 336) fled to Taiwan to establish a new base for the Republic of China (ROC), a measure initially conceived as a stopgap until KMT forces could recapture the "mainland."[10] In an effort to quell possible pro-Communist and pro-independence activities, the governor of the Taiwan Provincial Government, Chen Cheng (陳誠), again declared martial law on the island. This initiative gave virtually unlimited authority to Chiang and the military, critical to the process of consolidating the KMT's power and disciplining an increasingly discontented population in turmoil. Martial law prohibited the formation of opposition political parties and endowed the KMT with absolute control of mass media. The ensuing decades, known today as the White Terror (白色恐怖), also saw severe restrictions on civil and political rights: Taiwan's peoples enjoyed neither freedom of speech nor freedom of assembly, and thousands were tried in military courts, jailed, and executed under suspicion of dissident activity.

Under KMT hegemony, Hoklo and Hakka peoples assumed a new collective identity as "Native Taiwanese," or *benshengren* (本省人, lit. "people from within the province"), that opposed the collective identity of the "Mainlanders," or *waishengren* (外省人, lit. "people from outside the province").[11] The term *bensheng* elided much of the ethnic and linguistic variation within the prewar Han group and further obscured the identities of Indigenous peoples, especially those who had previously been absorbed into the Hoklo through marriage, assimilation, and other forms of identity change.[12] Likewise, the *waisheng* appellation suggested some degree of homogeneity among the heterogeneous Mainlander population, which had origins in multiple regions of China. The *bensheng-waisheng* framework also marginalized Indigenous peoples' experience of Taiwan as a settler-colony. Throughout the period of martial law, the KMT's repressive and discriminatory policies fostered a sense of animosity between these groups, even as it ramped up efforts to enforce on the island's peoples a uniform and coherent "Chinese" identity—itself an imaginary construction subordinated to a political purpose.

Chiang's claims to sovereignty over China while in exile on Taiwan necessitated an array of campaigns aimed at fostering a sense of common history and culture on both sides of the Taiwan Strait. Advancement of Mandarin as the national language—as opposed to Japanese, Hoklo, Hakka, or any of numerous Indigenous tongues—was critical to this objective. Beginning in the 1960s, the Chinese Cultural Renaissance Movement (中華文化復興運動) strenuously promoted modalities of artistic expression thought to embody Confucian values and the spirit of "traditional" China, especially Peking opera (referred to as *guoju* 國劇, lit. "national opera") and the canonical works and styles of classical Chinese literature (Lin 2005).[13] Cultural policy elevated Chinese national culture above local cultural forms and languages. Attendant to these policies, non-Mandarin cultural production and the public use of non-Mandarin languages were vigorously suppressed. Corporal punishment and fines were imposed on children for violating local language bans in school,[14] and the Bureau of Culture established laws that limited non-Mandarin programming to less than one hour per day on each of the three state-owned television channels.[15]

The Chiang regime's execution of these policies was bolstered by support from Washington, DC. An abiding political, economic, and military relationship between the United States and ROC had begun with their joint membership in the Allied Forces during the Second World War and continued through the Chinese Civil War. Following the KMT defeat in 1949, the United States endorsed the continued legitimacy of the Party as it decamped to Taiwan. Economic reforms instituted by the KMT beginning in the 1950s—with considerable financial, logistical, and military assistance from the United States—created the necessary conditions for rapid industrialization and the growth of an export-oriented capitalist economy. American investments in Taiwan as an "unsinkable aircraft carrier" during the Cold War intensified with the PRC's entry into the Korean

War. The United States dispatched military units to the Taiwan Strait, where they remained until Richard Nixon terminated formal diplomatic relations with the ROC in favor of rapprochement with the PRC in 1979.[16]

Demands for liberalization and the end of one-party rule intensified through the end of the 1970s and mid-1980s, as the ROC's declining international status in the wake of the PRC's rise undermined the KMT's legitimacy.[17] This period marked the emergence of the Taiwan Localization Movement (台灣本土化運動), which called for recognition of a distinctive "Taiwanese" cultural identity as well as the public embrace of non-Mandarin languages and expressive forms. In the political domain, this was accompanied by the growth of the Tangwai (黨外, lit. "outside the party"), a movement comprising predominantly *bensheng* politicians, elected locally, who opposed the KMT. Forming opposition political parties was illegal under martial law, but the Tangwai became increasingly intrepid in its pro-democracy activities, leading to a series of brutal reprisals from the KMT and the imprisonment of the movement's primary leadership in 1980. Undeterred, members of the Tangwai formed the Democratic Progressive Party (民進黨, or DPP) in 1986. Chiang Ching-kuo (蔣經國), who assumed the presidency after the death of his father Chiang Kai-shek in 1975, officially declared the end of martial law in 1987. Shortly after the junior Chiang's passing in 1988, successor president Lee Teng-hui (李登輝) legalized the formation of opposition political parties in 1989 under the Law on the Organization of Civil Groups (Fell 2018, 36), which granted the DPP and other opposition parties formal rights to political participation. Liberalization and the consolidation of democratic processes progressed over the course of the next several years.

The period immediately following the end of martial law saw dramatic transformations in relations among ethnic communities on the island, intimately linked to shifts in the increasingly fraught political discourse about Taiwan's national identity. The Hoklo far outnumbered the Hakka in the general population and within the Tangwai, a phenomenon that reinforced exclusionary perceptions of national and ethnic "Taiwaneseness" as tantamount to Hoklo-ness, but the first *bensheng* president of the ROC, Lee Teng-hui of the KMT, was Hakka.[18] Lee, who was democratically elected in 1996, promoted yet another identity classification, "New Taiwanese" (新台灣人), which integrated Indigenous peoples, *benshengren*, and *waishengren* into a single community. In an English-language article for *Foreign Affairs*, Lee characterized the "New Taiwanese" as "those who are willing to fight for the prosperity and survival of their country, regardless of when they or their forebears arrived on Taiwan and regardless of their provincial heritage or native language" (1999, 9). As anthropologist Robert Edmondson notes, while this construction conflicted with claims to "ethnonational Taiwaneseness based on opposition and political re-form," it suggested the possibility of detente after years of conflict among multiple ethnic communities (2002, 38).

Remaking Narrative and Knowledge after Authoritarianism

This book begins its story in the immediate aftermath of martial law, a time at which Taiwan's budding MCs first emerged to critique the KMT's decomposing state power apparatus, spin tales from their perspectives as members of marginalized ethnic communities, and rehabilitate and reimagine previously suppressed local musical forms. Their art, which from its inception employed multiple local languages and sampled diverse local soundscapes, sounded Taiwan's complex colonial history and its unremitting cultural heterogeneity. In venerating the local, early rappers aspired to reckoning with the damage wrought by martial law and earlier suppressions to local systems of knowledge. As authoritarianism loosened its grip, they asked: What languages and lifeways have been lost? Whose stories along with them? The post-authoritarian condition demanded new ways of understanding Taiwan's history untethered from the grand narratives of either Japanese imperialists or the KMT.[19] These grand narratives were, of course, not fated to vanish overnight, but rather to become the locus for long-standing debates—in politics, education, and art—about the meanings and makings of received histories, as well as their modes of transmission.[20]

Tracing the contours of the rap scene through interviews, archival findings, and music analysis, *Renegade Rhymes* explores how senior members of the community have continued to forge identities for themselves as knowledge producers, whose task is the critical interrogation of their time and place. Some have arrived at this role by way of their interactions with global hip-hop culture, which incorporates "knowledge" as one of its essential elements, alongside rapping (or emceeing, MCing), DJing (or dee-jaying), breaking (or b-boying/b-girling), and graffiti.[21] As delineated in the 1970s by the Universal Zulu Nation, "knowledge" encompasses the simultaneous pursuit of self-actualization and of awareness about hip-hop's history, ideals, and ethics.[22] Rappers' aspirations to knowledge production in Taiwan realize a convergence between the imperatives of hip-hop and the demands of post-authoritarianism. As I show, they leverage the affordances of rap as narrative music in their continued efforts to address key epistemic questions amid social, political, and economic change.

Although in this effort I draw on relevant foundational scholarship in narratology (e.g., Genette 1980, Bakhtin 1981, Zhou 1996, Gu 2006), my remit is not narrative theory. On the contrary, narratologists have sometimes advocated for limiting the purview of "narrative" in ways that would constrain the study of some musics. In the classic *Story and Discourse: Narrative Structure in Fiction and Film* (1978), which musicologist David Nicholls observes is one of the very few works of narratology to acknowledge music's narrative potential (2007, 297), the film and literary critic Seymour Chatman defines narratives as necessarily comprising both "story" and "discourse."[23] Chatman posits that stories are in turn composed of both events (actions, happenings) and existents (characters, settings), while discourses are "the means through which the story is transmitted" (Chatman 1978, 9). Certainly, there are many musical works that corroborate these notions of narrative in that they introduce characters who perform actions in time, but there are yet many others that constitute more impressionistic descriptions of persons, places, or things. Scholars of popular music have been more flexible in their approaches to understanding how songs are narrative or story-like. Imani Perry, for example, writes of rap as having different "formats," including narrative, exhortation/proclamation, description, battle, and allegory (2004, 77–101). Even though only one of these—"narrative"—necessarily includes characters that perform actions and undergo a traversal of time, all are invoked to tell tales. Aaron Fox considers how the notion of "a song with a story to it" "creates a conceptual space for a locally meaningful narrativity to emerge in the process of interpretation or 'relating to' the song" for country music artists and audiences in Texas (2004, 161).[24] Keith Negus's conception of popular songs as narrative likewise rests on the senses in which they are "intercontextual" and "participate in the wider cultural dialogues through which historical understanding is narrated" (2012, 368).

My approach to rap in Taiwan builds on these more pliant frameworks: some musical activity lends itself to analysis as narrative in the narrower sense, while discerning the storytelling qualities of other activity requires consideration of its position in various "social and semiotic chains of narrative meaning" (Negus 2012, 373). To this end, I deploy "narrative" and "story" more or less interchangeably, according to the norms of colloquial speech among my research associates, who do not differentiate in conversation between these English words or the Mandarin *gushi* (故事; tale, story, narrative). Likewise, I do not limit my discussions of narrative to musical works. Digging down to its roots in the Latin *gnarus*—"knowing" or "knowledgeable"—this book uses "narrative" to refer expansively to the modes of knowledge and cognitive schema that mediate perceptions of the world.[25] I emphasize the importance of narration as the process of sharing or transmitting such ideas. Storytelling is, after all, a fundamentally social act, with the capacity to build bridges between subjects, foster understanding between them, and bind them into a community of common fate.

Such bridge-building serves as a critical bulwark against isolation, which rappers navigate both as national subjects and, relatedly, as individuals living under neoliberal capitalism in an era of economic globalization. Taiwan has been diplomatically isolated from much of the world since the ROC's expulsion from the United Nations in 1971,[26] and the island's tenuous position in world polity has only grown more tenuous in recent years. Currently, only fourteen countries and the Holy See maintain formal diplomatic relations with the ROC, which represents a loss of seven allies since 2016. A robust economy—and a foreign policy that has historically relied heavily on tactics of "aid diplomacy" (Tubilewicz and Guilloux 2011)—buttresses Taiwan's claims to sovereignty. Writing two decades ago on "Globalisation and the (In)significance of Taiwan," Shu-Mei Shih observed that "for Taiwan to have an increasingly globalised economy is to keep ahead of the development game, and to have a more globalised culture is to displace Sinocentric influence and invent new forms of transculture.... Nowhere do we see such an intimate conjunction of ideological, economic, political and discursive rationales for globalisation as in Taiwan. For Taiwan, globalisation has to be, period" (2003, 146). The island's relentless pursuit of economic competitiveness, however, has come at a cost to workers—especially young workers—who are charged with negotiating the corrosive effects of neoliberalism on workplace cultures and educational settings (Chiang 2015). *Renegade Rhymes* observes the coincidence of Taiwan's entry into post-authoritarianism with its neoliberal transformation, and listens for the opportunities that rap presents to rethink the nature of associational life and to regenerate community under these circumstances.

Locating Myself in the Story

Throughout the research process, my presence in spaces for performance, instruction, competition, and casual socialization allowed me to observe firsthand the many ways in which narrative gives rise to sociality within the community. I traveled to Taiwan for fieldwork from August 2009 to December 2011, and then again in October 2013, July–August 2015, July 2016, December 2016, July–August 2017, September 2018, and finally January–June 2021. Although I regularly ventured out to locations all over the island, I was always based in Taipei, living with my husband's parents in their apartment in the eastern part of the city, while my husband remained for the most part back home in the United States. My family life has always represented an important context for my work in Taiwan, as it was my early relationship with my husband that brought me to the island for the first time in 2000 (Schweig 2019). It was sometimes difficult to balance my activities as an ethnomusicologist with domestic obligations during periods of fieldwork, but I also found the two to be mutually nourishing roles. In my day-to-day life as a daughter-in-law, I ran errands, assisted with household work, participated in important family events such as weddings and funerals, and socialized with family and family friends. Family activities imparted a sense of the rhythms of daily life for other young people in the capital city and allowed me to establish meaningful relationships outside the immediate confines of my research project.

I undertook many of my research activities during the evenings, when most live performances happen and when my research associates were free from their own work, school, and domestic obligations. I conducted both formal and informal interviews with musicians, fans, music producers, record distributors, shop owners, critics, and other scholars. We conversed in either Mandarin or English, whichever language the parties involved decided would be both most expedient and most pleasurable.[27] As my relationships with musicians deepened over the years and I spent more time in the process of what Clifford Geertz (2000) famously referred to as "deep hanging out," opportunities for informal conversations proliferated. I attended any and all rap-related events that I could during fieldwork stints, including concerts, public lectures, fan club events, and university hip-hop club meetings. I observed performances in as many kinds of settings as possible, including but not limited to clubs and festivals, university campuses, political events, and shopping malls. Curious about changes in performance practice and variations in audience dynamics outside of Taiwan, I followed Kou Chou Ching overseas to shows at the Mosaic Music Festival in Singapore and Telus TaiwanFest in Vancouver, and attended performances in New York City by artists such as Dwagie, MJ116 (頑童), BR, Xiao Ren (小人), and Soft Lipa (蛋堡). Social media became an important venue in which to make new contacts and maintain relationships with research associates, both during and after times spent in Taiwan. It also admitted a degree of reciprocity, in the sense that my research associates could access some personal and professional information about me prior to and following our meetings.

My identity, as shared online or in person, of course impinged on our interactions. Although one musician expressed his surprise upon our meeting that I was not Black (as he admitted he expected someone researching rap to be), my status as a white American went unremarked by the vast majority of my research associates, who are well aware that hip-hop's circulation throughout the world was prefigured by its circulation beyond its racial communities of origin in the United States. There can be little question, at the same time, that the racial capital associated with whiteness in Taiwan removed barriers to access in my research activities. I did not have to expend precious energy answering questions about my racial identity or combating pernicious racist stereotypes, many of which owe their continuance in Taiwan to the influence of white supremacist US popular culture. My identity as a cisgender, heterosexual woman prompted the most overt questioning. Artists often seemed perplexed by my interest in their predominantly male community, both because my research transgressed gendered social norms and because many simply assumed that a woman scholar would find their activities uninteresting. For some of my research associates, the fact that I am both an ethnomusicologist and connected to Taiwan through family seemed to explain implicitly my interest in their particular work and milieu—they often referred to me as a "daughter-in-law of Taiwan" (台灣媳婦) when encouraging my research efforts or introducing me to others. When my husband came to visit Taiwan on his breaks from school and work, he would occasionally accompany me to performances and once or twice participated in informal interviews; our daughter joined me in fieldwork after her birth in 2013. Although I cannot know with any certainty the effect that their presence had on my interactions with research associates, it did seem to open pathways for discussion about views on family, marriage, and child-rearing, which are central concerns for young people on the island today and which I address extensively in this book.

More directly consequential to my fieldwork outcomes, perhaps, was my position as first a student and later a teacher. My earliest academic interests in East Asian history, which I studied along with music during my undergraduate years, were motivated by recognition of the gaps in my own Eurocentric and Americentric educational upbringing—both the mainstream education I received in predominantly white American public schools and the Jewish education I received at our local Reform synagogue. I can recall just one brief lesson in sixth grade that mentioned Chiang Kai-shek, whose primary historical significance, as my textbook described it, was as a key American ally during the Cold War. It was not until the summer after high school that I began digging into books on the Pacific War and realized the extent to which my understanding of World War II privileged the European over the Pacific theater (even though my own paternal grandfather had been stationed in Okinawa). I had never heard of the Chinese Civil War, let alone the ROC's decampment to Taiwan, the 2-28 Incident, or the White Terror. My desire to remediate this lack of knowledge planted the seed for my academic and then professional path in ethnomusicology, throughout which I have continued to ask questions about received knowledge and selective remembering in the creation of historical narrative. I would come to discover that these same questions energize many of my research associates in their creative work, bearing fruit not just in music but also in their deep and prolonged engagement with politics and education.

Many of my professional relationships in Taiwan were inscribed in the circles of higher education. I found that my continued association with university life through a postdoctoral fellowship and then a faculty position provided numerous unexpected opportunities to engage with artists who themselves possessed or were in the process of pursuing advanced degrees. In some cases, we moved in parallel through dissertation writing and applications for jobs in the professoriate. Even as I gleaned invaluable insights from my time with them, I was privileged to serve as an interlocutor as they pursued their own academic projects. One example of the scholarly recursion that has developed between us can be found in chapter 3, which cites a 2020 publication by Professor Hao-li Lin (林浩立), aka MC Teacher Lin (林老師), which in turn cites the 2016 journal article that was the basis for the chapter. I have welcomed this element of reciprocity and intertextuality in our relationship, unique as it is to the circumstances and demographics of the community.

Exchanging accounts of personal experience, whether of academic work or life in general, is a defining feature of the ethnographic research process. The stories we shared over coffee, beer, and millet wine overlapped and intertwined with the stories emergent in rap performances, including those I first encountered at the 921.87 Rap Benefit Concert. As I conversed with my research associates about their childhoods, relationships, educations, workplace experiences, and views on politics, I slowly arrived at an understanding of the broader narratives that engender such stories and in which such stories are embedded. From the outset, it was clear that I had been granted admission to a conversation already in progress—a common experience for ethnographers, no doubt, but underscored here by the insistently academic nature of this particular network of artists and audiences. As I have sought to learn from musicians who are scholars of their own practice, I approach this topic with commensurate humility. Following their example, I recognize "expertise"—in rap, in ethnomusicology, in scholarship—as an aspiration rather than a destination.

Overview of the Book

Renegade Rhymes is organized along a fundamentally chronological arc. It begins and ends at moments of historic upheaval that compelled rappers to articulate their relationships to the past and their collective hopes for the future. The chapters in between develop progressively the conceptual and aesthetic frameworks that structure these articulations. The first part, "Polyphonic Histories," comprises two chapters that approach the history of rap in Taiwan as itself a narrative construction, subject to revision and reinterpretation at the hands of multiple authors. Drawing on recordings, archival resources, and interviews with established and emerging artists, I propose three distinct but overlapping histories, each unlocked by a different local gloss for "rap": *xiha* (嘻哈), a Mandarin transliteration of "hip-hop"; *raoshe* (饒舌), Mandarin for "rhapsodizing tongue"; and *liām-kua* (唸歌), Hoklo for "song reading" or "songs with narration." Attending to all three glosses permits an appropriately expansive account of rap in Taiwan that recognizes multiple centers of gravity: American and global hip-hop, Taiwan's domestic popular music industry, and local musical narrative tradition. These chapters do more than provide background; they also illustrate how desires to rethink historical narrative after the end of authoritarianism— and to draw different through lines from past to present—have crystallized in community discourse about the origins of rap itself.

The second part, "Narratives and Knowledge," explores over the course of its three constituent chapters interventions that members of the rap community have made to reshape the conditions under which they live and learn. Chapter 3, "Masculinity Politics and Rap's Fraternal Order," examines how artists have invoked the masculine ethos of rap in their efforts to produce new forms of post-authoritarian social reality. I posit the scene's male dominance as an intuitive response to a series of sociocultural, political, and economic disjunctures that have unsettled gender roles on the island since the end of martial law. In the context of these changes, rap artists have reimagined and refashioned Confucian gender regimes and notions of intragroup hierarchy to create meaningful new spaces for male sociality, avenues for male self-empowerment, and opportunities for the articulation of masculine identities not readily audible in the island's mainstream popular musics.

Building on this discussion of gender and power, chapter 4, "Performing Musical Knowledge Work," considers the myriad ways in which artists valorize and localize rap's discursive associations with knowledge, such that authority accrues to those who demonstrate the greatest prowess as teachers and scholars. Their pedagogical activities encompass songwriting, projects with university hip-hop clubs and creative collectives, conferences, exhibitions, and contributions to a Taiwan-specific digital platform called the Professional Technology Temple (PTT). Through these activities, community members acquire social capital, claim narrative agency, and carve out a meaningful existence within the constraints of neoliberal capitalism.

Chapter 5, "We Are So Strong, We Are Writing History," examines a corpus of rap songs about Taiwan's past, contextualizing them within fractious debates about the contents of the national history curriculum that began in the immediate post–martial law period and have continued into the present. These pieces make audible rap's constitution of historical narrative as a fundamentally social activity, in contradistinction to historical interventions in literature and film, and to the conventional teaching of history in the school system.

An epilogue listens for rap at the 2014 Sunflower Student Movement protests, a landmark in the island's process of democratic consolidation. Hearing symmetries between artists' affective responses following Sunflower and those following Typhoon Morakot, I contemplate rap as history of the present. I reflect briefly on the evolution of the scene, in light of accelerating neoliberalization and continued challenges to Taiwan's sovereign status. For the senior artists in the community, circumstances may change, but the imperatives of rap do not. There remain many lessons to teach and many stories to tell.

PART ONE

Polyphonic Histories

1
IT DEPENDS ON HOW YOU
DEFINE "RAP" . . .

At his workshop in Tainan City, I asked Dwagie to provide an account of the history of Taiwan rap. By this point, in September 2010, he had borne witness to the music's development for more than a decade, and journalists consulted him frequently as an authority on the island's vibrant underground scene. I wondered if he would find the request straightforward—tedious, even—but he met it with a furrowed brow and downward gaze, signaling that it merited prolonged contemplation. A white plastic pedestal fan oscillated back and forth a few feet from where we sat, its dull whir the only sound in an otherwise silent space. After a while, he leaned forward, stroked his chin, and said with the gravitas of one preparing to recount a saga: "Actually, the beginning...the beginning...well, it depends on how you define 'rap'" (interview, September 26, 2010).

In my attempts to discern rap's history in Taiwan, I ran headlong into a dizzying array of timelines and wildly divergent ideas about which events had proven formative to the community. Talk of history frequently circulates around artists, who write songs that imagine musically the local and national past, and who commit substantial energy to studying the developmental trajectories of US hip-hop. Most agreed on the general shape of rap's history in Taiwan within the past twenty years, noting especially the role of Dwagie and Taipei-based MC Hotdog in popularizing and legitimizing rap as not just an adjunct to other styles, as it had been for some time, but rather as an independent and self-sufficient project. With respect to the years prior to these artists' 1998 debuts, however, their accounts were more mutable. The profusion of histories communicated to me—and their frequently fragmentary and partial characters—echoed the multiplicity of terms artists used to refer to the music.[1] Dwagie's comments further underscored this idea, that how one recounts rap's history in Taiwan depends to a great extent on what one understands the word "rap" to mean.

There are at least three glosses that exist for "rap" on the island, and each unfolds a distinct story.[2] As *xiha* (嘻哈), a Mandarin transliteration of "hip-hop," rap is an ethos with roots in Black and Latinx cultural practices. Those who refer to rap as *xiha* emphasize the formative influence of a composite hip-hop culture that traveled to Taiwan from the United States via television, radio, and record imports beginning in the mid-1980s. As *raoshe* (饒舌), a Mandarin term I translate as "rhapsodizing tongue," rap is a musical technique that demands verbal agility of its performers. *Raoshe* highlights the contributions of politically incisive multi-genre musicians who first experimented with Mandarin- and Hoklo-language rap after the end of martial law. This term frames rap as a mode of performance that can be alloyed creatively with other locally significant musics. As *liām-kua* (唸歌), Hoklo for "song reading" or "songs with narration," rap is a species of narrative performance with affinities to local storysinging traditions. Those who understand rap in terms of *liām-kua* sometimes refer to the genre as a refashioned, modernized manifestation of narrative practices that date to the Ming and Qing Dynasties. That rap operates by these several aliases enriches a discussion of its present life in Taiwan and complicates the project of identifying its origins.

Patently polysemic, rap permits its adherents on the island to inscribe within it a variety of meanings that in turn open onto many pasts. With this in mind, I write the history of rap here and in the following chapter in a way that is neither linear nor singular, to provide ample bandwidth for the reconciliation of multiple, sometimes contradictory voices.[3] In this endeavor, I make recourse to "polyphony," a stylistic delineation common to both music scholarship and literary criticism. In musical contexts, polyphony can denote a compositional texture with two or more simultaneous but melodically independent lines. In literature, Bakhtin (1984) used "polyphony" to describe how multiple characters in a novel may possess individual perspectives that are not subordinated to the author's.[4] In both senses, the term is an apt metaphor for the kind of heterogeneous historical narrative toward which Dwagie initially gestured in our conversation. A polyphonic history of Taiwan rap—admitting of the separate and overlapping trajectories of *xiha*, *raoshe*, and *liām-kua*—underscores artists' regard for democratic modes of participation in the scene. It is likewise a compelling conceptual analogue for the political and cultural milieu of the immediate post–martial law period, a time in which the dominant metanarratives of the authoritarian state gave way to a swell of independent voices collaborating and competing to shape the island's future.

The Multiple Migrations of Hip-Hop and the Birth of *Xiha*

Identifying Taiwan rap as *xiha* affirms the island's status as a node in hip-hop's cosmopolitan formation, a position enabled by the liberalization of Taiwan's media environment after the end of martial law and throughout the process of democratization. In this period, engagement with hip-hop prompted two parallel and interrelated processes. First, artists and producers began to explore ways of making hip-hop legible to Taiwanese audiences, writing and releasing recordings that adapted and reworked rap sounds and hip-hop culture. Second, fans and practitioners of a nascent *xiha* formed networks that spanned university clubs, creative collectives, and online communities, ultimately generating new modes of sociality for young people at a time when sociality needed to be constructed anew. Today, many of the core performance practices, aesthetic preferences, and rituals of Taiwan's "rap community"—which I define expansively as comprising those who make or otherwise participate in rap—remain audibly and visibly wedded to global hip-hop cultural practice.

The dawn of hip-hop in Taiwan coincided precisely with the twilight of martial law. As the story has often been told by musicians, scholars, and critics, hip-hop culture first converged on the streets of the South Bronx in the early to mid-1970s.[5] A multimodal form of creative expression forged by Black and Latinx youth[6] in response to the privations of life in post-industrial, post–Civil Rights–era New York, hip-hop gained traction across the United States and in a variety of global contexts by the early 1980s.[7] Radio, film, and television supported hip-hop's pre-Internet expansion, particularly as rap songs filtered into the current of popular culture streaming outward from North America. In 1979 the Sugarhill Gang's single "Rapper's Delight" cracked the *Billboard* Top 40 and became a fixture of radio playlists and a crowd favorite in discos and dance halls around the world. Following closely on its heels, the 1982 film *Wild Style* served as an initial point of contact with a broader hip-hop culture for many outside the United States. Shot on a shoestring budget and distributed by an independent studio, the film played in theaters from Athens to Tokyo, introducing international audiences to visionary artists like Grandmaster Flash, Fab Five Freddy, and the Rock Steady Crew, and showcasing rap, turntablism, graffiti, and breaking as elements of a composite hip-hop cultural experience.[8] Television was slower to capitalize on the growing audience for what was by the mid-1980s a certifiably global phenomenon: hip-hop debuted on MTV in 1986 with a cover of Aerosmith's "Walk This Way" by Queens-based rappers Run-D.M.C. and gained widespread exposure with the 1988 premiere of *Yo! MTV Raps*, which became the network's highest-rated show within months (Chang 2005, 419). It was broadcast on several of MTV's overseas sister channels and spawned similar programs abroad, like the German Viva network's *Freestyle* (Von Dirke 2004, 96–98).

Tapping into these early signals posed a challenge to audiences based in Taiwan. The government and military held a monopoly over broadcast media from the end of the 1940s until the early 1990s, using radio and television to shore up established social and political agendas.[9] Radio stations were subject to federal jurisdiction, and television was restricted to sanctioned content on three channels operated by the central government, the KMT, and the military. Free-to-air entertainment options were relatively limited at this time: a handful of variety shows and singing contests nurtured the growth of the local Mandopop industry, and *Billboard*-type programs devoted airtime to mainstream artists like Michael Jackson and Madonna. Dance halls were forbidden and nightly curfews enforced, curbing dissemination of popular musics in concert, club, and party environments. Those who caught wind of hip-hop—either through travels abroad or English-language radio—leaned on black-market hawkers and importers to procure recordings and visual media.

DJ Chicano Chien (簡光廷), a founding figure of the Taipei *xiha* scene, seemed gleeful when recalling that much of his initial contact with US hip-hop culture in the late 1980s resulted from illicit activity. His first encounter with turntablism, he told me, was at an underground dance club, the albums he purchased were locally manufactured pirated versions, and his primary access to music videos was a neighbor's bootleg satellite television hookup. DJ Chicano was inspired to begin collecting hip-hop recordings after seeing the video for Young MC's 1989 track "Bust a Move" on *Yo! MTV Raps,* which he accessed via the aforementioned satellite connection. Exhilarated by the performance, he immediately traveled to Ximending, Taipei's epicenter of youth culture and a hub for entertainment-related businesses. Failing to find a pirated copy of *Stone Cold Rhymin'*, the album on which "Bust a Move" appeared, he located a record shop that agreed to place a special order. Although its proprietor chastised DJ Chicano for wanting to spend his money on a pricey American rap import—fifty to a hundred times more expensive than the pirated music most kids his age were buying on the street—DJ Chicano was undeterred. Once he had the album in hand, he pored over the liner notes, ravenous for clues about what he ought to buy next: "The cover of the vinyl said who had done what, who the producer was, who Young MC wanted to thank. . . . He wanted to thank many other rap artists, and I saw he had written about people called Eric B. & Rakim, DJ Jazzy Jeff, and so on. And so I went to look for these people and slowly started to buy more and more" (DJ Chicano Chien interview, June 14, 2011). Other first-generation members of Taiwan's underground scene impart similar stories about their attempts to access rap recordings at the end of the 1980s, remarking repeatedly on how difficult they were to locate, how expensive they were to import, and how their purchase often elicited expressions of bemusement from shop owners who simply could not fathom hip-hop's appeal.

DJ Chicano and his contemporaries were willing to expend significant time, effort, and money overcoming obstacles to access, and they reveled in the detective work of tracking down new artists to enjoy. Even with their varying degrees of English proficiency, they were as energized by the musical qualities of hip-hop as by their haphazard understanding of its textual (and contextual) meanings. But these dedicated listeners were, by their own account, a rarity among Taiwanese audiences, who overwhelmingly found hip-hop mystifying in terms of its cultural, linguistic, and musical modes of expression. Metaphors, puns, and plays on words that animate rap lyrics often aspire to obfuscation, challenging even lifelong English speakers to decipher their coded meanings.[10] For the most part, local audiences did not have the requisite English fluency, let alone the familiarity with African American Vernacular English, to participate in this challenge. They were also unacquainted with the stratified layers of Black cultural history upon which hip-hop was constructed: the dozens, the comic routines of Pigmeat Markham, the spoken word poetry of Gil Scott-Heron, and the philosophical teachings of the Universal Zulu Nation, for example, were more or less unknown on the island.

That said, the story of global hip-hop substantiates the music's ability to transcend linguistic and cultural boundaries. The more significant obstacle for Taiwanese audiences, as MC Teacher Lin of the group Tripoets (參劈) has speculated, was a lack of familiarity with the musical styles that helped give rise to hip-hop:

> In America, rap music developed from the music that DJs played in dance halls. But because of long-standing restrictions on dance implemented under martial law, dance halls were considered illegal places of gathering. It was only in 1988 after the lifting of martial law ... that dance halls and DJs began appearing in Taiwan in earnest. In the era of dance restrictions, Taiwan missed out on the golden age of disco taking place elsewhere. And it was precisely the rousing rhythms and melodies of disco, soul, and funk that provided an important musical foundation for rap music.[11]
> (Lin, Mo, and Shortee 2008, 13)

Describing the aftereffects of martial law strictures, Lin imagines that rap emerged, for Taiwan's listeners, seemingly out of nowhere, a sonic bolt from the blue rendered doubly foreign by its linguistic and musical novelty.

Despite these roadblocks to hip-hop's circulation in Taiwan, youth audiences readily consumed American cultural exports that showcased other aspects of hip-hop culture. In particular, as Tripoets' MC Ill Mo (老莫) told me, the early part of the decade saw the formation of a number of dance groups inspired by American movies like *Flashdance* (1983) (interview, March 3, 2010). That film, which featured a memorable sequence in which the groundbreaking Rock Steady Crew moved to the Jimmy Castor Bunch's "It's Just Begun," played widely in cinemas on the island. Young people gathered in schoolyards and parks to emulate the Crew's techniques and experiment with toprock, downrock, freeze, and power-move dance elements. While martial law prohibitions drove dance halls underground, they did not seem to discourage street dance, likely because it transpired out in the open primarily during daylight hours. Authorities could monitor rehearsals on the steps of the Sun Yat-sen Memorial Hall or in the airy avenues of Ximending more easily, with less concern for the potentially illicit activities—drug trafficking, sex work, or political organizing—that might have accompanied dancing behind closed doors. This is a tradition that continues into the present. Public spaces remain popular sites for high school and university street dance clubs to rehearse their routines.

For the most part, Taiwan's budding b-boys and b-girls were unaware of street dance as part of a larger hip-hop movement and therefore did not associate it with either rap or turntablism. The Rock Steady Crew's performance in *Flashdance* was accompanied not by rap but by funk music, and indie films like *Wild Style* that foregrounded hip-hop's integrated elements never played in Taiwan's theaters. DJ Chicano remembered that through the early 1990s, dancers in Taipei frequently approached him for music recommendations: "People who were breaking at that time, they had no idea what kind of music they should be using. They didn't really know about hip-hop. They would come and ask me [because I was learning to be a DJ], and I would suggest that they use music from the '70s and '80s like James Brown. They'd reply 'Right, right! We were watching a foreign dance video and they used that kind of music, but we didn't know what it was or how to find it'" (interview, June 14, 2011). According to George Chang (張兆志), who hosted a variety of shows dedicated to dance music on MTV Taiwan from 1995 until 2005, the island's youth gained access to knowledge about dance from programs they watched on bootleg satellite television and imported instructional videos (interview, June 22, 2011).

Japan, already home to a vibrant street dance scene in the 1980s, was the source of many of these videos, which guided amateurs through the basics as they had been absorbed through contact with American hip-hop and pop music culture in Tokyo.

Even unmoored from a sense of hip-hop culture as the synthesis of several elements, street dance amassed an enthusiastic following in Taiwan. By the 1990s, the island's burgeoning dance scene had developed a reputation in the Asia-Pacific region for its vitality and creativity. Reporters from overseas television networks like the Japan Broadcasting Corporation (NHK) began traveling to Taipei to film up-and-coming crews on the streets of Ximending (George Chang interview, June 22, 2011). As the trend developed, television talent shows like *Five Lights Contest* (五燈獎), broadcast every Saturday on the government-owned Taiwan Television Enterprise channel, established "hot dance" (熱門舞蹈) competitions that brought crews like the 800 Dragons and Gestapo (蓋世太保) to national prominence (Li 2007, 81). The phenomenal growth and sustained popularity of street dance in Taiwan showed music industry executives that hip-hop, packaged as commercial dance music, could be marketed successfully to local audiences. As several dance groups attained celebrity status, record companies hoping to capitalize on their popularity contracted them to produce albums as well.

"Then You Gotta Do It Like the Taiwanese": Processes of Localization

By far the most successful of these dancer-cum-musician acts was the LA Boyz, which consisted of clean-cut, California-bred, Taiwanese American brothers Jeff Huang (黃立成) and Stanley Huang (黃立行), and their cousin Steven Lin (林智文). The group was groomed by record label executive Ni Chonghua (倪重華)—who had worked with an array of critically acclaimed rock artists and would later serve as general manager of MTV Taiwan—to make waves as the island's first *xiha* teen idols. Ni spotted the trio performing on the *Five Lights Contest* and brought them together with rapper-composer Jerry Lo (羅百吉), also originally from California, to record their first album *SHIAM!* 閃 in 1992 (Ni Chonghua interview, August 23, 2010). The team fashioned an image for the LA Boyz capitalizing on perceptions of their Americanness as hip, cosmopolitan, and proximal to "authentic" (i.e., Black) hip-hop culture.

The group sought to make hip-hop comprehensible to local audiences by performing in a mixture of elementary English, Hoklo, and Mandarin. This compound emerged organically from the language competencies of the LA Boyz themselves, who had grown up in the United States (although in Irvine rather than Los Angeles) speaking English, but who conversed with their grandparents almost exclusively in Hoklo (Ni Chong-hua interview, August 23, 2010). They hewed closely to existing models of mainstream success in the United States, most notably artists like pre-teen rap duo Kris Kross. The title track of their second album, *Jump* (跳), went so far as to lift the title of Kris Kross's "Jump," employ much of the same rhyming vocabulary, and mimic many of its more distinctive musical gestures. The songs are virtually identical, apart from several lines in the first verse that propose a Taiwanese spin on hip-hop:

> I am jumping and I'm humping and I'm pumping to the beat
> and I never ever met a rapper faster than me
> with the big fat blabber mouth rappers of the '90s
> Jerry's gonna make his rap funky in Chinese
> first you gotta start off with the ABCs
> then you gotta learn it like the Taiwanese
> bopomofo[12] sure sounds easy to me
> but then you gotta spell it LA BOYZ!

Performed by Steven Lin, the verse begins by reproducing Kris Kross's rousing and boastful refrain "I got you jumpin' and bumpin' and pumpin', movin' all around," but shifts swiftly to the mission of making rap "funky in Chinese." That Lin declares this mission in English rather than Hoklo or Mandarin of course invites the question of whether the song's audience was imagined to consist of local listeners or other Taiwanese Americans like the LA Boyz themselves. In terms of sales it ultimately mattered very little—"Jump" was a smash hit on the island.

I interviewed Ni, twenty years removed from his experiences working with the LA Boyz. He lit up with pride when remembering that period of his career, so I was surprised to hear him characterize the group's early work as "fake" hip-hop (interview, August 23, 2010). Their performances, he explained matter-of-factly, lacked the gravitas of the American models on which they drew so brazenly, and the group's reliance on professional songwriters for material conflicted with hip-hop's imperative to realness. In other words, the LA Boyz were a commercial "idol act" (偶像團體), engineered to break through to a broad, untapped consumer base the way that MC Hammer and Vanilla Ice had in the United States. While later Taiwan rap artists would acknowledge their debt to the music's predominantly Black innovators, the LA Boyz, as Grace Wang observes, "decontextualized the music and culture into an innocuous form of dance, fashion and speech" and "disassociated themselves from the costs of blackness, disenfranchisement, and racism" (2014, 153). These critiques notwithstanding, many current members of the Taiwan rap scene credit the LA Boyz with demonstrating that hip-hop could be produced by and for people in Taiwan. Furthermore, they were the first on the island to consolidate rap, dance, and turntablism as elements of an integrated hip-hop aesthetic.

Ni tried his hand at reproducing the LA Boyz phenomenon with another dance-focused hip-hop act made up of seven teenagers from Taipei, called The Party (樂派體). The group did not ascend to the lofty heights of its predecessor but achieved modest success with the 1994 single "Monkey on My Back" (Monkey 在我背). Diverging from the LA Boyz, The Party performed primarily in Mandarin interspersed with occasional English catchphrases ("awwww yeah!"), countering the perception that local rap music could be performed convincingly only by Taiwanese Americans and in the English language. Tracks like "Monkey on My Back," which sampled Kool and the Gang's "Jungle Boogie" (1973), evinced a new awareness of the musical styles that brought about hip-hop in the United States and a desire to employ them in original compositions. Although the group performed for a scant few years and released only one full-length album, they occupied an important transitional space in the development of *xiha*.

Like the LA Boyz, The Party relied on some of Taiwan's most experienced pop lyricists, composers, and arrangers for material, including Jerry Lo, C. Y. Kong (江志仁), David Tao (陶喆), and He Qihong (何啟宏). But, as Ni explained, The Party and the LA Boyz posed different songwriting challenges: "We couldn't write anything too 'Taiwan-style' for the LA Boyz, because they were foreigners. We had to write things in an American style. The Party was local, so we had to search for lyrics with a little more depth" (interview, August 23, 2010). In other words, the limited overlap between the linguistic capabilities of the LA Boyz and those of their intended audience relegated them to simple, mutually comprehensible texts. The Party, acquainted with local cultural norms and capable of using idiomatic Mandarin, could more easily sell what Ni called "Taiwan-style" words and music. Ni called on thirty-year-old Zhu Yuexin (朱約信), a folk singer-songwriter, to contribute his local sensibilities to the project. But while Zhu collaborated successfully with the group for "Monkey on My Back" and several other tracks, Ni told me that he turned his other compositions away: "Zhu Yuexin wrote some songs and showed them to me, and I immediately knew they were completely inappropriate for The Party. So, I told him to come and meet me and I said, 'These words won't do.' And he was quite depressed.... But then I said, 'You should perform them, your own style suits them'" (interview, August 23, 2010). The three albums that resulted from this exchange, Zhu's *Funny Rap* series

(笑魁唸歌), departed significantly from the commercial, dance-oriented sound of the LA Boyz and The Party. Lyrically sophisticated and musically adventurous, they charted a radically different course for *xiha* in Taiwan.

A bookish singer-songwriter from Tainan who held a day job as a deacon for the Presbyterian Church, Zhu was an unlikely rap star. To perform the songs he had originally composed for The Party, he contrived a bold new persona called "Jutoupi" (豬頭皮)—literally "Pig Headskin"—an alter-ego whose adopted surname Zhu (豬, "pig") punned his actual family surname "Zhu" (朱). As a creative artist, Jutoupi was as engaged with social and political activism as Zhu Yuexin but far more mischievous, a trickster figure who brought his acerbic wit to bear on controversial topics like electoral fraud, safe sex, the vagaries of Taiwanese identity politics, and the island's ambiguous position in world polity. The first album in the *Funny Rap* series was released in 1994, a challenging year in which lawmakers worked to consolidate democratic processes through open gubernatorial and mayoral elections, the government loosened its grip on mass media, and the public engaged in a series of bitter debates about the future of Taiwan sovereignty. In a time of social and political instability, Jutoupi shed the carefree pop aesthetic of the LA Boyz and The Party to create music that acknowledged and reflected this tumult.

In response to the social and political changes sweeping Taiwan in the mid-1990s, the theme of madness suffused the *Funny Rap* series and found rich expression in Jutoupi's textual and musical designs. A sense of chaos engendered by this madness is apparent even in the liner notes, where a series of titles both refer directly to the idea of insanity and *are* "insane" by virtue of their linguistic inconstancy. To offer one example, Jutoupi provides the English title *Jutoupi's Funny Rap* for the first album in the series, but its Mandarin name *Wo shi shenjingbing* (我是神經病) glosses as "I Am Insane." The first track on the album goes by that same Mandarin title, but Jutoupi provides a second alternative English translation that conjures an even more decisive sense of turmoil: "You Sick Suck Nutz Psycho Mania Crazy Taipei City." Rapid code-switching among seven languages—Hoklo, Mandarin, Hakka, English, Japanese, French, and Bunun—further augments the sense of mayhem, particularly as dynamic wordplay multiplies into numerous cross-linguistic puns that compel listeners to question precisely what it is they have just heard.[13] Jutoupi's sonic sensibilities induce similar feelings of delirium: in collaboration with Jerry Lo, he drew samples from a variety of disparate sources, including Japanese popular songs from the 1930s, Hoklo and Hakka folk tunes, Mandarin *shidaiqu*, American rock and jazz, and Taiwanese Indigenous musics, among others. Taken together, the narrative content of the songs, their languages of performance, and their musical features all speak to a feeling of dizzy disarray.

Jutoupi's rise to fame coincided with substantial changes to the island's media landscape: in 1993 liberal reforms precipitated the end of the government monopoly over mass media. New radio frequencies were released, and multichannel cable and satellite television service providers officially entered the Taiwan market such that the number of entertainment options available to consumers skyrocketed virtually overnight.[14] At the same time, rap artists in the United States proliferated, diversified stylistically, and made incursions into the mainstream. Adam Bradley and Andrew DuBois identify 1993 and 1994 as a "second-wave hip-hop golden age" (2010, 330) marked by the release of "psychologically compelling" and "formally sophisticated" (325) works like the Wu-Tang Clan's *Enter the Wu-Tang (36 Chambers)*, A Tribe Called Quest's *Midnight Marauders*, Snoop Dogg's *Doggystyle*, De La Soul's *Buhlōōne Mind State*, Nas's *Illmatic*, and Common's *Resurrection*. Jutoupi's approach to rap as a field for linguistic play and sampling as a process of intertextual allusion mirrored these contemporary expansions in rap's thematic and stylistic ambitions across the Pacific.

While senior members of Taiwan's rap scene consider Jutoupi a *xiha* innovator, Zhu Yuexin balked at that characterization when we discussed his work just after a 2010 performance in Ximending. Prior to the *Funny Rap* series, Zhu was a folk singer and activist; today he performs mostly pop, electronica, and Christian rock. His adventures as Jutoupi were a happy accident, he told me, arising from his activities as a songwriter for hire rather than a deeply considered investment in *xiha*: "We studied De La Soul and Public Enemy, but it wasn't like we listened to them and thought, 'Ah, we have to make [*xiha*] music.' It was the social concerns they wrote about, the attitude of their songwriting, their techniques that we could learn and insert into funk, folk, rap, anything" (interview, October 10, 2010). Zhu took the sociopolitical engagement of Public Enemy and the sophisticated digital sampling of De La Soul as stylistic models, but stopped short of claiming a hip-hop lineage. Indeed, within the *Funny Rap* soundscape, hip-hop seems less a constituting force than one among many musical references. Music critic and radio DJ Ma Shih-fang (馬世芳) concurs that those who purchased Jutoupi's albums did not necessarily hear the music as *xiha*: "[Audiences] just thought it was interesting music, hilarious music, because he sampled a lot of old Japanese pop songs and foreign pop songs from all over the world.... So together [with Jerry Lo] they made a new kind of music which was blending different kinds of music.... It was very interesting to listen to" (interview, January 18, 2010). Ma attributes Jutoupi's appeal to this fundamental puzzle: Was he a *xiha* artist invoking Taiwanese folk sounds and Japanese pop, or a folk-pop artist sampling *xiha*? Whatever the answer, later performers would cite Zhu as a formative influence and credit him with bringing hip-hop aesthetics into spirited dialogue with local languages and sounds.

Spreading Community Roots and an Island-Wide *Xiha* Scene

Concurrent with these early forays into *xiha*, a burgeoning club scene continued to grow the presence of American rap music in Taiwan. Multinational music retailers like Tower Records and smaller independent music shops opened for business, and a number of DJs doggedly pursued imported recordings and promoted hip-hop in club environments whenever possible. DJ Chicano and his high school classmates Sam and Goldie formed a consortium of dancers and DJs called Doobiest, named in tribute to California underground rap outfit Funkdoobiest. They organized a series of monthly parties in Taipei bringing together DJs, street dancers, and graffiti artists, as well as non-performers who were passionate about hip-hop. If Taiwan had missed out on developing an active club scene under martial law, as Teacher Lin suggests, these events effected some degree of remediation. DJ, b-boy, and rapper Shortee (小個) of the Tripoets, who was a member of the Doobiest crew, recalled that the parties were popular among performers and fans alike: "Everyone wanted to go—it was a must at that time" (interview, March 3, 2010).

As a community coalesced in Taipei, those living in other parts of the island sought alternative means of identifying and engaging others who shared their interests. In 1997, eager to connect with fellow fans, MC Teacher Lin and a high school classmate started an Internet forum devoted to discussion of all things hip-hop. Called Master U, it was a beacon for its founders, who lived in central Taiwan and felt isolated in their musical tastes. Teacher Lin reminisced: "Back then I seriously thought I was the only one listening to hip-hop music in Taiwan because Taichung was very far away from Taipei, information-wise. So, I always thought I was alone until we started the Internet forum. We got some guys posting news and music, like twenty of them. And that's when I knew I wasn't alone" (interview, October 18, 2010). Compared to genres like Mandopop, which accounted for the majority of Taiwan's USD170 million popular music market around this time (Guy 2001, 358), the audience for hip-hop was minuscule. Master U provided individuals outside of major urban areas with a mechanism for locating kindred spirits. Those who signed on, almost exclusively teenage boys, were highly motivated participants, posting reactions to the latest releases, dissecting the history of hip-hop in the United States, and debating the merits of its most distinguished practitioners. For fans who struggled to understand rap lyrics and English-language articles about hip-hop, Master U was a welcome forum for learning. Both the Doobiest events and the forum transformed the experience of listening to rap music in Taiwan: a once-solitary activity gave way to a communal exchange of knowledge and values, with the clout of a social network.

Marcyliena Morgan has examined the importance of community in the production and consumption of American hip-hop, describing a system of core and long-term members whose participation and periodic regeneration are critical to sustaining hip-hop culture (2009, 55–59). The inception of both Doobiest events and Master U generated a core in Taiwan that behaved much as Morgan describes. Participants networked, studied American as well as Japanese and Korean models, and shared their findings with enthusiasm. Many developed over time into the long-term members that populate today's rap scene, and some experimented with their own approaches to making rap music by writing lyrics and workshopping them with others online. Unique standards for evaluation arose from these efforts, as participants merged knowledge of hip-hop criticism gleaned from American sources with their own definitions of success. Master U has since receded into the abyss of the Internet, replaced by newer discussion groups and social networking technologies, so it is not possible to reconstruct the precise process by which users came to understand certain kinds of approaches as successful and others as unsuccessful. The work of two key participants in the forum—Yao Zhongren (姚中仁), better known as MC Hotdog, and Tseng Kuan Jung (曾冠榕), better known as Dwagie—provides our best documentation of the techniques and styles that commanded widespread respect. To those who understand rap in terms of its identity as hip-hop, these individuals are frequently referred to as Taiwan's first bona fide *xiha* MCs.

Peering out behind his trademark oversize glasses and dragging on a cigarette, MC Hotdog struck me as mellow and amiable when we first met up in 2010. Although his present-day onstage persona is one of mature, swaggering confidence (see fig. 1.1), he summoned youthful earnestness as he recalled his early passion for American hip-hop and his desire to give it a powerful Mandarin-language voice. Born and raised in Taipei, MC Hotdog began writing lyrics as a high school student in the mid-1990s. He purchased a Roland MC-505 MIDI sequencer and tried his hand at recording original material and performing, first for classmates at the prestigious Taipei Municipal Jienguo High School, and then on the campus of Fu Jen Catholic University, where he enrolled for college (interview, August 12, 2010). As word of his music spread on the Internet and students began to download his homemade tracks, MC Hotdog was emboldened to take his act onto the nightclub circuit. There, he was spotted by executives from independent record label Magic Stone (魔岩唱片公司), who helped him

FIG. 1.1. MC Hotdog performs in Taipei, May 21, 2011. Photograph by author.

to make a high-quality demo and arranged for a performance with his frequent Master U collaborator Dwagie at Spring Scream (春吶音樂祭), a major annual outdoor music festival in southern Taiwan.[15] The exposure was a boon to his popularity on the island, and before long Magic Stone signed both MC Hotdog and Dwagie. Together with Taiwanese American rappers 168 and Witness (黃崇旭), singer and producer J. Wu, and DJ Xiao Si (小四), they formed a crew known as Big Circus (大馬戲團), which Magic Stone ultimately developed as a subsidiary label (Witness interview, May 24, 2011). Continuously honing his material in pubs, live houses, and nightclubs, MC Hotdog released four consecutive EPs in 2001, which sold hundreds of thousands of legitimate copies in Taiwan and an unknown but possibly greater number of black-market copies both locally and in the PRC. Following a brief hiatus from 2003 to 2005 to complete his military service, MC Hotdog returned to performing and relentless touring, often with pop artist Chang Chen-yue (張震嶽). Since 2006 he has released four additional full-length studio albums.[16]

MC Hotdog's sound has undergone a number of transformations over the past two decades, but early songs like 2001's "Let Me Rap" (讓我 rap), "Korean Wave Invasion" (韓流來襲), "Cram, Cram, Cram" (補補補), and "My Life" (我的生活) provide an indication of the broader stylistic changes afoot as *xiha* came into its own at the turn of the millennium. Diverging from the pop stylings of the LA Boyz and the madcap antics of Jutoupi, these tracks revealed a new affinity for hard-core hip-hop after the fashion of the Notorious B.I.G., Tupac Shakur, and Wu-Tang Clan. Adopting a less congenial stance than his predecessors, the rapper's voice seethed with frustration; his lyrics were alternately somber and truculent, riddled with English and Mandarin expletives. In "Let Me Rap" and "Korean Wave Invasion," he accused Taiwan's commercial music industry of privileging physical beauty over artistry and, in the latter track, invited pop stars with a purported propensity for vapid speech—or "shit from the mouth"—to come and "suck [his] dick."[17] "Cram, Cram, Cram" addressed the intense social pressure to succeed within the bounds of Taiwan's rigid educational system, encouraging listeners to boycott the national high school examination and resist spending their youth as passive "studying machines" (讀書機器).

In addition to its emphasis on social critique, MC Hotdog's early work established rap in Taiwan as a forum for the realization of personal narratives, especially ones characterized by conflict. "My Life" describes his path to becoming a musician, a story marked by deviation from parental expectations, financial struggle, and ongoing episodes of doubt and disappointment. In this excerpt, the rapper introduces his "dog" persona not with bravado but with self-laceration:

走在西門町　看到很多流浪漢
感嘆地笑一笑怎會有種親切感
原本流浪漢的身邊都有一隻流浪狗
只是沒有錢幫狗植入晶片他就一無所有
我也是流浪狗　嘴裡含著麥克風想問
誰又真正的在乎我

walking in Ximending, I saw many drifters
and laughed and sighed at how much my life is like theirs
every drifter had a stray dog
but without the money to microchip it, he really had nothing
I'm like a stray dog, with a microphone in my mouth, and I wonder
who really cares about me?

Alienated as a consequence of his unconventional life path, MC Hotdog encapsulates his experience in the melancholic, isolated image of the stray dog and the vagrant who is too poor to claim him. Expressions of estrangement and nonconformism pervade MC Hotdog's early music, which invokes hip-hop ideals of heterodoxy and realism to explore the challenges and conflicts inherent in the lives of Taiwanese youth.

Dwagie, with whom MC Hotdog collaborated regularly, has also exerted a profound influence on the *xiha* scene, particularly in the south of the island. Born and raised in Tainan, he was enrolled in the judo program at the Taipei College of Physical Education when he first began to consider work as a professional musician. Having made a name for himself as a knowledgeable and creative participant on Master U, he was eager to start writing songs "using my own language [Hoklo] and dealing with the life going on around me" (interview, September 26, 2010). Dwagie made his debut with MC Hotdog at Spring Scream in 2000 and signed with Magic Stone Records as a member of the Big Circus crew. In late 2002, he released his first full-length album, *Lotus from the Tongue* (舌粲蓮花), which featured his now-signature track "Taiwan Song" (台灣 Song).[18] When Magic Stone, prey to the island's weakening commercial music industry, dismantled its operations in 2003, Dwagie returned to his hometown of Tainan and began connecting with other rappers throughout the city, arranging group activities and performances in hopes of forming a local hip-hop community. His efforts bore fruit in the Kung Fu Entertainment (人人有功練) collective,[19] today the physical and spiritual center of *xiha* in Tainan. With a brick-and-mortar office housing a school and recording studio for aspiring rappers as well as dedicated spaces for writing and socializing, Kung Fu Entertainment is where Dwagie and I met to engage in our first discussion of Taiwan rap history.

Despite his ongoing associations with MC Hotdog and the pair's shared roots in Master U, Dwagie's music has long suggested a different set of objectives. While MC Hotdog's early songs meditated on the vicissitudes of daily life for young people in Taiwan and directed their critiques at a vacuous corporate popular culture, Dwagie swiftly carved out an identity for himself as a social and political activist. *Lotus from the Tongue* is performed almost exclusively in Hoklo, with limited Mandarin and English interjections, and on tracks like "Taiwan Song" the artist advocates forcefully for a consensus on the ontological reality of Taiwanese identity and a *xiha* with corresponding local specificities:

你甘有聽到這條歌　恭喜啦
這就是正港的台灣 hip-hop
[...]
這是啥米歌　台灣爽
是叨位最爽　台灣爽
吃是台灣米　(誰)　喝是台灣水　(你)
生是台灣人　(我)　死是台灣鬼　(他)
這是啥米歌　台灣爽
是叨位最爽　台灣爽
台灣人的愛　(這)　台灣人的愛　(那)
台灣人的愛　都在台灣之聲

if you haven't heard this song, congratulations!
this is real Taiwan hip-hop
[...]
what song is this, Taiwan song
where do you belong, Taiwan song
what you eat is Taiwanese rice (who?) what you drink is Taiwanese water
   (you!)
live as a Taiwanese person (me!) die as a Taiwanese spirit (he!)
what song is this, Taiwan song
where do you belong, Taiwan song
the love of Taiwanese people (here!) the love of Taiwanese people
   (there!)
the love of Taiwanese people is in the voices of Taiwan

Dwagie hoped that these rousing lyrics would inspire listeners to "stop being ashamed of being Taiwanese" (Perrin 2004). He wrote against both the residual effects of martial law–era Sinicization policies and growing anxieties about the island's ability to maintain its sovereignty against a rising tide of PRC political and economic influence. Against this backdrop, Dwagie's determination to keep *xiha* real established it as a new vehicle for political engagement. His elemental references to rice, water, life, and death invoked a nativist literary sensibility, and he adopted a strident, pro-Taiwan tenor in dialogue with a consolidated Taiwanese cultural nationalism emergent in the 1990s.[20]

MC Hotdog and Dwagie are widely recognized as initiating the development of an underground rap scene in Taiwan. Teacher Lin credits MC Hotdog especially with inspiring an island-wide *xiha* movement: "Taiwan underground rap started around 1998, and at that time southern Taiwan had Tainan-based youth group E.A.C. (East Assassin Clan), central Taiwan had T.T.M. (Top Trouble Makers), northern Taiwan had Big Circus. But strictly speaking, only one person was responsible for creating this trend, and that was MC Hotdog. Regardless of what you think of him, this historical distinction is certainly his" (Lin, Mo, and Shortee 2008, 19). Within a year of MC Hotdog's debut, numerous groups aspiring to similar renown emerged. Along with E.A.C. and T.T.M., Lin's first crew, known as O.G.C. (Original Gangstaz Club), came together at this time, along with another called D.G.B. (Da Ghetto Brothers). Gesturing toward a sense of community, most groups from this period assumed three-word English monikers evoking a hard-core American hip-hop ethos, which they rendered as acronyms following a practice that Lin has self-deprecatingly called "the legend of the three English letters" (三個英文字母傳奇) (21). All featured at least five members, if not more, and all developed, like MC

FIG. 1.2. Ill Mo (*left*) and Shortee (*right*) of the Tripoets performing in Taipei, May 21, 2011. Photograph by author.

Hotdog and Dwagie, outside the corporate music industry. As these artists evolved themselves into long-term community members, a new genera- tion arose with groups like the Tripoets, Da Ximen (大囍門), and Kou Chou Ching, as well as solo artists RPG, Manchuker (滿人), Soft Lipa, and GoRDoN (國蛋), among many others. As time has passed and the rap community has grown, diverse affiliations that cross generational lines have also developed. For example, the Tripoets (see fig. 1.2) and younger artists BR (aka "Buzz Rhyme") and PoeTek (熊仔, aka "Kumachan") now represent a subset of the core community dubbed "academic rappers" (學院派), referring to their matriculation to competitive colleges, pen- chant for musical and lyrical erudition, and/or shared history in extracur- ricular *xiha* clubs.

Beyond the underground rap scene, *xiha* styles and gestures also de- veloped a discernible presence in mainstream music in Taiwan. Record companies tried and failed to sell straight rap music to mass audiences in the early 2000s, when local label Alfa Music invested millions of New Taiwan Dollars to develop a gangsta-style rap group called Iron Bamboo (鐵竹堂). Like the LA Boyz and The Party before them, group mem- bers did not write much of their own material but relied instead on the assistance of hit-makers like Mandopop megastar Jay Chou's (周杰倫) songwriting partner Fang Wenshan (方文山). A formula that worked during the early '90s, however, seemed to hit a sour note after the turn of the millennium—sales were poor and the group ultimately disbanded.[21] In 2001, after several years in the United States building a successful tech startup, LA Boyz rapper Jeff Huang returned to the island and the music industry. Together with business associate Bobby Sheng and Korean American hip-hop and R&B artist Jae Chong, he founded MACHI Entertainment Group. Although not a *xiha* label per se, MACHI nevertheless represented a number of high-profile pop artists in Taiwan who identified with a hip-hop aesthetic, including Jay Chou and Van Ness Wu (吳建豪). Moreover, MACHI also became home to the Machi Crew (麻吉), a rap group composed of nearly a dozen performers that Huang founded in 2003. One of a small number of *xiha* acts on the island to gain major label support in the early 2000s, they have released several hit singles and collaborated in 2006 with American hip-hop icon Missy Elliott on "Jump, Work It!!!" which remixed her song "Work It" with an updated version of the LA Boyz hit "Jump." More recently, hip-hop labels True Color (本色音樂), KAO!INC. (顏社), and Ainoko Entertainment (混血兒娛樂) have blurred the lines between the underground and mainstream music industries, incubating the careers of artists like Soft Lipa, Miss Ko (葛仲珊), MJ116, 911 (玖壹壹), and Leo Wang (Leo王), who have received industry accolades, media coverage, and lucrative corporate endorsements. Some have even transitioned into relationships with multinationals, including BCW, who is signed to Universal Music Taiwan, and PoeTek, who is signed to Sony Music Taiwan.

Taiwan rap is a phenomenon distinguished by its multiple, rich historical legacies, but there can be little question that the *xiha* narrative predominates among members of the current scene, many of whom themselves participated as key actors in *xiha*'s development. From their youthful attempts to procure pirated recordings to their establishment of local networks for the exchange of knowledge, their prevailing memories are of efforts to connect through hip-hop with one another and with the world beyond Taiwan. In recent years, enterprising members of the community have traveled abroad to perform—sometimes with financial support from the government, which sees popular music as an important tool for the cultivation of soft power (Kuo 2011)—and have also invited overseas artists to visit Taiwan for collaboration.

I observed one such collaborative effort on July 22, 2017, when Dwagie and his colleagues from Kung Fu Entertainment convened what they called the "Asia Hip-Hop Summit" (亞洲嘻哈高峰會). Consisting of a variety of lecture-demonstrations that took place at locations in the south, middle, and north of the island, the Asia Hip-Hop Summit culminated in a conference-style panel discussion and concert in Taipei featuring

FIG. 1.3. Screen capture from field video of the Asia Hip-Hop Summit, July 22, 2017. Photograph by author.

delegate-performers from South Korea (Flowsik), Japan (Anarchy), Vietnam (Suboi), the United States (SteelyOne and Kool Kid Dre), and Taiwan (PoeTek) (see fig. 1.3). With Ill Mo's support as Mandarin-English translator, participants discussed their relationships to hip-hop culture and approaches to rhyming, and explored the topics of communication and collaboration across geopolitical and linguistic divides. In Dwagie's opening address (delivered in English), he reflected specifically on the historical arc of Taiwan's engagement with hip-hop, highlighting the themes of isolation and connection:

> Have no doubt, we are all connected today because of hip-hop. It's hard to imagine today that we [from Taiwan] can all stand together on the same stage with all the best rappers from all over Asia. I remember in the past, in the early days of hip-hop in Taiwan, we had to subscribe by mail to *The Source* magazine, sometimes we had to ask our friends in the US to record shows on BET [Black Entertainment Television] and send us the videotapes to Taiwan. There was a joke we said at that time: Hello Kitty was more popular than Snoop Doggy Dogg. But who knows today? Asian hip-hop can march slowly into Europe and America and Westerners will gradually know in Asia there's more than just Big Bang and Jackie Chan.... Even myself, I got to collaborate with Wu-Tang, Nas, the Dalai Lama. I made it to CNN, BBC, *Time Magazine*. Performed at the NBA Brooklyn Nets game. Also, a huge shout-out to my sister, our special guest today, Suboi! She rapped in front of Obama—that's so sick!

So we are all coming together here today to make something happen, to tell the world: Asian hip-hop is going to take the world by storm.

Notably, Dwagie emphasizes artists' forays not only into global popular culture, but also into the realm of global politics. Representing their respective homelands, artists can navigate the pathways of global hip-hop to access spaces traditionally reserved for diplomats and government officials. In other words, there is more at stake in the *xiha* narrative than proving that Taiwanese artists can converse in the global musical vernacular. Community members who grapple with Taiwan's ambiguous geopolitical status and ongoing existential uncertainty can take solace in an incipient hip-hop nationhood, forging transregional and translocal alliances with hip-hop heads around the world.

2
... BECAUSE OTHERS MIGHT DEFINE IT DIFFERENTLY

Cast in terms of *xiha*, rap indexes Taiwan's location in the global circulation of hip-hop culture. Other terms used to describe the music presume different centers of gravity. Rap as *raoshe* ("rhapsodizing tongue") takes a rambling path through the landscape of Taiwan's prolific and polymorphous popular music industry. Artists identified with the island's rock, pop, and folk scenes have since the mid-1980s employed rap-style vocal techniques in their compositions, often without direct reference to hip-hop aesthetics and, more importantly, without claiming membership in any particular *xiha* community. Their performances reflect a broader syncretic impulse in Taiwanese popular song, which has from its inception embraced the borrowing and refashioning of musical ideas from other places. The technique of *raoshe* is understood to be present in but prior to *xiha* cultural practice, untethering rap from its strict associations with hip-hop. Its lineage pulls from a broader musical culture characterized not only by its position in numerous "circuits of media and migration" (Jones 2016, 73), but also by a history of colonial encounter and attendant social, cultural, and political transformations.[1]

One such transformation was the cultural revivalism and literary nativism of the mid-1970s that laid the groundwork for latter-day rappers to claim dual lineage in *xiha* and the local narrative tradition *liām-kua*. Since Hoklo-language rap first emerged just after the end of martial law, it has drawn comparisons to *liām-kua*, widely regarded as one of Taiwan's most representative traditional *shuochang* arts. Although different in their formal and functional particulars, rap and *liām-kua* share similar features, including a storytelling ethos, a fundamentally improvisatory nature, and the use of speech-song vocal techniques. Artists working in both genres have typically employed narrative as a vessel for social critique, communicating complex and sometimes controversial messages through allegory and metaphor, as well as through musical sound. Predominantly Hoklo-language rappers in Taiwan have capitalized on these commonalities, repositioning an ostensibly foreign art form as a logical extension, or perhaps continuation, of local cultural tradition.[2] Beyond adapting rap to local specificities, they posit *liām-kua* as a grassroots political project in which they are simply the newest in a long line of participants.

Writing the alternate histories of *raoshe* and *liām-kua* requires that we adopt perspectives on rap that are at once more expansive temporally and more focused spatially than the history of rap as *xiha*. Current participants in the scene, such as those whose voices I foregrounded in chapter 1, invoke *raoshe* and *liām-kua* narratives speculatively and creatively, in ways that engender their own journeys into the study of history and their own ruminations on the relationship between past and present.

Syncretic Soundings in Taiwan's Popular Music Industry

Scholars and artists alike often trace the emergence of the popular music industry in Taiwan generally to the Japanese colonial period and specifically to the release of the 1932 song "Peach Blossom Weeps Blood" (桃花泣血記) by lyricist Zhan Tianma (詹天馬) and composer Wang Yunfeng (王雲峰).[3] The Hoklo-language theme to a silent film from Shanghai, it was recorded in Tokyo by performers from Taiwan and quickly found favor on the streets of Taipei (then Taihoku). With its pentatonic vocal line and diatonic accompaniment performed by Western strings, winds, brass, accordion, and piano, the song bears clear sonic traces of its transnational, transcultural genesis. Its sound was firmly in step—and in conversation—with developments in the urban popular music scenes of China and Japan, where artists in vogue fused idiomatic features of local folk songs and popular ballads with jazz, blues, Hollywood film music, and Latin dance styles.[4]

The Hoklo popular song business thrived until 1937, when Japan entered into war with China and the Japanese colonial government banned the use of local languages. During this period, a number of Hoklo songs were translated into Japanese and appropriated by colonial authorities for political propaganda (Guy 2008, 69).[5] The island's culture industries were subject to the vicissitudes of politics for decades to come; the end of the Second World War heralded Taiwan's turnover to China, and Chiang Kai-shek's Nationalist government imposed its own restrictions on the language, narrative content, and musical ethos of popular songs. As Nancy Guy has noted, the post-turnover period "witnessed a further decline in the production of Taiwanese popular music. The postwar economic downturn, coupled with the Nationalists' efforts to restrict and disparage local Taiwanese culture, drove many talented artists away from creative endeavors" (Guy 2001, 356). In a reversal of previous circumstances, by the 1950s Taiwanese musicians had begun adapting Japanese tunes and translating them into Hoklo for the local market, propagating what music historian Zhuang Yongming (莊永明) (1994) and others have called "songs of mixed blood" (混血歌曲).[6] Even as laws limited the number of non-Mandarin songs that could be broadcast on television and radio in a given day, artists continued to produce these songs, which, in their clear derivation from the Japanese ballad form *enka*, bore the deep sonic imprint of the Japanese colonial legacy on Taiwan. Likewise, early recordings that issued from the Indigenous recording industry, which developed around 1960 and targeted the island's Indigenous market, featured Indigenous tunes performed with instrumental accompaniments and stylistic flourishes consistent with the *enka* style (Tan 2008, 226).

"Mixture" has consistently defined the island's popular music in the years since, as local sounds have continuously churned, converged, and combined with musics circulating among Taipei and Shanghai, Hong Kong, Tokyo, Paris, New York, London, Buenos Aires, and Havana. The 1.2 million refugees who accompanied the Republic of China's decampment to Taiwan at the end of the 1940s were fond of Mandarin-language pop tunes that originated in the cosmopolitan Shanghai of the 1920s.[7] So-called *haipai* (海派, lit. "Shanghai-style") Mandarin pop songs quickly established a foothold on the island, fostered by a political environment that restricted local cultural expression. These songs were, of course, already self-consciously hybrid when they arrived on Taiwanese shores, amalgams of jazz, Latin American dance styles, Hollywood and Broadway music, and Chinese folk sounds.[8] Both Taiwan and Hong Kong, which also absorbed refugees from China following the war, became centers of *haipai* pop music consumption and production until the genre fell out of fashion toward the end of the 1960s.

Waning interest in *haipai* tunes coincided not only with the graying of the first-generation Chinese émigré population, but also with a deepening American military presence on the island following the First Taiwan Strait Crisis.[9] The years between 1957 and 1979 saw an injection of European and American popular music into the local soundscape via the Armed Forces Network Taiwan (AFNT), an officially sanctioned English-language radio station operated by the American military. AFNT played classical music, jazz, and the hits of the day, from Elvis Presley to Sammy Davis Jr. Its primary mandate was to serve the American military community, but AFNT also did the ancillary work of promoting a positive image of American cultural and political ideals to locals. When the United States withdrew forces from the island in 1979, the American Chamber of Commerce and local community and business leaders successfully lobbied President Chiang Ching-kuo to keep the station on the air. After this time AFNT started a new life as International Community Radio Taipei (ICRT), operated by the Taiwan government and overseen by a board of trustees of mixed American and Taiwanese representation.[10]

The listening environment on the island normalized the intermingling of all the aforementioned musical styles, and we might posit the genre known as "Mandopop," which began developing in Taiwan in the mid-1950s (S. Chen 2020), as one product of their synthesis.[11] Teresa Teng (鄧麗君), Mandopop's most notable luminary, was famously versatile: she performed confidently in multiple languages and seamlessly blended *haipai, enka,* and Euro-American pop stylings in dozens of hit records from the 1960s until her death in 1995. Mandopop continues to demonstrate a significant degree of stylistic diversity today. David Tao introduced rhythm-and-blues-inflected Mandopop to Sinophone audiences in the mid-1990s. His soulful interpretations of Hoklo popular songs from the 1930s, including "Awaiting the Spring Breeze" (望春風), and 1940s Mandarin pop tunes like "Fragrance of the Night" (夜來香) feature melismatic flourishes and blue notes characteristic of gospel and R&B, anticipating Mandopop's later widespread appropriation of Black American popular idioms. Jay Chou, whose songs also evince the profound influence of Black music, has experimented with both American country and western (i.e., "Cowboy on the Run," 牛仔很忙) and various Chinese folk (or folk-derived) styles (i.e., "Blue and White Porcelain," 青花瓷).

Early Forays into *Raoshe*

Given Mandopop's high tolerance for musical mixture, it is unsurprising that the first commercial rap song in Taiwan, "Yes, Sir!" (報告班長), was recorded by Mandopop star Harlem Yu (庾澄慶). Released in June 1987, just a month before the official cessation of martial law and five years before the LA Boyz made their debut, it was the eponymous theme to a martial film (軍教片) about draftees coming of age in the ROC's standing army. Although the song itself advances no specific political agenda, its lyrics seemed tailor-made to induce nostalgia among listeners who had completed compulsory military service, required of males between the ages of eighteen and thirty-six since 1951.[12] A pop singer by trade, Yu had never rapped prior to writing and recording the song and in fact considered it a bold attempt at integrating a new "way of singing" (唱法) into an otherwise standard Mandarin rock ditty (Yu 1987). Yu is typically credited with being the first to use the term *raoshe* and has often introduced the song in live performances as "the first Chinese-language *raoshe* song"

(第一個中文饒舌歌).[13] Apart from the chanted, rhymed lyrics, however, "Yes, Sir!" lacks any of the hallmarks of hip-hop—Yu's voice is accompanied by a rock band rather than a DJ; there are no audible traces of funk, soul, dub, or disco; and Yu makes no lyrical references to hip-hop cultural practice. "Yes, Sir!" was well received by audiences and remains a fan favorite, but Yu's flirtations with the vocal technique were short-lived—he returned to singing exclusively on subsequent albums.

The lifting of martial law in July 1987 brought to an end nearly four decades of KMT hegemony and ushered in both a consolidation of democratic processes and restoration of many previously suspended civil rights. This political seismic shift was of clear import to artists as it initiated the dismantling of policies that had long restricted local cultural and linguistic practices. Music had been subject to stringent government controls throughout the period of martial law; between 1949 and 1987, more than a thousand songs were censored by government agencies for a wide variety of reasons, including expressing left-leaning sentiments (意識左傾) or bitterness and grief (幽怨哀傷) (Chen 2008, 283–84).[14] Hoklo-language popular music, which bore the indelible imprint of the melancholy Japanese *enka*, had been especially vulnerable to censorship as the KMT enforced a strict policy of monolingualism and sought to eradicate lingering signs of Japanese influence.

The more liberal environment following the end of martial law galvanized artists for the first time in decades to engage political themes in their work, write lyrics in previously suppressed languages, and rehabilitate and reimagine local cultural forms. Musicians who came to be identified with the New Taiwanese Song Movement (新台語歌運動) were leaders in this regard, casting off the shackles of Mandarin monolingualism and calling for alternatives to the *enka*-inflected sounds of the Hoklo popular songs that came before.[15] They cultivated a critical acumen with regard to politics, history, and local cultural practice. In developing what they felt would be a distinctly local sound, however, they did not merely look inward. On the contrary, as literature scholar Liao Ping-hui has argued, culture producers in the post–martial law period responded to their "double marginalization" from "the periphery of China to the margins of the world" by becoming "strongly desirous of transnational codes and technologies" that signified participation in the global order (1997, 57–58). Remixing the past rather than breaking from it entirely, they merged rap, rock, new wave, and traditional Taiwanese song forms. The product was a dual exercise in musical cosmopolitanism and local cultural revival that spoke powerfully to post–martial law desires for a Taiwan-centered musical (post)modernity.

Raoshe manifested as a particularly powerful resource for creative experimentation in the New Taiwanese Songs of Blacklist Workshop

(黑名單工作室), a collective of musicians comprising Wang Minghui (王明輝), Chen Zhuhui (陳主惠), Chen Ming-chang (陳明章), American Keith Stuart (司徒松), and several others. The group's name—a reference to surveillance measures carried out during martial law by the Garrison Command—was a provocation in itself, a bold declaration of intent to speak the previously unspeakable. The nine tracks on Blacklist Workshop's watershed 1989 album *Songs of Madness* (抓狂歌) gave voice to lower-middle-class protestations against social injustice and epistemic violence. The group was audacious in its choice of lyrical themes in songs like "Imperial Taipei" (台北帝國) and "Taxi" (計程車), providing, as Andrew F. Jones has put it, "epic and politically pointed testimony to the tribulations of modern Taiwanese history, confronting issues as diverse as Japanese and US colonialism, KMT repression, and the decidedly mixed blessings of the island's breakneck economic development, all through a defiantly local lens" (2005, 61). Several years before Jutoupi's *Funny Rap* series took up the theme of insanity, *Songs of Madness* deployed rap as a musical technique to sound a society in the midst of chaotic metamorphosis: multiple voices performed in multiple languages and invoked multiple musical traditions as they clamored for recognition.

One of four rap tracks on the album, "Democracy Bumpkin" (民主阿草), claims the distinction of having been among the last songs banned by Taiwan's broadcast media (Chen 2008, 896–97). Opening with the sound of a military band playing an out-of-tune rendition of the Republic of China government national anthem, the piece follows a group of young farmers who come from the countryside to indulge in the urbane luxuries of Taipei City, only to encounter a political protest. They profess no interest in politics and beseech a police officer to let them pass, in the process observing the activities of a pro-democracy agitator standing nearby:

人伊要來抗議那個老法統
老法統唉呀無天理
霸佔國會變把戲
歸陣閒閒在吃死米
有的嘛老搆強未喘氣
咱政府驚伊呀擋不著
咱的稅金乎伊拿去吊點滴
全世界攏在笑伊未見笑

he wants to protest against the old political system
the old political system is truly unreasonable
occupying the Congress playing tricks
a whole group of them idle just wasting rice

some are now so old they can hardly breathe
our government fears they can't live forever
so they take taxpayers' money to pay for IV injections
the outside world is laughing at their shamelessness[16]

The lyrics in this excerpt refer to the seemingly endless tenures of KMT officials elected before the retreat to Taiwan who clung to hopes of "recapturing the mainland" well into the 1980s, consuming resources ("wasting rice"), and undergoing medical treatments ("IV injections") to prolong their political life spans. New elections could not be held, and their abiding presence in the government ensured the entrenchment of the KMT's political interests, even as Taiwan inched toward a consolidated democratic system with more diverse representation.[17] As the song reaches its conclusion, the anthem returns, this time interwoven with the "Walkürenritt" leitmotif from Wagner's *Die Walküre.* The union of the two strains is deliciously derisive, underscoring the chasm between the government's heroic self-image and its actual decrepitude. Songs like "Democracy Bumpkin" demonstrated Blacklist Workshop's commitment to opposition politics at the end of the 1980s, and their adoption of *raoshe* magnified the subversiveness of their message. By privileging lyric over melody, it provided a means of foregrounding the group's extensive use of Hoklo, the suppressed language of Taiwan's disenfranchised majority. Rap also allowed the group to embrace the tonemic contours of the Hoklo language and to deliver their powerfully critical lyrics in a way that emphasized semantic comprehensibility over conformity to a superimposed melody.

In a section of the liner notes to *Songs of Madness*, Blacklist Workshop writes whimsically in the style of pharmaceutical instructions. Recalling the formative 1921 essay "Bedside Examination" (臨床講義), in which Taiwanese writer, physician, and political activist Chiang Wei-shui (蔣渭水) imagined Taiwan as a patient suffering from a variety of social and cultural afflictions, Blacklist Workshop suggests that the group's work be received as an antidote to a similar politics-induced malady. They write that "this album uses Western rap and rock genres, and is refined and ground with local specialty culture to help improve blood flow and reduce inflammation and toxicity."[18] This combination of musical styles, they suggest, can help cure those who suffer from excessive nostalgia (懷舊) for Taiwan's past, stubborn attachment (執著) to notions of local culture, apathy (冷感) toward social issues, and depression (鬱卒) induced by not being able to speak one's mind (Blacklist Workshop 1989). Unlike the artists discussed in the previous chapter, who understand rap in terms of a hip-hop ethos and as a self-sufficient enterprise, Blacklist Workshop

envisioned rap as part of the larger project of inventing a stylistically omnivorous New Taiwanese Song.

Beyond Blacklist Workshop, other singer-songwriters associated with
New Taiwanese Song—including Lim Giong (林強) and Jutoupi—also incorporated rap into their musical arsenal. Although Lim is known primarily as a folk rock musician, his 1992 song "Bullets at Hot Spring Village"
(溫泉鄉的槍子) about a grisly mafia murder in Taipei's Beitou District,
employs a rapping vocal style to deliver an intricate story in the local
vernacular. As discussed, Jutoupi began his career as a folk singer but
achieved notoriety through his three *Funny Rap* albums. It is interesting
to note that Ni Chonghua, who discovered and produced the LA Boyz
and The Party as well as Jutoupi, also participated in the genesis of New
Taiwanese Song. Prior to his tenure as general manager of MTV Taiwan,
he ran the independent label Mandala Works (真言社), on which all the
aforementioned albums were released. Although I parse the history of
rap into distinct *xiha* and *raoshe* narratives, Ni's presence in both strands
reflects how they intersected in the early 1990s at the level of production
and distribution.

Since the late 1990s, Mandopop artists such as Jay Chou and Wang
Leehom (王力宏) have continued to perform *raoshe* as an adjunct to other
styles in their work; indeed, much of their output might better be termed
"Mandohop" to acknowledge its deep debt to hip-hop aesthetics. Chou,
for many years the world's most popular Mandopop artist, frequently
fuses rap with sounds that index traditional Chinese musics, rock, pop,
and R&B, as in hits like "The Herbalist's Manual" (本草綱目), "Red Imitation" (紅模仿), and "Checkmate" (將軍).[19] Chou is in fact so well known
for his distinctive, near-monotone style of *raoshe* that indie band Totem
(圖騰樂團), led by Indigenous 'Amis singer-songwriter Suming (舒米
恩), mimics it in a satirical 2006 Mandarin- and 'Amis-language song
called "I Am Not Jay Chou" (我不是周杰倫). Notably, Totem also experi-
ments with *raoshe* elsewhere on the group's 2006 album *Over There I Sing*
(我在那邊唱) on tracks that commingle rap, Latin, and Indigenous sounds.

While the majority of Wang Leehom's songs follow David Tao in their
invocation of R&B, Wang first began incorporating rap into his music in
the late 1990s. His 2000 album *Forever's First Day* (永遠的第一天) includes a cover of the 1978 Hou Dejian (侯德健) song "Descendants of the
Dragon" (龍的傳人), to which Wang added an autobiographical English-
language rap bridge about a couple—his parents—who emigrates to the
United States from Taiwan in search of greater educational and economic
opportunity.[20] Since recording "Descendants of the Dragon," Wang has
frequently employed *raoshe* in songs exploring the cultural dynamics of
Chinese diasporic identity. In the liner notes to his 2004 album *Shangri-la*

(心中的日月), he unveiled what he called his "chinked-out" style, which "repossesses the word [chink]" to describe "a sound that is international, and at the same time, Chinese." According to Wang, *Shangri-la* drew on "China's most precious and untapped resources, the musics of its 'shao shu min zu,' or ethnic minorities" to create "an R&B/hip-hop album that…the whole world can identify as being Chinese" (Wang 2004).[21] Songs like "Heroes of Earth" (蓋世英雄) and "Beside the Plum Blossoms" (在梅邊) juxtapose rap with Peking and Kun opera-style singing, articulating simultaneously Chinese nationalist and globalist aspirations.

Across the syncretic popular music landscape of Taiwan, rap is present as a musical technique in songs by artists associated with the island's rock, folk, and pop music scenes. Defining "rap" purely in terms of a globally circulating hip-hop culture, and "rappers" as artists who are committed exclusively to the performance of rap music, obscures the heterogeneous assortment of performers who have generated effects and meanings from rap. It is possible both to trace an unbroken lineage from Taiwan rap back to a broader global hip-hop and to recognize rap's fragmented presence as *raoshe* within the disparate popular music currents on the island. The next part of this chapter examines the specific current of *liām-kua*, which, refashioned and amplified by roots-seeking scholars and musicians in the mid-1970s, has since found a place in the lexicon of Taiwan rap.

Resignifying Rap as Local Narrative Tradition in *Liām-kua*

Rappers, particularly those working in the Hoklo language, appropriated the traditional narrative song genre *liām-kua* as both sound and symbol in the years following the end of martial law. Their resignification calls to mind Cheryl L. Keyes's notion of "cultural reversioning," "the foregrounding (consciously and unconsciously) of African-centered concepts" in rap (2002, 21). Although Keyes is resolute in her understanding of rap as "indigenous to the United States," her analyses of rap's musical and performative features consider its antecedents in the varied oral traditions of Africa, African America, and the Caribbean. She offers "cultural reversioning" as a way of thinking through the processes by which performers position themselves as alternately proximal to and removed from traditional influences. Taiwan rap's historical ties to *liām-kua* likewise occasions consideration of the ways in which musicians can be said to "signify on" local narrative tradition in their performances, to play with and profit from similarities between the genres. Theorized extensively by Henry Louis Gates (1988), "signifyin(g)" describes African American ritual practices of wordplay. In signifyin(g), individuals deploy strategies of indirection, misdirection, reversal, and double-meaning in everyday speech and storytelling acts—techniques that Taiwan's rappers share with their American counterparts as well as traditional narrative performers.

Liām-kua is a member of the *shuochang* family of traditional Chinese musical narrative performance genres. It finds its roots in a style of *shuochang* called *jinge* (錦歌), which traveled to Taiwan during the Ming and Qing Dynasties with migrants from Fujian and Guangdong Provinces, but acquired unique characteristics over the course of several centuries on the island (Chen 2008, 350–52). Until about the 1960s, *liām-kua* flourished as a form of popular entertainment for members of Taiwan's largely agrarian society. In urban and rural settings alike, it was performed by beggars, itinerant blind musicians, and traveling medicine sellers to rapt audiences hungry for amusements to fill the quiet evening hours. Before the advent of mass media, these presentations served not only as pleasant distractions from the responsibilities of work and family life, but also as technologies for the dissemination of information and the teaching of morals and ethics.

Although *liām-kua* performance practice has changed over time and varies with location, in the present day it is typically performed by a vocal soloist who accompanies him- or herself on an instrument, more often than not a *yueqin* (月琴, "moon lute"); supplemental instrumentalists may also be present in some cases, thickening the musical texture (see fig. 2.1). Yang Hsiu-ching (楊秀卿), a blind *yueqin* player and perhaps the most famous living performer of *liām-kua*, often takes the stage with her husband, who accompanies her on the bowed instrument *daguangxian* (大廣弦). Following the imperative of *shuochang* genres to tell a tale, musicians are tasked with balancing "a semantically intelligible linguistic communication of the storyline (according to the tonal requirements of the language) with the aesthetic needs of the delivery style in the act of performance" (Lawson 2011, 7–8). *Liām-kua* artists remain seated, do not wear costumes related to the content of their songs, and do not typically gesture physically. Their performances are primarily sung but may also include long spoken interludes. Vocal melodies are derived from a limited number of tune types—for example, the "Seven-Character Tune" (七字調), "River and Lake Tune" (江湖調), and "Duma Tune" (都馬調)—the contours of which bend and flex to accommodate the tones of Hoklo. The most celebrated *liām-kua* performers are virtuosic in their abilities to improvise within these constraints.[22]

Throughout much of the Japanese colonial period, the genre enjoyed consistent patronage on the island. Indeed, *liām-kua* performances were among the first targets of record companies in Taiwan, predating the emergence of Hoklo popular songs by several years (Huang 2006, 15). Publishers in Shanghai and Fujian conducted a brisk trade in *liām-kua*

FIG. 2.1. *Liām-kua* performers at Bangka Park (艋舺公園) in Taipei, December 5, 2009. Photograph by author.

songbooks (歌仔冊) for public consumption (Tsai Hsin-hsin [蔡欣欣] interview, June 9, 2011).[23] As part of Japan's attempts to consolidate its rule over Taiwan, however, colonial authorities clamped down on both trade with China and the expression of local languages and cultural forms at the end of the 1930s. Things did not improve much following the end of the war; while KMT administrators did not ban the performance of *liām-kua* outright, policies promoting Mandarin as the national tongue enervated the production of Hoklo culture.

As the island transitioned to an industrial economy and forms of mass-mediated popular entertainment proliferated, *liām-kua* continued to recede from public awareness, sustained only through the efforts of enthusiasts and a small number of accomplished older artists. Other *shuochang* arts, such as ballad-singing from the Hengchun Peninsula region in southern Taiwan (恆春歌謠), languished similarly during that period.[24] Although their performance practices are somewhat similar, Hengchun folk songs use a different set of fixed tunes (調) than *liām-kua*, and scholars typically consider them as distinct genres. Nevertheless, it is my experience that laypeople do not distinguish between the two in everyday parlance, but refer to all local *shuochang* genres as either *shuochang*, *liām-kua*, or *minyao* (民謠, folk ballads).

In spite of challenges to their survival, these musical narrative traditions did not vanish entirely but resurfaced instead on the concert stage. In 1966 ethnomusicologists Hsu Tsang-houei (許常惠) and Shih Wei-liang (史惟亮) embarked on a major project to survey the full range of musics of the island, including those of Hoklo, Hakka, and Indigenous peoples.[25] A year into this project, they stumbled upon Chen Da (陳達), an elderly, impoverished ballad singer from Hengchun who had been performing in that area for decades. Proclaiming him the soul of Taiwanese folk music, Hsu invited Chen to Taipei to record in 1971 and again in 1977, as well as to perform in a number of landmark concerts. The results of this collaboration—among them the albums *Folk Musician Chen Da and His Songs* (民族樂手陳達和他的歌) and *Chen Da and Hengchun Tune Shuochang* (陳達與恆春調說唱)—were highly influential to young nativist intellectuals steeped at that time in debates about Taiwan consciousness and its implications for the future of musical and literary culture on the island (Liu 2010, 548).

Many of these intellectuals were participants in the Modern Folk Song Movement (現代民歌運動), which emerged in the mid-1970s in part as a response to American cultural imperialism on the island. In brief, the movement encompassed a heterogeneous assortment of artists working to reclaim domestic popular music from the totalizing influence of both foreign and commercial interests. Musicians Yang Xian (楊弦), Li Shuangzi (李雙澤), and Ara Kimbo (aka Hu Defu 胡德夫) inspired students throughout the island to take up their acoustic guitars and, as a popular slogan from the period put it, "sing their own songs" (唱自己的歌).[26] Their efforts to define a local sound generated a number of different strategies: although cultural production during the earlier stages of the movement aligned closely with state-sanctioned nationalist ideologies—promoting the performance of "new Chinese folk songs" rather than American-style pop music—this "quickly gave way to 'Taiwanese folk songs,' with local references accentuated" (Chang 2004, 105). When we spoke in 2010, music critic Ma Shih-fang noted Hsu Tsang-houei's "rediscovery" of Chen Da as a watershed moment in the development of the island's new folk sounds. Ma witnessed this history firsthand alongside his mother, Tao Xiaoqing (陶曉清), a professional broadcaster and pivotal figure in the Modern Folk Song Movement:

We rediscovered Chen Da back in the '70s. . . . He made his first field recording back in the late '60s. But back then not too many people knew him except for the small circle of musicologists. And it wasn't until the mid-'70s that Chen Da became a household name, and that was because some younger people invited him to come to Taipei to play in a folk club and younger people recognized his music, and then listened to his record. They were so shocked. At first they, you know, they listened to records from the US, they knew Mississippi John Hurt, they knew Robert Johnson . . . but after Chen Da they suddenly realized we have our own, and he's even cooler than Mississippi John Hurt! Some old guy playing his *yueqin*. . . . So Chen Da was kind of an icon. After he was gone, people from the folk movement, and later Chen Ming-chang [of Blacklist Workshop], later the New Taiwanese Song Movement, and later Taiwanese hip-hop and Taiwanese rock, they all went back to Chen Da. (interview, January 18, 2010)

So even as *liām-kua* and the *shuochang* arts gradually shed their mantle as popular forms of entertainment in the latter half of the twentieth century, nativist proponents of modern folk music invested them with symbolic capital as authentic loci of Taiwanese folk culture. In such an atmosphere, celebrated practitioners like Chen Da ascended to icon status and came to exert tremendous influence on the creation of new music during the 1970s and '80s.

Hearing/Voicing *Liām-kua* in Rap

Blacklist Workshop's Chen Ming-chang was in his early twenties when Chen Da galvanized the new folk scene, and he became aware of the celebrated performer's work through the Cloud Gate Dance Theater's (雲門舞集) 1979 production *Heritage* (薪傳), to which Chen Da had contributed music. In a 2011 magazine article, Chen Ming-chang describes his initial response to hearing Chen Da's work: "I discovered that what I was lacking [in my music] was precisely an emotional connection to the land, some reflection on local culture. When I looked back at the Mandarin-language songs I had done in the past, I was immediately really shocked" (Guo 2011). Chen has often spoken about the influence of traditional musical narrative genres on his compositions; much of his work following Blacklist Workshop has referenced Chen Da or other narrative singers in some way, and he is now himself a celebrated performer and teacher of *yueqin*.

   Liām-kua was a natural source of inspiration for Blacklist Workshop, as well as for Jutoupi and other musicians who played key roles in the development of rap music via New Taiwanese Song. Not only did *liām-kua* have political salience as a representation of an "authentic" Taiwanese expressive culture, but it also modeled techniques for embracing the tonemic contours of Hoklo and thereby rendering an intelligible communication of lyrics. *Liām-kua* is an example of what Chao Yuen Ren (趙元任) classified as a "singsong" style, which demands that its practitioners articulate lexical tones in musical performance (1956, 52–59). Many performers of Hoklo popular songs produced after the 1930s had departed from this practice, preferring to marry pentatonic vocal lines and diatonic accompaniments without particular regard for preserving speech tone.[27] Performer and *liām-kua* scholar Wang Chen-yi (王振義) opines that in the 1950s and '60s, "many [Hoklo] songs were written in a way that tended to compromise the [Hoklo] language's tonal or musical quality, and the results sometimes made your flesh creep" (Gao 2007).[28] For participants in New Taiwanese Song, the *liām-kua* style of performance offered the possibility of a corrective to this situation, that is, the restoration of greater semantic comprehensibility.

Because the "singsong" storytelling quality of *liām-kua* called to mind the American hip-hop that had begun to infiltrate Taiwan's airwaves by the end of the 1980s, Blacklist Workshop had the opportunity to suggest that *liām-kua*-style performance could speak to contemporary topics and appeal to contemporary sensibilities. As Chen Ming-chang remarked in a 2000 interview published in the English-language periodical *Taiwan Review*, "Rap versions of Taiwanese songs were new at that time, and listeners probably found them fresh. . . . They dealt with things like the grief you get driving a taxi for a living. They had a strong local cultural flavor because they were essentially storytelling, true-to-life dramas" (Her 2000).[29] Affirming this hypothesis, music critic Lin Zonghong (林宗弘), who recognized the influence of local musical narrative traditions in *Songs of Madness*, wrote in a 1993 article about the album: "The songs blend black reggae music, rap, and Taiwan's *tsáp-liām-á* (雜念仔), a tune type employed in narrative genres like *liām-kua* and Taiwanese opera style to portray the many facades of modern Taiwanese society" (Lin 2009, 38–39). The rap tracks on *Songs of Madness* do not sound exactly like traditional *liām-kua*, but they clearly bear the imprint of the tradition in at least three respects. First, they are predominantly in the Hoklo language and carefully preserve the tonemic inflection of lyrics. Second, they provide incisive social commentary and seek to inspire reflection on moral and ethical problems. Last, they are fully narrative, with vividly rendered characters and unfolding storylines.

Blacklist Workshop alluded sonically to *liām-kua* but used the English term "rap" to describe their particular brand of speech-song vocal performance; Zhu Yuexin, recording as Jutoupi, made an even more direct reference to narrative song by titling his series of albums—which I have thus far referred to by their English name *Funny Rap*—*Funny Liām-kua*. None of the three-dozen or so rap tracks that Jutoupi recorded between 1994 and 1995 abide by the musical conventions of traditional *liām-kua*, but they retain its flavors in a manner similar to Blacklist Workshop's *Songs of Madness*. When I interviewed Zhu in 2010, he referred to a link between rap and *liām-kua* just a few moments into our conversation: "The concept of 'rap' already existed in old Taiwanese 'folksongs,' [for instance in] *liām-kua*." He then sang a short tune and imitated the plucking sound of *yueqin* vocally before continuing: "That's *qigai diao* [乞丐調], the 'Beggar's Tune,' that's what it is. It's like 'Mississippi blues.' . . . Way back when it had a little [of rap], it was like 'speech,' not so 'melodic,' [it was] *shuochang* . . ." (interview, October 10, 2010).[30] In Zhu's formulation, rap is a "concept"

(概念) rather than a genre, defined as an integrated speech-song technique that has a life prior to and apart from contemporary hip-hop. While he frames rap and *liām-kua* as independent exercises, Zhu suggested to me that rap is comprehensible to him as a Taiwanese listener in part because of its consonance with the *liām-kua* tradition. His argument that rap "already existed in old Taiwanese folksongs" attributes to *liām-kua* a prescient quality, a sense of latent modernity and inherent compatibility with global cosmopolitan trends. Zhu's reference to the Mississippi blues calls to mind Ma Shih-fang's statements regarding the reception of Chen Da's music in the 1970s, when listeners "suddenly realized we have our own, and he's even cooler than Mississippi John Hurt!" Zhu and Ma posit *liām-kua* as echoing or even anticipating the forms of African American expressive culture that ultimately informed the development of hip-hop. Their perspectives bind the histories of these three genres—*liām-kua*, blues, and rap—closely together.

For all the similarities between their two projects, Jutoupi's rapprochement with both *liām-kua* and hip-hop is more explicit than Blacklist Workshop's. The title *Funny Liām-kua* makes the series' intentions quite plain, and Jutoupi's vocalizations mobilize certain idiomatic features of *liām-kua* performance that are absent from *Songs of Madness*. For example, on the track "Taiwan Language Battle" (IF U 惦惦 NO BODY SAY U 矮狗), Jutoupi plays the parts of multiple characters the way a traditional *liām-kua* performer might, by changing the register and timbre of his voice in imitation of different personalities. The song describes a journey into the heart of Taipei, wherein the narrator notes that he is surrounded by signage in foreign languages, advertising everything from pachinko parlors and karaoke to Kentucky Fried Chicken and Tower Records. As he steeps in this pointedly colonial visual cacophony, he overhears conversations among speakers of Japanese-accented English, Taiwanese Mandarin, and official standard Mandarin.[31] One female character is performed by a guest vocalist, but Jutoupi takes on the rest himself, as in this excerpt:

S1: 同學你幾歲阿 / S2: 我洗腳水啦
S3: 老師你鑰匙掉了 / S4: 沒有關係
S5: How old are you? / S6: 阿ㄋㄛ I'm dirty.

S1: Classmate, how old are you? / S2: That's my footbath water.
S3: Teacher, you dropped your keys / S4: It doesn't matter.
S5: How old are you? / S6: Well, I'm dirty.

Jutoupi assumes the roles of all six speakers here, each attempting some part of an exchange that generates a comical misunderstanding. In the first, a student (S1) speaking official standard Mandarin asks another student (S2) his age, to which the other student intends to respond "I'm nineteen years old" (我十九歲啦, *wo shijiu sui la*). Because of his thick Hoklo accent, however, the utterance sounds more like the nonsense phrase "That's my footbath water" (我洗腳水啦, *wo xijiao shui la*). In the second, a student (S3) intends to tell his teacher "You dropped your keys" (你鑰匙掉了, *ni yaoshi diaole*). Again, because of his accent—especially his tendency to substitute the retroflex sibilant with a dental sibilant—it sounds more as if he is prophesying, "You're going to die" (你要死掉了, *ni yao sidiaole*), to which the teacher responds (S4) nonchalantly, "It doesn't matter" (沒有關係, *meiyou guanxi*). Finally, a fluent English speaker (S5) asks the age of someone with a heavy Japanese accent (S6), who intends to respond that he is thirty but stumbles over the voiceless dental fricative such that he declares himself to have a personal hygiene problem. The song's lyrics highlight the difficulties of communicating about even the most prosaic things in Taiwan's multilingual society, subtly critiquing the KMT's attempts to "standardize" speech on the island through imposition of Mandarin as the national language.[32]

Jutoupi's performance of multiple characters in rapid succession calls to mind the rhythms of comic *liām-kua*, but the track's use of extended vocal techniques—beatboxing, specifically—places it equally in the sound world of hip-hop. In "Taiwan Language Battle," Jutoupi beatboxes for much of the song's duration, impersonating the sounds of a snare drum, hi-hat, and bass drum, as well as vocally approximating the sound of a DJ scratching a record. To this end, he employs an array of techniques, including lip oscillations, inhalations, and growls. The use of beatboxing accompaniment as opposed to a traditional instrument such as *yueqin* creates a novel backdrop for Jutoupi's *liām-kua* stylings. Moreover, his combination of these disparate elements represents sonically the processes of modernization, globalization, and hybridization that the lyrics so neatly describe.

"Real Taiwan-Style *Liām-kua*" aka "Taiwan Traditional Hip Hop Style"

Following in Jutoupi's footsteps, Taipei-based Kou Chou Ching has described their music in Hoklo as "real Taiwan-style *liām-kua*" (正港台灣味唸歌) and in English as "Taiwan traditional hip hop style" (see fig. 2.2).[33] The group—two MCs, a DJ, and two instrumentalists with backgrounds in traditional musics—formed in 2003 and attracted a significant underground following on the island. Like both Blacklist Workshop and Jutoupi, the music of Kou Chou Ching reflects the group's close engagement with social justice and human rights advocacy, and group

FIG. 2.2. Kou Chou Ching promotional material, featuring the Hoklo phrase "real Taiwan-style *liām-kua*" (正港台灣味唸歌) and the English "Taiwan traditional hip hop style." Image produced by Djebala, courtesy of Kou Chou Ching.

members are outspoken in their support for Taiwan's sovereignty. As such, their work reflects an abiding interest in local cultural practice in both its form and content. They are recognized for their use of multiple local languages in their songs—especially Hoklo and Hakka—and their predilection for sampling from historic recordings. When I interviewed MC Fan Chiang, a member of the group until 2014, he described his notion of hip-hop not as a formula for emulating American artists, but as a set of guidelines for (re)discovering and (re)deploying local sonic artifacts in compositions that comment on issues of local importance. Invoking *liām-kua* in their translation of "hip-hop," Kou Chou Ching channels that genre's long-standing significance as both a source of such commentary and a potent symbol of Taiwanese cultural heritage:

> Most elderly people, when it comes to this [hip-hop], don't really understand it, they think, "I don't know what you're talking about." But actually when these elderly people were young, they listened to something similar, and it was this thing, *liām-kua*, that we are always talking about. It's actually very similar, although in terms of the music it's something different, actually very similar. It has things very similar to "rap," very similar to "old-school rap." And it also has "freestyle," it is very improvisational [follow your heart/mind-like], because it doesn't have set lyrics. It's improvisational, whatever you think of you just recite it. Then you've got to rhyme, got to rhyme, got to rhyme....[34] (Fan Chiang interview, April 7, 2010)

Fan Chiang suggests that *liām-kua* and hip-hop share qualities that make the two forms mutually comprehensible even if they developed independently of one another. Based on their exposure to *liām-kua*, he opines, older audiences should be able to access Kou Chou Ching's brand of "real Taiwan-style hip hop," which features vocals that shift back and forth along the speech-song continuum and implements similar kinds of improvisation and rhyme. Acknowledging that they are different in their particulars, Fan Chiang nevertheless constructs hip-hop as a continuation of local tradition.

The group further cultivates this relationship through the hip-hop practice of sampling from and citing traditional musics, including *liām-kua* and pieces associated with other *shuochang* genres. For example, their song "Against Nature" (逆天) samples Chen Da's *yueqin* accompaniment from his "Laborer's Song" (長工歌), and "Tiu Tiu Thinking Of" (丟丟思想起) builds its groove on repeating melodic fragments from the children's folk tune "Tiu-tiu-tâng" (丟丟銅) and the Hengchun *shuochang* tune "Thinking Of…" (思想起). In each of these, traditional narrative song is interpolated into Kou Chou Ching's newer narratives about environmental degradation and the loss of childhood innocence, respectively. Layers upon layers of stories blur the line between traditional narrative and contemporary rap practices.

The below transcription (musical example 2.1) of an excerpt from the 2007 track "Good Appetite" (好嘴斗) provides a glimpse of the group's approach to integrating "real Taiwan-style *liām-kua*" with a sample from a narrative song, the celebrated Uncle Qilin's (其麟伯) "Improvisation on the Burning of a Fishnet-Drying Hut" (火燒罟寮隨興曲). "Good Appetite" explores the decline of Taiwanese open-air banquet culture, as the custom of setting up outdoor tables to commemorate major life-cycle events has gradually given way to indoor celebrations at luxury hotels and catering facilities. Kou Chou Ching's lyrics mourn the loss of the tactile pleasures of community and the cultural practices that have traditionally attended outdoor festivities, including performances of Taiwanese opera and *beiguan* (北管) music.[35] One measure of Uncle Qilin's *yueqin* accompaniment (m. 1) is fodder for an ostinato figure that repeats for the duration of the piece. It is doubled every so often by *suona* (嗩吶) (mm. 2–3 and 6–7), a double-reed horn, performed by one of the group's two instrumentalists. The resulting effect is one of persistent nostalgia—a traditional sound that, in repetition, seems to mark the passing of time as surely as a ticking clock. For those attentive to the sample's original context, highlighted in the liner notes to the album on which "Good Appetite" appears, the intertextual interplay between Uncle Qilin's narrative and Kou Chou Ching's provides perspective on the time period during which outdoor banquets were common. Indeed, "Improvisation on the Burning of a Fishnet-Drying Hut" is not about the joys of life in a simpler time, but about the bitterness of lost

MUSICAL EXAMPLE 2.1. Transcription of an excerpt from Kou Chou Ching's "Good Appetite" (好嘴斗), approx. 1:20–1:40.

love and the tragic outcomes of a poor marriage in a rural seaside village. As Fish Lin and Fan Chiang rap about the olden days, when those living in agrarian Taiwan labored hard and had less to eat, the sample reminds informed listeners that outdoor banquets traditionally punctuated lives of privation and struggle. Uncle Qilin's voice, which appears at m. 8 and then sporadically throughout the song, seems to call out from the past, anointing Kou Chou Ching his successors in storytelling.

Rap informed by traditional narrative performance is not the sole province of musicians who perform in Hoklo. Taipei-based rapper Manchuker, for example, suggests that the roots of Mandarin hip-hop also lie in a concatenated network of theatrical and *shuochang* styles:

> Chinese people had hip-hop a long time ago, Chinese people had rap a long time ago, Chinese people had R&B a long time ago. It's just that we never updated our skill, we never updated our style. . . . Like before, like those Chinese operas, *jingju, xiangsheng*—they're all hip-hop! They were telling the stories of society, just like how American people do with R&B and hip-hop these days. So it's already in our blood. We just have to find a new way to express it. (interview, September 21, 2010)

Manchuker propounds a sense of continuity among the narrative impulses of hip-hop and Chinese genres like *jingju* (京劇, Peking opera) and *xiangsheng* (相聲, cross-talk). He does not merely localize rap music but claims it as already local. To Manchuker, rap music—whether we call it *xiha, raoshe*, or *liām-kua*—constitutes an "update" of something "already in our blood." By this logic, rap fulfills a crucial role once performed by traditional narrative genres, to tell "the stories of society."

The broader consequences of this kind of resignification for traditional musics remains to be seen. Tony Mitchell and Alastair Pennycook write about similar assertions by Indigenous Australian, Maori, Somalian, and Senegalese rappers in terms of "modes of self-fashioning" and argue that taking such claims seriously can open up new ways of thinking about global hip-hops not as adaptations (or bastardizations) of a pure and originary hip-hop with immaculate roots in the South Bronx, but as something with the potential to "radically [reshape] the ways in which we can understand global and local cultural and linguistic formations" (2009, 40). Moreover, attention to the ways that rappers invoke local oral-poetic and musical narrative forms can tell us something about the ways in which local traditions travel and transform (34). As the community of traditional *liām-kua* performers grays and younger generations decline to replace them, it is entirely possible that rap will subsume *liām-kua* in the minds of listeners as Taiwan's musical storytelling genre par excellence.

Conversations I had with scholars and performers of traditional arts in Taiwan revealed, perhaps unsurprisingly, resistance to this idea. One Taipei-based musicologist with whom I chatted about this project asserted that rappers were simply confused about *liām-kua* and lacked sufficient musical training to understand its difference from their art. In an interview on a televised traditional arts variety program, presenter Xu Gengxiu (許耿修) asked *liām-kua* performer Zhou Dingbang (周定邦) whether *liām-kua* bears any relation to "today's popular Western *raoshe*" (現在西洋流行的饒舌), to which Zhou responded in no uncertain terms and with no further elaboration: "They are completely different" (完全不同) (Kunshan Television 2009). I have found to the contrary that rappers readily acknowledge the distinctions—formal and functional, musical and methodological—between rap and *liām-kua*. Their music does not conflate the two; rather, it serves as a starting point from which listeners may choose to navigate multiple paths of exploration—to traditional musics, hip-hop, or the sonorous spaces in between.

As they have unfolded, chapters 1 and 2 have advanced complementary historiographies. The first centers the words and ideas of members of the current rap scene and foregrounds ethnographically their many and varied contributions to *xiha*'s development. The second proposes ways of creatively contextualizing rap in the *longue durée* of local popular (*raoshe*) and traditional (*liām-kua*) music histories. Together, these chapters uplift a history of rap that is multivalent and multivocal, and that declines to suggest a greater stylistic or ideological homogeneity among past and present rap artists than truly exists. By distilling the passionate, protean stories imparted to me into separate but overlapping narratives, I attempt to elucidate the myriad pathways by which rap has acquired its current multifaceted character. My goal is not to legitimate one discourse at the expense of the others but to demonstrate that all are equally sensible means of describing the music's development on the island—in other words, to synchronize the polyphony. As a conceptual category, rap permits its performers in Taiwan to inscribe within it a variety of meanings that in turn open onto many pasts. *Xiha, raoshe*, and *liām-kua* are often used interchangeably, impressionistically, and evocatively by members of the community. One can deploy *raoshe* in *xiha*; just as in the English "rap" and "hip-hop," those terms often appear as synonyms even if "hip-hop" refers more technically to a composite cultural movement and "rap" to specific musical practices. Likewise, as Kou Chou Ching demonstrates, *liām-kua* can be conceived as a way of doing *xiha* locally.

Participants in rap—which has operated for most of its existence outside the purview of the corporate music industry—labored to create the conditions of their own audibility after the end of government censorship and media monopolies. Although artists diverge in their understanding of rap's relationship to local and global pasts, they express a common desire to exert a measure of control over how their work is received, interpreted, and interpellated into different ideological structures. Their accounts of the music's history vary not merely as a function of linguistic determinism but also in accordance with the reorganization of cultural, political, and economic capital that transpired after the end of martial law and through subsequent processes of democratization and neoliberalization. What one calls rap in Taiwan is therefore not an exact science—indeed, we might posit rap instead as a "rich semiotic mode" (Turino 1999, 237), capable of conferring diverse meanings. Rap has the capacity to reach audiences however receptive they may be to it: some gravitate to the sense of community it offers, some to the feelings of pleasure and/or power it induces, and some to the civic and political engagement it catalyzes.

PART TWO
Narratives and Knowledge

3
MASCULINITY POLITICS AND RAP'S FRATERNAL ORDER

In the crisp early morning hours, Dwagie stood on a broad thoroughfare in the Neihu District of Taipei, his back to a crowd of about two hundred people. Still and reverent, most in the crowd kept their eyes firmly affixed to the MC, but Dwagie turned his attention to music video director Lai Yingzai (賴映仔), perched atop a weatherworn blue dolly jib and wielding a large digital camera some fifty yards away. As Lai bellowed, "Action!" Dwagie led everyone behind him in a slow, deliberate procession down the street toward the camera. After a minute or two, all parties halted, doubled back to their original positions, and stood silently once again. This sequence of events repeated itself at least a dozen more times during the course of a 2010 video shoot for the song "Change Taiwan" (改變台灣), which was written and recorded on commission from the DPP in advance of the 2010 municipal elections.[1] Dwagie had invited fellow performers and members of university *xiha* clubs from the island's largest municipalities to appear in the clip with the goal of encouraging young people from those areas to vote. Released on the Internet several weeks later, the final cut incorporated the footage of the processing crowd to dramatic effect: as Dwagie rapped in his characteristically gruff voice, "Young soldiers, remember these words, one day we will change Taiwan," he had at his back a *xiha gens d'armes*, marching forward in slow motion, eyes steely, heads held high (see fig. 3.1).

Scant information about these "young soldiers" could be inferred from their appearance alone. Some were attired in ways that hinted at their places of origin. Those who had come from the southern city of Tainan wore black baseball caps emblazoned with the sign of Tainan-native Dwagie's creative collective, Kung Fu Entertainment: the character *gong* (功, "achievement" or "merit") embroidered in yellow.[2] Similarly, those from Taichung City in central Taiwan donned red caps reading "911," the

FIG. 3.1. Participants film a scene for Dwagie's "Change Taiwan" video, October 17, 2010. Photograph by author.

name of a popular local crew, in white. Aside from their hometowns, the only discernible unifying feature of the two hundred individuals on parade that morning was that nearly all—like the crowd at the 921.87 Rap Benefit Concert the previous year—appeared to be young men.[3] Although Dwagie had not indicated a gender preference in his online request for participation in the shoot, men alone had answered the call. The turnout, he later told me, did not surprise him. With the exception of one artist—Miss KO, at that time a Taiwanese American newcomer to the scene—there were no professional women *xiha* MCs on the island, and only a handful of professional women *xiha* DJs. Recording studios and rehearsal rooms I visited were clearly marked as spaces for male homosocial interaction by the presence of cisgender, heterosexual male audience-based magazines, video game consoles emitting the rat-a-tat-tat of gunfire, and cigarettes sending ribbons of tarry smoke into the air.[4] Among audiences at many rap concerts and community events, small clusters of women stood out conspicuously in vast fields of men. *Xiha* clubs, the extracurricular organizations around which the rap community coheres at the island's universities, had an almost exclusively male membership.

Given these demographics, the crowd following Dwagie in the video for "Change Taiwan" stood as striking physical evidence of an entrenched and established reality: rap music in Taiwan is made primarily by and for a community of young men. Artists and fans with whom I have spoken over the years have attributed this state of affairs to two primary conditions. First, they assert that the lack of female participation in the scene is in step with the perceived male-centricity of American hip-hop. Although women have been active participants in hip-hop from its beginnings— buried by "amnestic analyses" of Black popular music and culture (Rabaka 2012, 3)—the globally circulating hip-hop that *xiha* artists in Taiwan first embraced in the early 2000s was, indeed, masculinist in its leanings. Gender ideologies in the Taiwan rap scene are expressed in terms of fidelity to that norm, as well as to the hip-hop imperative to keep it real. Among rap artists and audiences in Taiwan, keeping it real manifests in acts of masculine agency characterized by unambiguous and sometimes confrontational expressions of pain, pleasure, anger, and desire. Second, community members often understand rap's gender practices as consonant with a Confucian paradigm that posits women as inherently *nei* (內, "inside")—reserved, refined, and introverted—and men as inherently *wai* (外, "outside")—audacious, coarse, and extroverted. Within this framework, women are cast not merely as constitutionally unsuited to performing rap music but also as fundamentally disinterested in the ugliness that often attends "keeping it real."

Rappers' tendency to rationalize the makeup of their community with recourse to Confucian gender-role discourses, linchpins of Cold War cultural and educational policy under KMT hegemony, seems at odds with their otherwise progressive politics. Just as Dwagie implored young listeners to "change Taiwan" by exercising their hard-won right to democratic participation, many other MCs lend their voices to causes identified in Taiwan with progressive worldviews, such as the environmental, antinuclear, transitional justice, and Indigenous rights movements, as well as, in some cases, the Taiwan independence movement.[5] And yet these same figures have, for the majority of *xiha*'s history, resisted the interpellation of feminist and queer politics that burgeoned on the island during the 1990s and 2000s in the twilight of authoritarian rule.[6] Even as those I interviewed expressed their admiration for American female MCs like Missy Elliott and Nicki Minaj, Canadian MC Eternia, and Japanese MC Miss Monday, they resolved that Taiwan rap is essentially men's music and that the rap scene is, at its core, a fraternal order.

Besides the scene's de facto exclusion of women, rap's male dominance responds to a series of sociocultural, political, and economic disjunctures that unsettled gender roles on the island over the course of the past three decades. During this time, marriage and fertility rates have declined precipitously, women's labor participation has increased, incomes have stagnated, and compulsory military service requirements, which served as rites of passage for young Taiwanese men following their initiation by the KMT in 1951, have been significantly reduced. In the context of these changes, rap has created meaningful new spaces for male sociality, avenues for male self-empowerment, and opportunities for the articulation of multiple masculine identities not readily audible in the island's mainstream popular musics. In other words, the rap scene has developed into a terrain of what R. W. Connell has termed "masculinity politics": "Those mobilizations and struggles where the meaning of masculine gender is at issue, and, with it, men's position in gender relations" (2005, 205). Masculinity politics matter because they are critical mechanisms for determining control over social resources and they exert a profound shaping force on the social environment. In both recordings and community events, artists invoke the masculine ethos of rap in their various efforts to alter social reality, to "change Taiwan."

To what end, this change? Community members do not advocate a return in Taiwan at large to the modes of social organization and gendered discourse promoted by the KMT's state power and ideological apparatus under martial law, or in any particular past preceding KMT hegemony. Rather, they reimagine Confucian gender regimes within the setting of Taiwan's present democracy. Through *xiha*-based coalition-building—by modeling and practicing solidarity, hospitality, and friendship with their male colleagues on the island—they claim the power to catalyze civic and political engagement.

"Insiders" and "Outsiders": Sounding Gender

Although women artists and fans are not actively and intentionally excluded from the Taiwan rap scene, their absence is often explained in terms of innate gendered preferences and abilities that dovetail with traditional worldviews. As Kay Kaufman Shelemay argues in her work on the male-dominated Syrian Jewish *pizmon* tradition, excavating women's silence can engender an understanding of gendered power relations within musical communities (2009, 269). Taiwanese women are not prohibited by doctrine from performing rap music, but, as Dwagie explained to me: "Taiwanese women are relatively traditional, and most don't really want to be like men. Because in Taiwan, after all, men are more outside [*wai*] and women are more inside [*nei*]. Women are more sensitive. Another thing is that everyone thinks rap has a lot of foul language, expresses dissatisfaction, and speaks about low and dirty things. So women are under the impression that it's like this, and they don't want to perform" (interview, September 26, 2010). Dwagie made recourse to a *nei-wai* binary in explaining the dearth of women in rap, but he also suggested that they have some agency in the matter: profanity and expressions of dissent are the province of men, and unless women are open to troubling the *nei-wai* boundary and assimilating masculine norms—he assumes that most are not—rap music holds little appeal. Artist after artist offered the same reasons for the lack of female participation in rap. Even Taipei-based DJ Noodles (麵麵), who holds the distinction of having been the first woman Disco Mix Club world championship finalist in 2006, told me with a deep sigh that rap is dominated by men because it has little to offer women: "Women find these matters boring. There's no enjoyment in it for them" (interview, February 6, 2010).[7]

The Confucian symbolic categories of *nei* and *wai* have long been important ordering principles in conceptions of gender throughout the Sinophone world, including Taiwan. As Teri Silvio writes on gender performance in the Taiwanese opera tradition, gender formations on the island "are intimately linked to structures of interiority and exteriority, public and private, speaking and writing, thing and word. These oppositions are discursively gendered; they also structure the experience of living within sexed bodies and gendered identities" (Silvio 1998, 23). Although once a means of representing the division between the "inner" realm of the imperial court and "outer" realm of the military, the relational *nei-wai* dyad gradually emerged as a "functional distinction that defines the propriety of two gender spheres and the normative gender division of labor" (Rosenlee 2004, 43, 56). In this paradigm, women became identified with interiority and the private. Traditional worldviews held that their chief task after marrying out of their natal families was to maintain domestic harmony in their new homes and produce sons to sustain a male chain of descent. Men, by contrast, became identified with exteriority and the public, charged with working outside the home and performing ancestral memorial rites.

The entrenchment of these gender roles owes much to the arrival of Confucianism in Taiwan with Hoklo and Hakka settlers. An ethical and political philosophical system based on the teachings of Confucius (c. 551–479 BCE), Confucianism nurtured the growth of a patriarchal society and attendant gendered kinship ideologies, relations, and practices in the many places where it took root. The patrifocality of Hoklo and Hakka settler communities was at odds with the gender ideologies and kinship systems of some of the island's Indigenous groups. The earliest Han travelers to Taiwan fixated in their writings on the extent to which Indigenous women seemed to occupy positions of power and influence on the island and ultimately set in motion forced assimilation campaigns to bring Indigenous gender ideologies in line with Confucian thinking (Teng 2001, 256).[8]

A countercurrent to patriarchy, an autonomous women's movement first materialized on the island during the Japanese colonial period. Those who claimed membership in the movement's moderate reformist wing advocated for legal protection from gender discrimination, equal pay for equal work, and for a general elevation of women's status in the private and public realms, even as its members continued to acknowledge explicitly the importance of the gendered qualities ascribed to them by Confucianism (Chang 2009, 9). Following Japan's defeat in the Second Sino-Japanese War, Taiwan was ceded to the Republic of China, at that time engaged in a protracted civil war against the Chinese Communists. Confucian ideology was a cornerstone of political rhetoric on both sides of that conflict: the Communists denounced Confucian values as feudal, and the KMT promoted them as foundational to the establishment of a peaceful and prosperous society. The initiation of universal military service for young men between the ages of eighteen and thirty-six in 1951, a response to both civil unrest on the island and the ongoing threat of war with the PRC, had a material impact on family processes, as it forced men to delay marriage and work until they fulfilled their obligations to the government (Thornton and Lin 1994, 112). At this time, women began to assume additional responsibilities outside the domestic realm, first assisting with work on family farms and then going to labor in factories and to serve in minor administrative roles (116–45). Chiang Kai-shek and wife, Soong May-ling, encouraged women to participate in the KMT effort to transform Taiwan's economy from an agricultural to an industrial one and recognized the necessity of their contributions to the labor force, but they continued to promote Confucian values in an attempt to counter Communist ideology (108) and bolster Sinocentric cultural policy.

The political climate under martial law suppressed further development of an autonomous women's movement independent of state control, and it was not until the 1970s that movements for gender and sexual equality patterned after liberal individualist models secured more mainstream support (D. Chang 2018, 93–94). In 1973 prominent feminist and pro-democracy activist Annette Lu (呂秀蓮) published her landmark *New Feminism* (新女性主義). The book, initially censored by the KMT but today a cornerstone of women's studies curricula in Taiwan (Rubinstein 2004, 252), reviews principles gleaned from Euro-American feminist movements and argues both for their application on the island and their adaptation to local specificities. In particular, Lu's brand of Taiwanese feminism maintained the importance of traditional gender roles within the family and of "upholding certain traditional standards of femininity, domesticity, female beauty, and chastity" (Tang and Teng 2016, 94) while also advocating for the equal treatment of men and women under the law.

Since the end of martial law and ensuing democratic consolidation, a number of women's organizations have materialized, focused on concerns as wide-ranging as sex trafficking, urban-rural disparities, Indigenous rights, environmentalism, radical feminism, and LGBTQIA rights.[9] The government has made efforts to enact policies that promote gender parity in education and employment, and that criminalize discrimination based on sexual orientation (*China Post* 2007). Although women remain underpaid relative to their male colleagues and pursue advanced degrees and executive management positions at significantly lower rates (Gao 2010), the overall female labor participation rate reached 51.4% in 2019; among women ages twenty-five to twenty-nine, that figure ballooned to 92.7%.[10] In recent years, a select group of women have secured powerful positions in political leadership on the island: Annette Lu served as vice president from 2000 to 2008, and Tsai Ing-wen (蔡英文) was elected the island's first female president in 2016, and then reelected to a second term in 2020. There are signs that traditional gender ideologies have given way in even the most conservative of venues: in 2009 the Ministry of the Interior revised existing guidelines to allow women to serve in the role of Sacrificial Official to Confucius, a government-compensated position that has traditionally been reserved for male descendants of the sage.

Despite these changes, rap scene discourse suggests that the way current community members think and feel about gender remains conservative.[11] Implicit in statements like Dwagie's and DJ Noodles's—which pointedly seek to *explain* rather than *endorse* gender asymmetry in the scene—are specific notions of the narrative themes and expressive modes that ought to be invoked in the performance of rap music, and an assumption that such "low and dirty things" are outside the realm of women's experience or interest. Moreover, artists posit specific sonic attributes as congruent with rap's thematic masculinity, especially forcefulness and loudness. At least two of the most celebrated voices in Taiwan rap, Dwagie's and MC Hotdog's, are frequently described as textured (質感的) or gravelly (沙啞), and powerful (有力).[12] Women are excluded from the rap sphere at least in part because they are assumed less capable of producing these kinds of sounds than men. On this matter, DJ Noodles opined: "For women, if you want to use rap techniques to express something besides just the meaning of the lyrics, well, it's not easy to make something that sounds good.... It's very difficult to use a woman's vocal tone to rap. It's hard to do it with power" (interview, February 6, 2010).

There is, of course, no physiological basis for the claim that women's voices are less powerful—however one hears "power"—than men's. The voice is neither innate nor immutable (Eidsheim 2019), and vocality is, as Katherine Meizel has shown, "both an embodied act and a constructive process" (2020, 11). I interpret the "woman's vocal tone" to which DJ Noodles referred, however, not as immanent in biology, but as emergent from a vocalizer's desire to be perceived in ways that are gendered by the listener. More specifically, she gestured at a form of habitus and style of communication prevalent among young, unmarried women in Taiwan known as *sajiao* (撒嬌). Defined as petulant or childlike coquetry, *sajiao* is associated with particular sounds and speech patterns, including nasalization and the use of prolonged sentence-final particles, which together have a distinctively whiny cadence (Chuang 2005, 22).[13] The feminine lilt of *sajiao*, and its connections to notions of youthful feminine attractiveness, opposes the masculine growl of rap. Its pervasiveness as a socially acceptable mode of speaking is part of what compels women to become singers or dancers, undertakings in which DJ Noodles suggested they are more evenly matched with men, rather than rappers.[14] It is perhaps for this reason that on the rare occasion that women's voices do surface in Taiwan rap songs, they usually deliver choruses rather than punch lines.

The characterization of women as disinterested in rap or lacking the constitution or will necessary for powerful performance is often expressed in terms of their inability or disinclination to keep it real. Although he has since collaborated on a number of occasions with his labelmate Miss Ko, KAO!INC.'s DJ Mr. Gin, told me in 2010:

> Hip-hop stuff, it's about life, the lyrics record your life or somebody else's life. You're telling a story, so you want to use appropriately realistic language and let people know that this song, its lyrics, they express strong things. Maybe some words need to be different for men and women. [...] There's a female group who rap in Kaohsiung, called "Candy Box" or "Toy Box" or something, but what they do sounds more like *shulaibao*. When women rap there's less of a sense of realism, it's more refined. Hip-hop should be pissed off! But they're so refined ... they just can't express that kind of stuff.[15] (interview, February 6, 2010)

DJ Mr. Gin suggested that "realism" (寫實) is an important quality of rap storytelling, and that expressing "strong" (強烈) things and being "pissed off" (氣死) are critical to the process of keeping it real. Although he could not recall with certainty the name of the group from the southern city of Kaohsiung, the English-language terms Mr. Gin summoned, "candy" and "toy," clearly impart a sense not of strength, but of sweetness and innocence—anathema to one who associates rap with toughness and temerity. His comments attested to a belief in the fundamental contrast and separation between the childlike nature of woman and the more mature, worldly character of man.

Claiming that what women "do sounds more like *shulaibao*," DJ Mr. Gin further underscored his claims that female artists sound amateurish and stylistically dislocated in rap. *Shulaibao* (數來寶, lit. "counting treasures"), a form of northern Chinese recited narrative poetry with roots in the Ming dynasty, is typically performed by a soloist or duo with no instrumental accompaniment apart from minimal percussion—usually one small and one large pair of clappers (板)—and features a patterned end-rhyming structure, on-beat accents, and markedly regular and straight rather than swung rhythms.[16] *Shulaibao* was originally the province of itinerant performers who would stop in front of shops to sing the praises of a vendor's goods in exchange for a small quantity of money. Today the subjects of *shulaibao* narratives run the gamut from the dramatic to the comedic, encompassing everything from historical stories to recitations of classic tales. In their bid to be understood by audiences, artists deliver lyrics in a deliberate fashion and enunciate the four tones of Mandarin in an exaggerated manner. To listeners in Taiwan, *shulaibao* bears a passing resemblance to rap, but rap that sounds overly stiff and simplistic, lacking the more virtuosic flows that characterize the styles of current popular artists. DJ Mr. Gin's follow-up that Taiwanese women are too "refined" (文雅) for rap echoed Dwagie's description of women as "traditional" (傳統), "sensitive" (溫柔), and irrepressibly *nei*.

Miss Ko attempted to both exploit and subvert these perceptions by anointing herself "the Teresa Teng of rap" (饒舌的鄧麗君) in her lyrics to the 2012 song "Break Him" (打破他), cowritten with and featuring MJ116 MC E.so (瘦子). The comparison with the late Teng (1953–1995), a star of the greatest luminosity throughout East and Southeast Asia, must have raised a few eyebrows: Teng was a celebrated performer of folk tunes and romantic ballads, and her voice and physical appearance were venerated as the apotheosis of feminine beauty and virtue—she was, in short, the antithesis of all things *xiha*. As Miss Ko told me, she invoked Teng because: "I think she's kind of like the mother of [pop music]. Well, not the mother, but everyone loves her and admires her.... You won't hear something bad about Teresa Teng. There's a lot of admiration and respect for her" (interview, March 25, 2014). By casting herself in Teng's likeness, Miss Ko hoped to redeem what she perceived as the generally negative image of rappers—especially female rappers—among the Taiwanese listening public: "I think the image associated with females in hip-hop is not particularly positive in America even, so I wanted to kind of associate [hip-hop] with [Teng]. [She's] someone that everyone knows, you know?" Miss Ko might have deployed the comparison with Teng as a defensive gesture, a way of both capitalizing on Teng's fame and asserting to listeners that she could claim skill as an MC and still identify as a woman.

Delivering the lyric "If hip-hop has an MVP, I'm the Teresa Teng of rap, motherfucker!" in a low vocal register without a hint of *sajiao* nasality, however, she also issued a reminder that Teng was a master of her craft, in addition to being a paragon of femininity.

Although she was first signed to the venerable indie *xiha* KAO!INC. label and shored up her credibility through collaborations with MC Hotdog and other respected senior community members, Miss Ko has only ever seemed to operate on the periphery of the *xiha* scene. This is perhaps as much a function of her Americanness as of her womanness—she arrived in Taipei from New York in 2012 already a college graduate and did not participate in the university hip-hop club rituals that have traditionally precipitated membership in the core *xiha* community. Additionally, like the LA Boyz and other American-born Taiwanese artists before her, she is not fluent in Mandarin or Hoklo to the degree that local performers are. Nevertheless, she managed to capture the interest of pop music industry gatekeepers almost immediately. Her debut album, *Knock Out*, secured the top position on the local music charts, and she was the first rapper to win Best New Artist at the 2013 Golden Melody Awards, often likened to the Grammy Awards for Sinophone and Formosan-language musicians. Having demonstrated her ability to record commercially successful music, she was signed by Universal Music Group in 2016. Since then, she has performed at Glastonbury and SXSW, signed lucrative endorsement deals with corporate juggernauts Nike and McDonald's, and was nominated for Artist of the Year at the 2017 Golden Melody Awards.

In spite of her commercial successes, she has struggled to earn the approval of rap's acolytes, as reflected in numerous Internet-based discussions that describe her lyrics and vocal performance as subpar. In a thread posted on August 7, 2017, titled "What's Wrong with Miss Ko" (Miss Ko 為什麼不行), a user named raymond5566 asked fellow netizens on a popular hip-hop bulletin board: "Only after seeing previous posts have I come to understand that everyone on the [hip-hop] board dislikes Miss Ko. As a rapper, Miss Ko has been nominated for the Golden Melody for female artist, a great achievement. Dwagie, Hotdog, Soft Lipa have all been nominated for male artist. With this as the standard, what's wrong with Miss Ko? I feel a little bad for her." A flurry of responses followed, for the most part exclaiming that Miss Ko's Mandarin is "rotten" (太爛了), that her 2017 song "Pizza" was "super terrible" (超難聽), and that she has "trash lyrics" (垃圾歌詞). A user with the handle "sclbtlove" responded with an epithet that seemed to encapsulate all the aforementioned critiques and reveal the gendered logics that perhaps underpinned them: "[She] plays at *shulaibao*" (數來寶型玩家).

The Roots of Rap as Men's Music

Rap has been marked as men's music since the release of Harlem Yu's "Yes, Sir!" in 1987. The song exploits similarities between the speech-song qualities of American rap music and the characteristic sounds of military drill commands as it extols the virtues of patriotism:

看我們的隊伍　雄壯威武
聽我們的歌聲　響徹雲霄
看我們的國旗　迎風飄揚
答數　一二三四
到了這裡你會成為頂天立地的大男孩
離開這裡你會成為成熟獨立的大男人

> see our battalion, mighty and majestic
> hear our song resounding
> see our nation's flag, fluttering in the wind
> count off, 1-2-3-4
> here you'll become an upstanding boy
> you'll leave here a mature, independent man

The song's conscription nostalgia—which portrays military service equally as civic duty and process of masculine-becoming—spoke directly to male listeners, as women typically stayed at home, joined the work-force, or matriculated to college at the same time that men were headed to the barracks. Sociologists Ying-Chao Kao and Herng-Dar Bih (2014) posit the "cultural gender meaning" of conscription as "more salient than its ostensible military purpose" in the post–Cold War era (181).[17] The KMT fostered pro-military sentiment in Taiwan during the early 1950s, when cross-strait tensions were at their peak, by linking military service to the development of a robust masculine identity. Official slogans ("Heroes are those who hold weapons and protect society"), popular songs, and nursery rhymes encouraged boys to develop martial sensibilities, to first serve their parents as good sons and then the state as good soldiers (180–81). Written in the years after the KMT relinquished its claims to sovereignty over China, the lyrics of "Yes, Sir!" do not reference battle but focus instead on how the experience of training transforms "boys" (男孩) into "upstanding" (頂天立地) and "mature, independent men" (成熟獨立的大男人).

Although Yu's flirtations with rap were short-lived and many current rappers and fans dismiss the song as more *shulaibao* than rap, there can be little question that "Yes, Sir!" helped codify Taiwan rap's associations with men. A string of all-male pop-oriented hip-hop groups, most notably the Party and the LA Boyz, followed Yu in the 1990s. Artists identified with New Taiwanese Song who experimented with rap—including Jutoupi, Lim Giong, and the majority of Blacklist Workshop—were likewise nearly all men. Tracks by the latter performers, which critiqued the KMT's authoritarian politics and shed light on the daily struggles of Taiwan's working class, did not address themselves specifically to male listeners but did reinforce the notion of rap as men's music, insofar as they were delivered in men's voices and framed by men's perspectives.

Members of the nascent *xiha* community that came together in the early 2000s venerated rap in their public discourse as quintessentially "Black music" (黑人音樂) and sought to demonstrate their fealty to hip-hop's innovators by self-consciously appropriating globally circulating models of Black American hip-hop masculinity in their dress and stage mannerisms. Both Dwagie and MC Hotdog—who in our conversations named artists like Biggie Smalls and Tupac, rather than local performers, as among their earliest and most critical influences—adopted more pugnacious postures than their pop-oriented and New Taiwanese Song–oriented predecessors. Donning baggy jeans, oversize T-shirts, baseball caps, and dark glasses, MC Hotdog bobbed and weaved like a boxer onstage, pausing intermittently to gesticulate broadly with his arms and hands. The young Dwagie sported Kangol-style bucket hats and thick gold chains, fashion trends popularized by and strongly associated with Black American men in hip-hop. More recently, he has transacted what Adriana Helbig terms "relational proximity" (2011, 127) to Black American hip-hop masculinity through recording collaborations with artists like Nas, Talib Kweli, and Raekwon of Wu-Tang Clan.[18] Taiwanese rappers' efforts to dress and "act" hip-hop in the halcyon days of *xiha* suggest a reflexive relationship to Blackness rooted in stereotyped notions of how Black American men clothe and comport themselves, as well as a desire to project ethno-racial hip-hop authenticity by proxy. When I raised this in conversations with senior artists, however, they repeatedly emphasized their awareness of hip-hop culture as rooted in the life experiences of Black and Latinx people and their engagements with Black masculinity in terms of a refusal to approach hip-hop as an "assimilative commodity" (Whaley 2006, 198) extractable from its Afro-diasporic foundations.[19]

Dwagie has further amplified a preexisting dialectic between Black American and East Asian martial arts masculine imaginaries, effectively closing a loop on Afro-Asian crossings in hip-hop popularized by the Wu-Tang Clan, dead prez, and Foxy Brown, among others, in the early 1990s.[20] A lifelong student of judo, Dwagie dubbed the all-male creative collective he founded in his native Tainan "Kung Fu Entertainment" and plays prominently with martial themes in his work. In the 2002 track "Forty-Four Fours" (四十四個四), for example, he boasts of his warrior-like abilities as an MC and samples "The General's Orders" (將軍令), the theme song of the perennially popular Huang Feihong (黃飛鴻) films, which take the eponymous Chinese revolutionary, martial artist, and folk hero as their subject.[21] To listeners familiar with the references to martial arts cinema that populated Wu-Tang's sound world beginning with their 1993 album *Enter the Wu-Tang (36 Chambers)*, "Forty-Four Fours" might have registered not only as a response to Wu-Tang's earlier call, but also as a riff on what Cheryl Keyes calls "cultural reversioning" (2002, 21), exchanging the foregrounding of African-centered concepts for Asian-centered ones.

In "Forty-Four Fours," Dwagie channels Method Man and GZA of Wu-Tang in his adoption of what music theorist Adam Krims calls a "percussion-effusive flow" (2000) but does so while capitalizing on particular properties of the Mandarin language. "Flow" is a way of describing an artist's integrated approach to rhythm and rhyme; the term "effusive" refers to a tendency to "spill over the rhythmic boundaries of the meter, the couplet, and, for that matter, of duple and quadruple groupings in general" (50). This spillage can be achieved through subdivision of the beat, staggering of syntax or rhymes, off-beat accenting, or by other means of creating polyrhythms. With percussion-effusive flows, the listener is given the impression that the MC is using his or her mouth as a percussion instrument, effecting "off-beat attacks with a sharply-attacked and crisp delivery that accentuates the countermetric gestures" (50–51). Dwagie's take on percussion effusiveness profits from Mandarin's remarkable capacity for homophonic punning, illustrated in the excerpt below. I render the lyrics of the first four lines of "Forty-Four Fours" first in characters, followed by romanization, and finally in translation; groups of rhyming/punning syllables are shaded in gray, while moments of alliteration are double-underlined:

1. 降龍十八式　十八銅人少林寺　獨孤九式　一生一世
2. 切～你的招式等級只不過是小姑娘再世　有眼不識泰山
3. 孫悟空在釋迦牟尼前放肆　放肆放肆　　五指山會被誰識破
   倒是要見識見識
4. 你們每個人都是近視　是不是　是不是　近視幾度

1. *xianglong shiba shi shibatong ren shaolin si dugu jiu shi yisheng yishi*
2. *tshè! nide zhaoshi dengji zhi buguo shi xiao guniang zai shi youyan bushi Taishan*

3. *Sun Wukong zai Shijiamoni qian fangsi fangsi fangsi Wuzhishan hui bei
   shei shipo daoshi yao jianshi jianshi*
4. *nimen meige ren dou shi jinshi shi bushi shi bushi jinshi jidu*

1. the Eighteen Subduing Dragon Moves, the Eighteen Copper Guardians
   of Shaolin Temple, the Nine Swords of Dugu, in one life
2. ha! you move like a little reincarnated girl, you have eyes but can't see
   I'm Tai Mountain
3. the Monkey King disrespected disrespected disrespected the Buddha,
   who will see through Five Finger Mountain? I'd like to see that
4. you all are nearsighted, right? right? how thick are your glasses?

Dwagie repeats the syllable *shi*, mapped to a number of different characters with different tonemic inflections and meanings (e.g., the second-tone
shi 十 that means "ten" and the fourth-tone *shi* 式 that means "moves"),
nineteen separate times, rhyming it occasionally with the syllables *si*
("temple"), *zhi* ("only"), *si* (the second syllable of "presumptuous"), and
zhi (the second syllable of the phrase "Five Finger Mountain"). The object
of interest in this sequence is less the like-sounding final stressed vowels
than the matching and alliterative initial consonants: *sh*, *zh*, and *s*. There
is a local, self-deprecating joke here in the spirit of Jutoupi's "Taiwan Language Battle," discussed in the previous chapter: these initial consonants
only register as alliterative because speakers of Taiwanese Mandarin and
Hoklo sometimes conflate alveolar and retroflex sibilants. Their repetition, strong articulation, and rhythmic placement against the meter gives
the impression that Dwagie is using his mouth, per Krims's description,
as a percussion instrument.

Additional occurrences of the *sh* sound as in *shao* (the first character
of "Shaolin"), *sheng* ("life"), *shan* ("mountain"), and *shei* ("who") further
contribute to the alliterative effect and also constitute vocal attacks, as
illustrated in musical example 3.1.

Although these attacks occur on strong beats in the first measure, they
shift thereafter unpredictably between strong and weak beats. Weak-beat
attacks occur notably at the end of measures 3, 4, 7, and 8, and at the junc-
tion of measures 5 and 6. They accentuate the countermetric gestures as is
characteristic of percussion-effusive flows, particularly at measures 5 and
6, where "*fangsi fangsi*" spills over the boundary of the bar line. Dwagie's
syntactic units are often dissociated from the meter, crossing bar lines
from measures 3 to 4 and 6 to 7.

Dwagie's rapid pacing and machine-gun-fire delivery in "Forty-Four
Fours" are practically pyrotechnical and an exercise in *wai* virtuosity. The
song is audibly inspired by tracks like "Bring Da Ruckus" on *Enter the*

♩ = 100

xiang-long shi - ba shi ‖ shi - ba-tong ren shao-lin si ‖ du - gu jiu shi ‖ yi-sheng yi - shi

tshè! ni - de zhao-shi deng - ji zhi bu-guo shi xiao gu niangzai shi ‖ you-yan bu - shi Tai shan

Sun Wu-kong zai Shi-jia-mo - ni qian fang-si fang-si fang-si Wu-zhi-shan hui bei shei shi-po dao - shi yao

jian-shi jian-shi ni-men mei-ge ren dou shi jin - shi shi bu - shi shi bu - shi jin - shi ji - du

MUSICAL EXAMPLE 3.1. Transcription of the first eight rapped measures of Dwagie's "Forty-Four Fours" (四十四個四), approximately 0:15–0:35.

Wu-Tang (36 Chambers), with its introductory sample of dialogue from the Hong Kong martial arts film *Shaolin vs. Wu Tang* (1983). Dwagie's percussion-effusive flow, however, derives its power—and hyperbolic humor—from features of local language use.

"Call Them Out on What? On Guava!": Staking Out Difference from Mandopop

Accruing associations of rap with masculinity, and masculinity with the real, paved the way for *xiha* artists to promulgate rap as a form of cultural resistance, a way of challenging what Mark Slobin terms the superculture: "The usual, the accepted, the statistically lopsided, the commercially successful, the statutory, the regulated, the most visible" (1993, 29). Straying from Confucian orthodoxy, they have invoked the masculine ethos of rap to express feelings of anger and resentment toward authority, not just traditional figures like teachers, parents, and politicians, but also those who hold sway over the regional pop music industry. Indeed, the sense of rap and rap musicians as "real" is inextricable from the sense of rap and rap musicians as "masculine," especially when held up in comparison to Mandopop's effete and impeccably coiffed idols, who have dominated the Taiwan charts for more than three decades. Male chart-toppers like Wang Leehom, Jam Hsiao (蕭敬騰), Wilber Pan (潘瑋柏), and JJ Lin (林俊傑) have frequently been characterized by fans as *wenrou* (溫柔), a term that glosses most closely to the English "sensitive," "warm," "soft," "tender," and/or "gentle."[22] Contrasting starkly with Taiwan's brusque and combative rappers, the *wenrou* man is deeply sentimental, unafraid to seem vulnerable performing his feelings of lovesickness and longing to mass audiences.[23]

The 2001 song "Korean Wave Invasion," which targets the public's infatuation with Mandopop and similarly lovelorn K-pop stars, demonstrates the feelings of contempt that songwriters MC Hotdog, Dwagie, and MC 168 harbored for Taiwan's and Korea's *wenrou* singing sensations at the turn of the millennium:

(大支)
台灣歌手怎麼唱都是在那邊愛來愛去　所以我在這裡一定要說真實的事情
現在的偶像歌手長的帥長的美麗　就等於可以上台去
什麼都不用會　但要保持笑嘻嘻　沒事幹時還要傻笑裝白癡
有時眼淚最好一兩滴　博取觀眾同情　那就是他們生存的道理

(熱狗)
在電視上看到只是表面　你在裝傻　還是你沒有發現
愛來愛去　實在太假　凍抹掉　所以現在要跳出來罵
我問你要罵什麼？　罵芭樂　你們沒有別的選擇　在這個環境下長大
每天吃芭樂　一定有一天你吃不下
你的排泄物　一定要拉　本來是從屁股　可是歌手是從嘴巴　shit from the mouth, shit from the mouth, shit from the mouth

(熱狗, 大支, MC 168)
操你媽個B 操你媽個B fuck Clon and H.O.T.
Yuki, A-Mei, Coco Lee, suck suck suck suck my dick
操你媽個B　操你媽個B fuck Clon and H.O.T.
Yuki, A-Mei, Coco Lee, suck suck suck suck my dick

(Dwagie)
why are Taiwanese singers always going on about love?
so I'm here to keep it real
today's idol singers are good-looking, that's how they get onstage
you don't have to do anything, just have to smile and giggle, if you've got nothing else just grin like an idiot
at times it's best to shed a tear or two, win over the audience, that's their means of survival

(MC Hotdog)

on TV you only see the surface, are you playing dumb or have you never
realized

their talk about love is totally fake, can't take it, so I'm here to call them
out

call them out on what? On guava! You haven't had choices, growing up
like that

each day eating guava, one day you'll get sick of it

you'll have to shit it out, and it should come from the ass, but with singers
it's from the mouth

shit from the mouth, shit from the mouth, shit from the mouth

(MC Hotdog, Dwagie, and MC 168)

fuck your mother, fuck your mother, fuck Clon and H.O.T.

Yuki, A-Mei, Coco Lee can suck suck suck suck, suck my dick

fuck your mother, fuck your mother, fuck Clon and H.O.T.

Yuki, A-Mei, Coco Lee can suck suck suck suck suck my dick

The lyrics, arresting in their profanity, take aim at performers whose claim
to stardom rests solely on their ability to sing love songs, smile vapidly,
and weep opportunistically for gullible audiences. They are, according to
the songwriters, shameless purveyors of *bala* (芭樂, lit. "guava"), Hoklo
slang in this context for mediocre and ultimately meaningless claptrap
that puns cleverly with the English "ballad." Things take a particularly
vitriolic turn at the chorus: against the repeating stereotyped nine-note
pentatonic figure known as the "oriental riff," voiced by a synthesizer, MC
Hotdog dares several specific female Mandopop (Yuki Hsu, A-Mei, and
Coco Lee) and male K-pop (Clon and H.O.T.) artists to perform fellatio on
him. The use of the "oriental riff" (see musical example 3.2), which traces
its roots to the early twentieth-century United States and has become a
globally ubiquitous musical orientalist trope, accentuates the performers'
lyrical accusations of falseness and foolishness.[24] The riff's banality underscores the jejune charm and immediate recognizability of the performers
in question as the rapper—who wants to "keep it real" (說真實的事情, lit.
"say true things")—suggests a punishment of sexual humiliation for their
crimes of artificiality. A constellation of associations in opposition to each
other emerges from this gesture: the feminine ethos and meaninglessness
of Mandopop counters—and is threatened with defilement by—the masculine ethos and meaningfulness of rap.

The misogynist and homophobic notes that ring out from "Korean
Wave Invasion" set it apart from the majority of Taiwan rap music, which

MUSICAL EXAMPLE 3.2. Transcription of the "oriental riff."

does not exhibit such qualities.[25] MC Teacher Lin interprets these anomalous features of the song as in tune with "the American gangsta rap legacy, by which we Taiwanese rappers were all strongly influenced in the beginning" (personal communication, January 29, 2016).[26] Lacking awareness of the histories of racism, economic disenfranchisement, and police brutality to which gangsta rap's performances of hegemonic masculinity responded in the United States (see hooks 1994, Folami 2007, Jeffries 2010, White 2011), they were uncritical, according to Lin, in their early efforts to "copy some of those raw and hard-core images" as they grappled with the process of finding their voices and places in Taiwan's own gendered social hierarchies. This is discernible in Dwagie's and MC Hotdog's phallocentric monikers—the Hoklo "Dwagie" means "big one" and the implications of "Hotdog" are obvious—which echo the canine-influenced names of American rap pioneers associated with the gangsta style, such as Snoop Dogg, Nate Dogg, and Tha Dogg Pound.[27] Certainly, their choice of stage names suggests a more-than-momentary interest in performing masculine sexual bravado, and the observation that "Korean Wave Invasion" was isolated in time (reflecting the earlier influence of gangsta rap) and some of its language derivative of American influences does not absolve it or the *xiha* scene of its sexism. It does, however, clarify the violent gestures within the track as, perhaps, one step in a prolonged process of consolidating masculine identities that has yielded more nuanced performances in later years.[28]

Another atypical feature of this track—its xenophobia, which contrasts sharply with the Taiwan rap community's generally collegial relationship to its Korean counterpart—also benefits from contextualization. Belying the specificity of its name, "Korean Wave Invasion" does not target Korea exclusively, or even primarily. The track is best understood in terms of the experience of rap artists within an early twenty-first-century regional pop culture industry that did not embrace them. Moreover, although the term "Korean Wave" is prominent in the title, the song expresses with greatest clarity the *xiha* community's dissatisfaction with Taiwan's musical superculture, which encompasses works by K-pop, Mandopop, and J-pop artists, as well as American and European pop artists. MC Hotdog, Dwagie, and MC 168—none of whom were considered "idol" handsome by industry standards at the time of the song's release—rail against the notion that one must be beautiful and act vacuous to flourish in the island's established star system. They perform from the position that life is not always pleasurable or uncomplicated, and that there are issues beyond romantic relationships that musicians can and ought to address. Nearly twenty years after the release of "Korean Wave Invasion," the generation of rap artists who followed MC Hotdog and Dwagie continued to remark in interviews on their feelings of marginalization from the mainstream popular music industry and their sense that there is little space in it for musicians whose work explores what they feel is real: darker, more introspective, critical, and often vindictive emotional states.

Engendering Complex Stories, Sounding Social Roles

Opposition to the romantic fixations of pop music has long been a marker of integrity among the island's rappers, before and after the release of "Korean Wave Invasion." Sexist and sexual language in that song notwithstanding, artists' attitudes toward sexuality and intimacy are not often easily discernible. Diverging clearly from the pop sphere, the *xiha* scene has historically been a venue in which cisgender heterosexual men are concerned primarily with speaking to other cisgender heterosexual men about issues other than their relationships with and feelings about women.[29]

Even tracks that at first listen seem to describe simple romantic and/ or sexual entanglements often, in fact, tell more complex stories about the gendered social roles their performers inhabit. For example, MC Hotdog's 2006 collaboration with rocker/rapper Chang Chen-yue, "I Love Taiwan Girls" (我愛台妹), generated compelling tensions with locally prevalent models of masculine gender performance when it was first released. The song casts MC Hotdog as a mack, a character described by Adam Krims as a "man whose confidence, prolificness, and (claimed) success with women mark him as a 'player'" (2000, 62). As one of the island's most commercially successful rappers and a revered progenitor of the scene, MC Hotdog plays the part more easily than others: because he *is* prolific, he has earned the right to be confident, even cocky, onstage. He also boasts more female fans than many of his colleagues—indeed, he has in the past reminded his followers on social media of this fact by posting sexually suggestive pictures that women have sent him. Prior to the release of "I Love Taiwan Girls," mack rap was relatively rare in Taiwan, perhaps because although the player has a long history in African American fiction, poetry, and film, he has no precise local equivalent. He does not share the sensitivity of the *wenrou* idol or the nobility ascribed to the romantic male characters featured in Chinese martial chivalry novels and films, and he bears little resemblance to the rough-and-tumble triad bosses and gangsters featured as stock characters in Hong Kong and Taiwan films.[30] MC Hotdog's persona in "I Love Taiwan Girls" is deliberately incongruous with all of these, inviting listeners to question the conditions of its (im)possibility.

The lyrics to "I Love Taiwan Girls" encompass repeated declarations of love—simultaneously mocking and affectionate—for women who embody stereotyped notions of predominantly Hoklo, rural, working-class femininity. Such women are known on the island by the name *taimei* (台妹), which marries the morpheme *tai* (台) of "Taiwan" with the morpheme *mei* (妹), which on its own means "younger sister" but here indicates more generally a young woman or girl without the connotation of kinship. As cultural archetypes, *taimei* are simultaneously fetishized and denigrated for dressing in provocative clothing, applying heavy cosmetics, using "vulgar" speech, and engaging in intemperate partying and drinking. In this excerpt from "I Love Taiwan Girls," MC Hotdog pleads with a *taimei* who has caught his eye to engage in a romantic dalliance:

(熱狗)
我不愛中國小姐　我愛台妹　萬萬歲
妳的檳榔2粒要100　好貴　有沒有含睡
如果能夠和妳共枕眠　更多更多的奶粉錢
我願意為妳貢獻　我不是愛現
請妳噴上一點點銷魂的香水
換上妳最性感的高跟鞋　人群之中　妳最亮眼
台妹來了　我是否和妳一拍即合
跟我去很多的不良場合
大家看到我都對我喊yes sir
因為我是公認最屌的rapper
台妹們　麻煩和我拍拖
我不是凱子　可是付錢　也不會囉唆
純情是什麼　我不懂　我的想法很邪惡　張震嶽他懂

(張震嶽)
我愛台妹　台妹愛我　對我來說　林志玲算什麼
我愛台妹　台妹愛我　對我來說　侯佩岑算什麼

(MC Hotdog)
I don't love Chinese girls, I love Taiwan girls, long live Taiwan girls
two betel nuts for $100 is expensive, does that include sex[31]
if I could share a pillow with you, I'd give you plenty of money for baby
　　formula
I'm willing to contribute, not that I'm bragging
put on your sexiest perfume

change into your hottest high heels, you'll stand out from the crowd
Taiwan girls on the scene, will we hit it off?
come with me to lots of sketchy places
everyone who sees me yells "Yes, sir!"
because everyone knows I'm the flyest rapper
Taiwan girls, why not go out with me?
I'm no sugar daddy, but I'll foot the bill
I'm no innocent, my thoughts are twisted, Chang Chen-yue gets me

(Chang Chen-yue)
I love Taiwan girls, Taiwan girls love me, what's Lin Chi-ling to me
I love Taiwan girls, Taiwan girls love me, what's Patty Hou to me

This verse, the second of three, begins on a patriotic note, with the narrator declaring that he has no affection for "Chinese girls," but is instead taken with the emphatically local *taimei*.[32] The MC then praises the particular *taimei* he is addressing for adorning herself in a manner that suggests one of the island's vaunted "betel nut beauties" (檳榔西施), young women who work at the side of the road in small, neon-lit betel nut shops, where their job is to lure in customers by wearing risqué clothing. The betel nut beauty is an iconic—if historically maligned—figure on the island, strongly identified with working-class culture. As he flatters the *taimei* in question, the rapper propositions her for sex and boasts that he would be able to help support financially any children that might arise from their congress. In a further attempt to seduce her, he then suggests that they would be like celebrities at any of the "sketchy places" (不良場合) to which he might take her—he is, after all, a famous rapper with fans at his beck and call. Finally, he reiterates that he has the financial resources to pay for the date and concludes by declaring to the listener that his advances do not stem from any romantic impulse; far from it, his thoughts are "twisted" (邪惡) in a way that surely his collaborator Chang Chen-yue, a fellow man, will understand. Chang Chen-yue chimes in on the two lines of the chorus that follow, singing out that he loves *taimei* and they return the sentiment, and suggesting that glamorous celebrity women like model-actress Lin Chi-ling (林志玲) and television presenter Patty Hou (侯佩岑) simply do not excite him to the same degree.

The other two verses of "I Love Taiwan Girls" further elaborate on the virtues of its object, the *taimei*, but the larger story the song tells regards the identity of its male subject. Indeed, as the "guidette" of Italian American working-class subculture is the female counterpart to the male "guido," so is the *taimei* the female counterpart to the male *taike* (台客). The origins of the term *taike*, which juxtaposes the morpheme *tai* (台) of

"Taiwan" with the morpheme *ke* (客), meaning "guest," have long been in dispute. Some say that Chinese migrants newly arrived in Taiwan after the war used it as a pejorative to refer to already-local men as, literally, "Taiwan guests"; others suggest that the *tai* refers to the Hoklo people, while the *ke* refers to the Mandarin term for the Hakka people, *kejiaren* (客家人, lit. "guest people"). Whatever the case may be, to refer to someone as *taike* imputes to them qualities of unworldliness, crudeness, and unintelligibility (ostensibly the result of poor Mandarin)—qualities that underpinned migrants' prejudicial claims to superiority over the local, majority-Hoklo population and reinforcement of the island's ethnopolitical hierarchy (Ho 2009, 566). The *taike* stereotype indexes a number of additional objects, states, and actions, including being from rural parts of south or central Taiwan, chewing betel nut, smoking, sporting tattoos, wearing cheap button-down shirts in floral patterns, and driving a motor scooter. The epithet provoked the ire of those aligned with hard-line pro-independence and nativist politics between the mid-1970s and early 2000s, who feared that its redemption would, as sociologist Tung-hung Ho puts it, "consume the Taiwanese as a collective subject, while also further deepening the position of its subjugation" (569). Nevertheless, recent years have seen numerous efforts to reclaim, redefine, and even commodify the appellation. Several prominent acts have worn their associations with *taike* culture as a badge of honor, including rock musician Wu Bai (伍佰) and post-punk band LTK Commune (濁水溪公社). Both Chang Chen-yue, who is of Indigenous 'Amis descent, and MC Hotdog, who has *waisheng* heritage on his father's side, also came to be identified with *taike* culture as the identity broadened beyond its core associations with Hoklo subjecthood to include men who are considered to embody a kind of earthy coolness, sport tattoos, and even wear hip-hop style clothing (Quartly 2006). Cementing their associations with *taike*, MC Hotdog and Chang Chen-yue were two of the headliners of the 2006 T.K. Rock Festival (台客搖滾嘉年華), an all-day concert that celebrated local popular music and exploited sounds and images associated with *taike* as part of its marketing campaign.

In performing "I Love Taiwan Girls," MC Hotdog and Chang Chen-yue reimagine the *taike* as a mack. Far from finding the identity shameful, they celebrate their lust for the *taimei* and the various activities and places she represents. They do not indulge their desires for her secretly, but call out proudly in the chorus, "I love *taimei*, *taimei* love me!" As it extols the *taike*'s affection for the *taimei*, the song superimposes the lyrical and musical gestures of the quintessential mack rap recording onto this identity. Mack rap—codified by Black American artists like Too $hort and LL Cool J—has a distinctive sound: eschewing the "stark, intricate,

or uneven" layering that marks other kinds of rap, it favors simple accompaniments with R&B accents (Krims 2000, 64). To this point, mack
rap recordings often feature sung choruses and live instrumentation that
is recorded through, rather than samples and beats that are layered and
looped by a sequencer (63–64). In this case, the band is Chang Chen-yue's
frequent collaborator Free9 (also known as Free Night), which consists
of guitars, bass, and drums, interpolating the accompaniment from the
Spinners' 1972 "I'll Be Around" and slightly transforming the opening
saxophone riffs from Glenn Frey's 1982 "The One You Love." The song's
lyrics also suggest mack rap, with its depictions of wealth and boasting
about sexual prowess. In the commercially successful American hip-hop
exported to Taiwan beginning in the late 1990s and early 2000s, images
of conspicuous consumption center the possession of luxury cars, fashion accessories, mansions, or yachts. In "I Love Taiwan Girls," however,
MC Hotdog boasts glibly that he has enough to cover the cost of baby
formula if necessary—an expenditure more in line with what he, a mere
taike, can afford.

In both "Korean Wave Invasion" and "I Love Taiwan Girls," MC Hotdog, Dwagie, and their collaborators tell stories that examine their self-
conceptions as young Taiwanese men. The latter is an exercise in creative
self-fashioning, an attempt to reimagine the previously maligned *taike* as
a kind of mack, a man of sexual dynamism, with confidence, charisma,
and cash to spare. The former explores their dissatisfaction with prevailing
models of masculinity in the music industry that exclude from participation men who are insufficiently *wenrou* to perform sentimental love songs
with conviction.

Rappers' strenuous efforts to differentiate themselves from pop stars
may veer at times toward gratuitous posturing but acquire greater gravitas
when one considers how the island's popular culture industries have historically mediated perceptions of Taiwan itself as debased and effeminate.
This phenomenon predates and runs deeper than contemporary Mandopop: writing about lyricist Zhou Tianwang (周添旺) and composer
Deng Yuxian's (鄧雨賢) 1934 song "Flower in the Rainy Night" (雨夜花),
Nancy Guy suggests that recordings from the golden age of the Hoklo
popular music industry under Japanese colonialism "offer evidence of
early expressions of the notion of Taiwan as a feminized victim" (2008,
69). The narrative of "Flower in the Rainy Night" centers on the plight of
a grief-stricken young woman who has been cast off by a cruel lover. Its
themes of shame, dejection, and abandonment are prominent in many
Hoklo popular songs of the same vintage. Guy speculates that Taiwan's
long history of colonization and its perpetual status as a nation without
a state have contributed to notions of the island as like "a woman who

has suffered multiple rapes" (70).[33] To this point, Hoklo popular music over the decades—also traversing *nakashi* (那卡西), *enka*, and later Tai-pop styles—furnishes multiple examples of songs that gesture toward and repeatedly gender this strain of trauma. Rappers, especially those positioned on the front lines of politics, often write and perform material that pushes back in ways both oblique and direct against this prevailing musical metanarrative.

Their reluctance to promulgate *wenrou* masculinity or to corroborate perceptions of Taiwan as "feminized victim" does not entirely preclude them, however, from imagining new modes of masculine performance that index the cerebral, sensitive, and sentimental. Teacher Lin regards Tainan-born Soft Lipa—whose English-language moniker is a cheeky reference to his own pillowy pout—as undertaking a particularly "unique" "project of masculinity" involving the construction of "flexible gendered viewpoints" to "[document] personal stories" (2020, 161–62). Enlivened by softly shimmering jazz instrumentals, these stories often describe impressionistically and in rich sensory detail mundane moments of everyday beauty: the fragrance of buttered toast, the feeling of a hot shower, the sound of insects chirping in the moonlight.

Soft Lipa's emotive style emerges in themes of longing and nurturance in his 2009 song "Homesickness" (鄉愁). In a dense latticework of rhymes, he describes acute feelings of urban alienation as experienced by a young man who has moved to the city in pursuit of job opportunities, but who longs for the familiar faces and comforts of his old home. A close reading of the song illuminates the aesthetic qualities and the technical prowess for which Soft Lipa is admired by his peers. Here, I render the lyrics of the first four lines of "Homesickness" first in characters, followed by romanization, and finally in translation; English letter markings classify sets of syllables that rhyme or pun:

```
            A        B    B C C      B A
1. 而對於每種背景離鄉的鄉愁都大致相同
      B A                   D A D A
2. 我將從你的回憶裡面找出其中一種
          B E F    E G B E G
3. 會讓你想哭的人不只講故事
          E F    B    E G
4. 也曾經照顧著你像是小護士


          A            B        B C    C       B A
1. er duiyu meizhong beijing li xiangde xiangchou dou dazhi xiangtong
```

```
     B   A                    D  A   D A
2. wo jiang cong nide huiyi limian zhaochu qizhong yizhong
         B  E  F     E G B    E G
3. hui rang ni xiang kude ren buzhi jiang gushi
            E  F    B       E G
4. ye cengjing zhaoguzhe ni xiang shi xiao hushi
```

1. and for folks from all walks of life, their homesickness is much the same
2. from your memories, I am going to find one kind among them
3. those you cry for did not just tell you stories
4. they once cared for you like little nurses

Soft Lipa's concatenation of end rhymes and internal rhymes conveys the sense of churning movement and ceaseless forward momentum that characterizes modern urban life. The end-rhyming syllables *tong* ("same") and *zhong* ("kind") of lines 1 and 2, and the end-rhyming *gushi* ("stories") and *hushi* ("nurses") of lines 3 and 4 are most readily audible, but are interspersed among numerous internal rhymes: the syllables *chou* (the second syllable of *xiangchou*, "homesickness") and *dou* ("all") in line 1, and the sequence of *ku* ("cry"), *bu* ("not"), *gu* (the first syllable of *gushi*, "stories"), *gu* (the second syllable of *zhaogu*, "cared for"), and *hu* (the first syllable of *hushi*, "nurses") in lines 3 and 4. A strong sense of tonal parallelism—which continues into the next verses—emerges in the sequence of fourth-tone syllables *bu*, *gu*, and *hu*, as well as in the sequence of first tone–second tone syllable pairings *xiangchou*, *xiangtong*, and *jiang cong*. The complex rhythmic patterns of Soft Lipa's vocal performance, shown in musical example 3.3, buoy a masterful flow.

By launching into the first verse two beats before the first transcribed measure, and by opening the lyrics in medias res ("And for folks from all walks of life..."), Soft Lipa generates a pressured, frenetic pace. His rhymes do not wait politely for the end of the measure: *xiangtong* closes a measure and is followed immediately by *jiang cong* at beginning of the next measure. Coinciding with the repeated rhythmic figure of two strong-beat eighth notes—in contrast with the preceding weak-beat eighth notes and subsequent rapid-fire sixteenth notes—this internal rhyme intensifies the underlying sense of urgency, pushing as it does across the boundary of the measure as well as the lyrical line break.

Intricately constructed, "Homesickness" demonstrates Soft Lipa's commitment to craft, both sonic and lyrical, that is a key component of the erudition to which so many in the community aspire. It is but one example from the rapper's vast catalogue of pieces that disarm listeners

MUSICAL EXAMPLE 3.3. Transcription of first five rapped measures of Soft Lipa's "Homesickness" (鄉愁), approx. 0:29–0:40.

with their beauty and dazzle them with their virtuosity. Although those I have interviewed frequently characterize the Tainan-born MC's rhythms and rhymes as poetic, effortless, and delicate, they are always quick to qualify this: Soft Lipa might sound soft-hearted, but he is still a force to be reckoned with, a maestro of the highest order.[34]

Rap as a Terrain of Masculinity Politics

Amid sweeping sociopolitical and economic disjuncture, Dwagie, MC Hotdog, Soft Lipa, and others engage in diverse efforts to determine what it means to be "masculine" on the island. These efforts manifest not just in the contrasting approaches of songs like "Korean Wave Invasion," "I Love Taiwan Girls," and "Homesickness," but also in the social structure of the rap community and the rituals around which its members gather. The performance of masculinity—and the process of demonstrating *wai-ness*—is a crucial aspect of membership for young men in the scene. This performance is by definition public, or "outside," occurring as it often does within the social context of university *xiha* club meetings. Community members undergo a graduated ascent within the hierarchy of these social organizations that constitutes, for all intents and purposes, a path to mature manhood. University clubs, although informally organized, assume tiered structures that include ranked leadership positions and offices. Their primary activities include lectures, public performances, and instruction in the art of MCing and DJing. Off-campus, creative collectives like Kung Fu Entertainment also offer classes to aspiring rappers who want to climb the community ladder. Many of the most influential artists in the scene were at one time participants in such activities and climbed the ranks by demonstrating their apprehension of superior *xiha* knowledge and/or performance skill.

The progression from neophyte to authority figure in clubs offers a means of both reproducing and disrupting the broader processes through which manhood has traditionally been achieved in Taiwan. Confucian values emphasize the importance of filial behavior; as anthropologist Avron Boretz has observed, young men on the island are traditionally "beholden to their fathers (including fictive fathers, those who stand in positions of power and authority) and elder brothers (including fictive brothers), expected to unquestioningly accept their subordination to their elders' authority and the collective interest."[35] It is only following marriage and child-rearing that they can hope to "enjoy the advantages of power due to all legitimate representatives of the social order" (2004, 175). On one hand, the hierarchical structures of clubs and creative collectives suggests capitulation to a similar system, wherein members who are less experienced or less knowledgeable are subject to the authority of those above them. On the other hand, involvement in the rap scene constitutes an alternative passage to manhood that controverts some of these norms. Rappers frequently challenge authority figures and voice their frustrations at power asymmetries in the music industry, school system, and government; MC Hotdog and Dwagie have, in fact, built their careers on such critique. Status in the community is conferred on individuals for their mastery of knowledge about rap or for their skill as musicians, not as the inevitable outcome of prolonged subjection to authority.

Alternative pathways to manhood might appeal to members of the rap community in light of sociopolitical and economic changes in progress in Taiwan since the first decade of the twenty-first century. As the government under Ma Ying-jeou established closer ties with Beijing and cross-strait economic integration increased during his administration, the standard two-year period of conscription was gradually reduced and new forms of "general substitute service"—including work at social services and domestic security—were introduced (Ministry of Foreign Affairs 2010). The Ministry of the Interior's plans to shift to an all-volunteer force would eliminate conscription altogether as a rite of passage. Marriage and child-rearing, two additional pillars of masculinity, have long been critical to achieving adult status according to traditional worldviews, but young people on the island today are either deferring these life-cycle events or forgoing them altogether. Joint processes of industrialization and economic expansion beginning in the 1950s altered the gendered division of labor, a transformation that gave rise to significant changes in the size, organization, and behavioral habits of the island's families. Since the mid-twentieth century, Taiwan's fertility rates have plummeted: the total fertility rate in 1951 was 7.040 compared to 1.049 in 2019.[36] As a sample population, the rap community embodies these broader trends to a striking extent. Among the many scene participants I have interviewed over the years, a small minority were married or had children by their early thirties.

If previous paths to adulthood—military service, marriage, and child-rearing—are not as readily navigable as they once seemed to be, the hierarchies and rituals of the rap community offer men a set of alternatives. They need not spend two years in the barracks, commit to a spousal partnership, move out of their parents' homes, or feather their own nests in order to be considered legitimate representatives of the social order by their peers in the community. (As I will discuss in chapter 4, the vicissitudes of the economy and Taiwan's culture of extreme overwork in some cases preclude these possibilities even when they are desired.) Hip-hop club activities provide a means to self-empowerment and pleasure outside the traditional structures of family and home. They are spaces in which to make casual and close friendships, as well as to form durable social ties. As life under neoliberalism augurs increasing social isolation, fragmentation, and precarity, they help to create what Judith Butler has described as the "social network of hands" (2009, 67), a vital existential support system.

These social ties are bolstered not just by convivial activities of shared learning and creative collaboration, but also by structural opportunities for competition. Ciphering—a feature of Taiwan *xiha* clubs as well as global hip-hop cultural practice—is paradigmatically *wai* in the demands it places on participants. In a cipher, a group of rappers gathers in a ring of three or more people who take turns freestyling. The exercise is often friendly, but there is something at stake—one must perform at an equal or higher level than others in the circle to avoid embarrassment. Likewise, rap battles, which pit two or more rappers against one another in a public contest, invite participants to demonstrate superior hip-hop skills and knowledge, and to assert dominance over their peers. Ciphers and battles socialize young artists into trumpeting their own skills, verbally attacking or mocking others, and giving and receiving public criticism.

I observed one such cipher at the video shoot for Dwagie's "Change Taiwan," involving a group of young men who gathered on the sidelines as the crew engaged in the time-consuming process of setting up different angles. As previously noted, the men who answered Dwagie's call for participation in the shoot were performers and members of *xiha* clubs from cities at that time preparing to hold municipal elections. This cipher comprised two artists affiliated with Tainan's Kung Fu Entertainment—R-Flow and Shao Ye (少爺)—and a beatboxer named Jimix (see fig. 3.2).

Although the atmosphere in the circle at first seemed congenial, the two rappers repeatedly angled their bodies and gestured confrontationally

FIG. 3.2. Shao Ye (*left*) and R-Flow (*right*) ciphering, October 17, 2010. Screen capture from field video by author.

at a third young man standing several feet away, called BR. Dangling a cigarette between his teeth, R-Flow motioned insistently to BR to join the cipher. R-Flow and Shao Ye were more mature, in terms of both their chronological ages and their length of tenure in the *xiha* scene; both were at that time senior members of their university *xiha* clubs and had been signed to indie labels. BR, then a junior member of his university's club, seemed intimidated by their invitation. Although he is now a respected presence in the *xiha* scene, he was a less experienced improviser at that time. His flow was clumsy and his voice shaky as he delivered an uninspired diss on the hairstyle of a young man standing nearby. His eyes darted around nervously as more onlookers drifted in the group's direction. As BR struggled to stay ahead of the beat, R-Flow motioned to yet another young MC named Professor H (韓森) to take BR's place. Professor H approached the group, and BR's expression immediately soured. Although he clearly did not appreciate the blunt suggestion that he should step aside, he assented to the substitution. As things in the circle heated up with the new trio, Dwagie wandered over and with a dramatic sweep of his hand put an end to the action. He proposed that those in the circle engage instead in a freestyle battle and asked the crowd who had gathered around to select two participants. Everyone laughed and all simultaneously pointed their fingers at BR, who put his head down sheepishly.

Unable to decline the invitation without further embarrassment, he agreed to participate. Dwagie selected his opponent, a young man with a sideways-facing baseball cap, whom I will call by the surname "Qiao." Although we were not acquainted, I had seen Qiao at a number of other community events in the course of my fieldwork on the island. He was also boyish and inexperienced—a good match for BR—and, from the chuckles his selection elicited, had a reputation for being something of a comedian. Qiao approached BR and everyone laughed as R-Flow sarcastically announced their meeting as an epic battle between the north (BR) and south (Qiao) of the island before counting them in—"Five, six, seven, eight!" BR went first. Although his voice was initially too quiet for me to discern the content of his improvisation, the hissing of the crowd suggested that he had elected to diss Qiao. Rapidly gaining confidence that he could dominate his opponent, BR's voice crescendoed, his tempo picked up, and he began moving physically in Qiao's direction. Once BR had finished vocalizing and retreated a few steps, Qiao hesitated for a few beats before improvising a few short lines about his love for Taiwan and his refusal to participate further in the battle because he had, as he remarked in English, "no beef" with BR. Qiao then seized BR's hand and began shaking it enthusiastically in an exaggerated gesture of submission. The crowd booed in Qiao's direction. Dwagie announced BR the winner by default and, smiling and laughing, everyone scattered back into the street, where it appeared the camera crew was ready to begin filming again.

Multiple levels of hierarchy were on display as this sequence of events unfolded. BR started out at the lowest echelon, subordinate to the more experienced R-Flow, Shao Ye, and, later, Professor H. R-Flow and Shao Ye teased BR as they drew him in and subsequently expelled him from the cipher. Dwagie's status in the community was readily apparent as the three MCs ceased their activities when he appeared, and all immediately agreed to his suggestion of a battle. Qiao performed poorly in competition, making BR look poised and audacious by comparison. Although reputations were clearly on the line for participants, at no point did the atmosphere seem clouded by hostility. On the contrary, these activities represented an opportunity for more junior members of the community to showcase their raw skills and to demonstrate the potential for further development. The ultimate goal, it seemed, was not intimidation but empowerment to greater participation. (In BR's case, this is an ambition fulfilled: nearly ten years after I observed this scene play out, he has climbed the ranks at Kung Fu Entertainment to tour with Dwagie and has released his own recordings.)

As this scene demonstrates, the rap community has created organizations and embraced rituals that serve as alternative incubator spaces for masculinity outside the structures of family and home. Contained within this terrain of masculinity politics are echoes of other vanishing rituals, sonic analogues to traditional rites of passage such as compulsory military service. The ability to handle a firearm or drive a tank seems increasingly less vital as the nature of warfare evolves, but the island's young MCs continue to write verses, engage in public displays of their skills, and attempt to ascend the ranks of leadership in clubs. They gird themselves not for eventual military confrontation but for wars of words with one another.

Confucian gender regimes retain currency in the rap scene, as evinced in both the discourse that surrounds the performance of rap music and in the hierarchies that structure social relations among community members. The particular masculinity politics at play in Taiwan rap, however, have undergone significant changes since the end of the 1980s, an apt reflection of rapidly transforming sociopolitical and economic conditions. In "Yes, Sir!" Harlem Yu reflected with nostalgia on the production of state-sanctioned masculinity, still a potent concept during the final months of martial law. Capitalizing on the similarities between the characteristic sounds of military drill commands and American rap music, Yu reveled in memories of the transition from boyhood to manhood, which he underwent in the company of friends and fellow conscripts primed for war. Dwagie and his contemporaries have promulgated a dissident masculinity, one that remains rooted in notions of *wai*-ness but derives power from its opposition to traditional authority figures—including those in the educational system, government, and music industry—and does not owe its continuation to family or state institutions. Yet others have explored their masculinity in different ways, by cultivating public images as *taike*, scholar-poets, and political pundits.

Only time will tell whether additional women artists or artists with nonbinary gender identities will gain a foothold in the community and, if they do, how their presence might transform the gender politics at play. Over the course of the last several years, female multi-genre musicians like Aristophanes (貍貓), Chen Hsien-Ching (陳嫺靜), and Abao (阿爆) have begun experimenting with rap techniques, but largely from outside the structures that I describe here as constituting the *xiha* community. Aristophanes, who has perhaps developed more of an international profile than a local one because of her collaboration with Canadian musician and visual artist Grimes, describes herself in multiple online articles as feeling like a perpetual outsider to *xiha*: "Maybe it's my personality. It's not really easy for me to make friends with rappers. It's hard for me to do that. We all rap in Mandarin but I think we're speaking two different languages. What I want to write, they don't really think those [things] can be songs.... I don't really care. I'm not really interested in what they like to talk about" (Lee 2019). Nevertheless, she remains optimistic that she might blaze a trail for others to follow: "The situation is still male dominated, but I believe that things are going to change. And I'm happy to be part of that change" (Creery 2018).

Likewise, young artist Yang Shuya (楊舒雅) gained online notoriety after the release of her 2019 track "Who Is in My Body?" (華康少女體內份子), which boldly cast the story of a love affair gone bad between a Chinese military officer and a young local woman as a metaphor for the KMT takeover of Taiwan. Yang is distinguished from the aforementioned women artists by her active membership in the *xiha* club at National Taiwan University, where she is currently in her third year of undergraduate studies. In an interview with a campus paper, Yang described her encounters with gender bias in the club when she first joined in 2018 (Xu, Li, and Ouyang 2020). Although some in the group were supportive and encouraging of her efforts, others were patronizing. Critiquing her performance in a cipher, one senior male club member told her that women were better off performing in "chill" (read: soft, down-tempo, ambient) styles. She argued back: "Why are women only supposed to do 'chill'? Women can also rap in ways that are fierce and fly!"[37] Galvanized by this and other incidents of sexism, her first original song addressed gender inequality in the community. She now tries to create an environment of support for other aspiring female rappers: "If the masculine culture in the rap circle can be changed, the girls in it will feel more comfortable. I think this is a very important thing." Nearly a decade after our first discussions about gender, it seems that Dwagie agrees: in 2021 he and Ill Mo collaborated with Yang on "1947 Overture" (1947序曲), a track commemorating the seventy-fourth anniversary of the 2-28 Incident.

It also remains to be seen how the refashioning of masculine identities and hierarchies currently underway in the rap scene might anticipate or organize new political subjectivities on the island. Artists like Dwagie are strategic in their attempts to cultivate qualities of democratic responsibility and civic nationalism in younger performers and audiences. *Xiha* clubs and creative collectives are the kinds of self-organized associations that in all likelihood would have been forbidden, or at least suppressed, under martial law. Voluntary and not built on family or kinship ties, these organizations "constitute a public sphere where individuals and groups interact to influence the publicly shared understandings that govern interrelationships in collective life," encouraging "horizontal ties of trust" that "facilitate social coordination" and ultimately form "the heart of stable democracy" (Weller 1999, 12–13). Part of a longer history of predominantly male, community-based associations, they occupy an intermediate space between family and state realms. Similarly constituted groups (e.g., women's interest groups, business clubs, baseball teams) multiplied after 1987 and since then have figured prominently in public conversations about the island's developmental trajectory (14). Their memberships may not espouse a particular politics, but they nevertheless play a role in inciting political change by encouraging forms of political participation like voting—as Dwagie did through his work on "Change Taiwan"—as well as fundraising, petitioning, and protesting.

Furthermore, the homosocial relations articulated with and through rap music activities can be said to constitute a rebuke to neoliberal rationalization on the island. While they are fundamentally unproductive in an economic sense, costing participants time and money to execute, they reward community members motivated by the prospect of camaraderie, self-empowerment, and the sharing of social space. Dwagie's young soldiers model is one approach to reconciliation in Taiwan between Confucian and democratic values, long regarded as mutually antagonistic by political pundits and scholars alike.[38] Their efforts to cultivate qualities of aggression and competition, and the premium they place on speaking truth to power as a fundamentally masculine imperative, have nurtured an energetic, community-wide engagement with democratic citizenship. To some members of the rap community, "Change Taiwan" is more than a catchphrase or chorus—it is a clarion call to action.

4
PERFORMING MUSICAL KNOWLEDGE WORK

In the summer of 2018, Kung Fu Entertainment posted a striking image to its Instagram account advertising a workshop for students on break from school (see fig. 4.1). The pedagogical impetus driving the workshop and similar university hip-hop club and creative collective-based educational programs rose humorously to its surface: at the center of the image was a digitally manipulated portrait of Confucius, adorned with a crown, pixelated sunglasses, and hands—which appeared cut and pasted from an image of a darker-skinned MC's body—throwing a backward "H" sign and holding a microphone.[1] The aged rice paper background of the space behind Confucius was embellished with a pale brown graffiti-style tag reading "Hip-Hop," as well as four black calligraphed characters—"in education, never weary" (有教不累, *you jiao bu lei*)—that rhyme and pun with the Confucian axiom "education for all, regardless of background" (有教無類, *you jiao wu lei*). The text below, in white, reiterated Kung Fu Entertainment's name and the title and date of the workshop, accompanied by *zhuyin fuhao* (注音符號), phonetic symbols used as literacy aids for young students in Taiwan.

The flyer's chimeric references were clearly tongue-in-cheek, a convivial jab at old-school artists' conscious self-fashioning as intellectuals in an old-fashioned and distinctly masculine tradition. But they communicated an earnest, tripartite message to their intended audience: Senior performers at this particular workshop would be pedagogues, perhaps with sagacious qualities; rap music and hip-hop culture are things to which one can devote academic attention; rap music and hip-hop culture are worthy of such attention. The shout-out to Confucius, teacher nonpareil, illuminated some of the threads that tether *xiha* both to locally prevalent models of learning and to local history.

FIG. 4.1. Advertisement for Kung Fu Entertainment summer workshop, 2018. Courtesy of Kung Fu Entertainment.

As I have shown, rap's community of learners reimagines traditional gender regimes to create new spaces for male sociality and to catalyze civic and political engagement. While the *nei-wai* dichotomy provides a symbolic framework for the feminine-masculine relations described in the previous chapter, a second theoretical formulation, the *wen-wu* (literary-martial, 文武) dyad that descends from Chinese philosophy and political culture, is useful for thinking about how masculine people relate to one another—and to themselves—within this community. *Wen* reflects the importance of gentleman-scholar (君子) figures in the writings of Confucius and in the *I Ching*, while *wu* reflects the historical and religious importance of Guan Yu (關羽), the legendary Han Dynasty general widely worshipped in Taiwan. The *wen-wu* paradigm of antiquity described the relationship between the civil (*wen*) and military (*wu*) branches of imperial government, but scholars have examined its utility in delineating notions of ideal masculinity in the PRC (Louie 2002, 2015) and contemporary Taiwan (Kao and Bih 2014), as well as in Japan and Korea (Benesch 2011).[2]

The gendered creative and social dynamics of the broader Taiwan rap scene, as represented in Kung Fu Entertainment's summer workshop advertisement, might be understood in terms of the *wen-wu* paradigm. Community discourses, rituals, and performance practices clearly invoke both martial virtues (i.e., battling, conscription nostalgia, explicit references to martial arts imaginaries) and civic ones (i.e., studying, teaching).[3] Individual songs and artists also balance *wen* and *wu* in strategic ways. At least some of the pleasure of Dwagie's music, for example, derives from its subjectively shifting *wen* and *wu* frequencies: On one wavelength, the martial themes of "Forty-Four Fours" are paradigmatically *wu*; on another, the clever wordplay and dense intertextual references are all *wen*. Teacher Lin has analyzed the Tripoets' relentless appeals to hypermasculine braggadocio and sexual innuendo on their 2008 album *The Beginning of Rhymes* (押韻的開始) not just as saber-rattling attempts to assert dominance over other artists or to channel a hard-core masculinity, but as efforts to showcase their hard-won knowledge of diverse hip-hop styles (2020, 164). Likewise, Soft Lipa might be described as having a predominantly *wen* sensibility, writing and performing cerebral, even arcane, compositions that testify to his narrative prowess and facility with flow.

Clubs and creative collectives cultivate both *wen* and *wu* qualities in participants, offering opportunities both for competition in the form of rap battles and for the acquisition of knowledge through study and mentorship. Events like the summer workshop are a cornerstone of Kung Fu Entertainment's operations and a critical part of how the collective ensures its continuation. In addition to organizing concerts and social activities and maintaining a strong social media presence, the group also conducts classes out of its headquarters in Tainan, in an alley near the busy intersection of Nanshiguohua Street and Minsheng Road. Theirs is a modest midrise structure, shabby-looking from the outside in the way that many buildings in post-industrial Taiwan are: clad in square tiles dingy from years without cleaning, draped with tattered awnings, and surrounded at the street level by haphazardly parked motor scooters. I was first invited to visit in September 2010, shortly after the group moved in. Their previous digs had grown too small to accommodate a growing number of students keen to learn how to rap under Dwagie's tutelage, and they had been compelled to seek out a new place with more space for classes. Dwagie's then-manager Sophie apologized for the state of the facilities, which they had not yet had the opportunity to thoroughly clean and arrange to their liking. Things were a mess when Kung Fu Entertainment moved in, she explained, but the recent incursion of Typhoon Fanapi had exacerbated the sense of disorder, breaking windows and leaving puddles of fetid water on the ground. As I wandered the facility, I traveled through a warren of rooms and corridors that were sparsely furnished but clearly designed to serve flexibly as spaces for socializing, music-making, and conducting business. The building's tabula rasa potential as a center for collaborative creative work was immediately apparent and, as a lifelong musician and student myself, I understood implicitly why it had appealed to the community-minded Dwagie and his crew.

One of the higher floors featured a room scattered with chairs, a dedicated area for classes. Dwagie did not set out to run a school when he started Kung Fu Entertainment in the early 2000s. At its beginnings, he told me, the organization comprised a group of friends who would occasionally go out, perhaps to a local teahouse or bookstore, and write songs together. As he began to take his career as a rapper more seriously and the association grew larger and more active, however, he sought space for a clubhouse, where members could socialize, compose songs, and record together. In due course, he was approached by outsiders who expressed a desire to study rap, and before long he was cast—happily, if unwittingly—into the role of pedagogue. In time, he enlisted others from the organization with the requisite experience and desire to pass their knowledge on to others. Those who register for classes now travel to the building once or twice a week, for a few months at a time. Dwagie views the practice of teaching as integral to the development of the Taiwan rap community and participants in Kung Fu Entertainment classes as prospective new group members. Some, he told me, are more rigorous in their approach to study than others: "I hope all of them [want to be part of the group], but some of them are just in it for the fun of it, they want to give it a try. There are also some who just don't have the patience to really create something new." Regardless of their intentions, he sees the classes as a form of civic engagement, providing youth with a structured alternative to illicit activity: "For the young ones, it's better than having them out drag racing, doing drugs" (interview, September 26, 2010).

Dwagie describes a process whereby young acolytes "prove [themselves]" and progress from level to level. Lessons focus on topics like song structure, crafting flow, arranging lyrics and structuring narrative, emotional expression, and international hip-hop trends and new techniques. After learning the basic tenets of rap and gaining confidence through exercises such as ciphers, they are encouraged to write and workshop original material with classmates.[4] Their success or failure in the program depends directly on the quality of the work they produce: "It's about your songs, it's about your performances. If they're good enough, then you can put them on the Kung Fu Entertainment websites. If they're not good enough, but you seem sincere and you can perform OK, then you can maybe perform at one of our shows." Once budding artists demonstrate

102 * CHAPTER FOUR

a degree of maturity as judged by their elders in the organization, they are encouraged to move beyond the confines of the building to perform for the public, in the flesh or virtually through online presentation (Dwagie interview, October 25, 2014). It is a very effective system—over the course of the past decade, I have observed Kung Fu Entertainment affiliates like PoeTek and BR mature from amateurs into auteurs in precisely this way.[5]

Enthusiasm for pedagogy—the work of *wen*—is by no means confined to Dwagie's sphere of influence but characterizes much rap-related activity beyond the streets of Tainan. Senior artists across the island valorize rap's discursive associations with knowledge on myriad fronts. The process of knowledge acquisition nourishes the performance of rap music. In the sociohistorical context of the United States, Marcyliena Morgan (2009) explores how everything from developing "everyday language creativity" (62), to demonstrating cultural insidership (74), to gaining membership in the core and long-term communities materializes from hip-hop devotees' dedication to learning as much as possible about the music's history, cultural significance, and aesthetic possibilities (55–62). The notion of learning as critical to hip-hop's growth and survival prevails among those who make the music as well as those who study it: the Universal Zulu Nation's formulation of hip-hop's fifth element places knowledge on equal footing in its importance with rap, DJing, graffiti, and dance.[6] In this view, knowledge plays a transformational role in hip-hop, guiding performers through their development and practice of the other elements. Moreover, through becoming knowledgeable about hip-hop and the broader world to which hip-hop is duty-bound to respond, the fifth-element principle teaches that community members can nurture the spread of peace and foster greater understanding between people.

To create and disseminate information about the rap world in Taiwan, and to transmit their creative practices to subsequent generations of performers, a number of senior artists, sometimes referred to as members of the aptly named "Old School" (老學校), engage in what I characterize in this chapter as "musical knowledge work." This heuristic signifies on sociologist Peter Drucker's (1959) classic formulation of knowledge workers as professional thinkers, whose job functions in post-industrial economies are distinguished by their emphasis on information manipulation and creative problem-solving.[7] Like Drucker's capable knowledge workers, enterprising MCs in this cohort tend to have high levels of educational attainment (sometimes, but not always, acquired at elite institutions), a desire for personal and professional self-direction, and previous preparation for careers in fields like design, engineering, medicine, architecture, law, and academic research. Prominent members of the Taiwan rap community, however, use the training they acquire in preparation for conventional knowledge work careers to communicate their mastery of musical and lyrical techniques and their knowledge of *xiha*/hip-hop history through classes, lectures, competitions, mentoring sessions, conferences, exhibitions, and contributions to a Taiwan-specific digital platform called the Professional Technology Temple (PTT). In these and other venues, many also extol the virtues of rap as a vehicle for teaching about non-hegemonic and counter-hegemonic histories, languages, and musics.

Naturally, musical knowledge workers diverge from conventional knowledge workers in a variety of ways, though perhaps none more significantly than in the financial expectations they attach to their undertakings. Except for a small number of performers, rap is not a lucrative endeavor, and most cannot support themselves with recourse to their artistic labors alone.[8] As members of a community formed initially through refusal—to participate in the corporate popular music industry and assimilate to Taiwan's hegemonic "auditory regimes" (Daughtry 2015)—their activities are seldom devised with the presumption of generating profit, even if the occasional artist with commercial appeal rises, phoenix-like, from their ranks. The products that rappers generate have historically performed the character of commodities more than they've functioned economically as such.[9] Albums, released on CD or vinyl as well as on the Internet, are produced to high standards, with carefully curated liner notes and compelling album art; live shows likewise manifest with quality sound equipment and sophisticated lighting design. With few exceptions, however, neither record nor ticket sales bring in much money, and they are not, as a general rule, expected by those involved to recoup the investments made in their production.[10] They are, in other words, fetish objects that hold subjective value for their creators and interested members of the rap community, but which do not often entice non-connoisseurs to pay their market-exchange prices. This is a matter of taste as well as a matter of scale: until recently, the audience for straight rap music was not sizable enough to pique the interest of the island's embattled mainstream record companies, and the companies themselves seemed incapable of producing acts that aroused the interests of mass audiences.[11] Moreover, the seemingly boundless PRC market has not historically represented the growth opportunity for the island's rappers that it has for Mandopop artists—the profane language, resistance rhetorics, and, in some cases, brazen support for Taiwan sovereignty that galvanize many *xiha* sounds and texts are clearly at odds with PRC government censorship edicts.[12] The four major local *xiha* labels—Kung Fu Entertainment, KAO!INC., True Color, and Ainoko—have made strides in cultivating both new talent and new potential listeners on the island, but the vast majority of musical activity in the scene is still undertaken by interested amateurs rather than seasoned professionals.

Although Kung Fu Entertainment and other organizations charge small fees for classes that reimburse overhead and materials, most of this work is performed on an essentially voluntary basis. When money is involved, there isn't much to speak of: for conducting a January 2019 Kung Fu Entertainment workshop, well-known performers Professor H and Rock Chen (洛克) charged tuition of NTD5,000 (approximately USD160) for sixteen hours of classroom time spread over eight weekends. Likewise, for a February 2019 workshop at the private experimental school Xue Xue Institute (學學) in Taipei conducted by Ill Mo, students paid just NTD1,800 (approximately USD58) for six hours of instruction spread over three weekends (Ill Mo personal communication, March 14, 2019).[13] Teaching for university clubs commands even less—an honorarium of perhaps NTD1,000–1,500 (approximately USD32–58) per two hours of instruction time. Under these financial circumstances, what is the draw of teaching? Why do artists invest so much time and energy in transmitting what they know to others? Is teaching just about keeping young people off the streets, as Dwagie suggests, or does it offer more elusive rewards?

In this chapter, I argue that rappers perform musical knowledge work as an adjunct to or replacement for conventional knowledge work, and as resistance to the market-oriented and individualizing practices and ideals that have proliferated on the island since the end of the 1980s.[14] While the resistance potential of hip-hop in the United States has sometimes been characterized as circumscribed by its complicity with neoliberalism, Taiwanese artists' financially unproductive activities sound a distinct note of rebuke to economic rationalization.[15] In teaching, researching, and mentoring about rap, they deploy skills developed for the purposes of achieving prosperity—with the affordances of technological tools developed in the service of national economic competitiveness—but use them to create little of appreciable value in the traditional economic sense. In addition to pleasure, their work ultimately generates narrative agency, a rapper's capacity to formulate and articulate his own subjectivity and to engender intersubjective relations. The Taiwan rap scene is, at its heart, an economy of such agency: those who earn it also claim the right to opine on issues that affect the broader community, to function in their milieu as pundits, oral historians, and chroniclers of quotidian struggles and joys. In recent years, artists have sometimes invoked this agency to narrate musically their frustrations about Taiwan's culture of overwork, the island's wage-stagnation crisis, and systemic barriers to homeownership and child-rearing—in other words, the ways in which conventional knowledge work has failed to meet the needs of their generation.

Studying *Xiha*, Producing Erudition

"In Taiwan, we have so many PhD rappers!" Ill Mo exclaimed as we first bonded over our shared experiences of graduate studies at a McDonald's in Taipei, on the cusp of the Lunar New Year (interview, February 12, 2010). The fast-food restaurant—a popular study spot—typically teemed with high school and college students, but it had emptied out in advance of the holiday break. Ill Mo was busy planning travel to his wife's parents' home on the second day of the new year, a traditional practice known as *hui niangjia* (回娘家), but he was happy to suspend preparations for an hour or two in order to meet another aspiring young scholar. Making his way through some French fries across the table from where I sat, he explained that he was busy completing coursework toward a PhD in English literature at Tamkang University, with plans to build on his previous MA thesis on Spike Lee's 2000 film *Bamboozled* from the Chinese Culture University. Similarly, his partner in the Tripoets, Teacher Lin, was preparing to depart for fieldwork in Fiji. A doctoral candidate in anthropology at the University of Pittsburgh, Lin was already in the thick of work on a dissertation exploring conservation, farming, and development in an Indigenous community on Taveuni Island. Caught up in his studies, he wasn't in Taiwan very often, which made recording and performing challenging for the group.

The Tripoets were not alone in trying to balance musical activities with academic pursuits. Chang Jui-chuan (often referred to as "Teacher Chang" [張老師] by fans and other artists) was pursuing a doctorate in English education at National Chengchi University when we first met in 2009, following his completion of a master's degree in writing, rhetoric, and discourse from DePaul University in Chicago; Fish Lin of Kou Chou Ching was writing a thesis for his master's degree in architectural preservation; and amateur MC Braindeath of Psycho Piggz was in the process of becoming a physician. Other senior performers had earned their bachelor's or master's degrees in Chinese literature, business administration, engineering, physical education, and graphic design. The academic credentials of the younger generation of artists were no less sterling, with many enrolled at competitive universities and prestigious high schools. PoeTek and BR, at the forefront of this younger generation, are sometimes referred to as "academic rappers" because they cut their teeth while earning degrees from the ultra-competitive National Taiwan University, but there have always been artists who could lay claim to academic excellence.[16]

The scholarly bent of the community was something I noticed early in the course of my work, as many musicians and fans were conversant in the task of conducting research and eager to help in whatever way they could. As I grappled initially with the logistics of fieldwork—fumbling with my digital recorder, asking anxiously if interviewees would sign consent forms—nervous sweat beads collecting on my brow were met with looks of recognition rather than consternation or confusion. This isn't to suggest that my interest in rap seemed natural or intuitive to those I contacted. On the contrary, my research associates, who usually imagined themselves as bit players in Taiwan's musical ecosystem, expressed bemusement as to the draw of this particular topic, especially for a white American woman without a heritage connection to the island. Over the years, we have bonded over our shared love for music, but our shared identities as academics have often furnished our greatest source of solidarity.

The intersection of rap and higher education in Taiwan is not coincidental. Although American hip-hop emerged initially from the marginalized space of the post-industrial ghetto—where its architects produced a new "alternative economy of recognition and prestige" (Austin 1998, 242)—hip-hop outside the United States has often first been the province of those with relatively greater socioeconomic advantage. Individuals with easiest access to communications technologies, especially the Internet, have also been most able to devote time and energy to the study of hip-hop history and techniques.[17] This is also the case in Taiwan: rappers overwhelmingly represent the island's middle socioeconomic strata, and most grew up in financially stable homes and have had or are pursuing some form of higher education. They do not hail from the blighted landscapes that populate what media studies scholar S. Craig Watkins (1998) has called the "ghettocentric imagination," but reside in the comfortable, compact dwellings stacked within urban Taiwan's numerous ramshackle midrise apartment buildings. Although some claim working-class backgrounds, the majority of those I interviewed described childhoods in households headed by elementary and secondary school teachers, professors, office workers, nurses, construction supervisors, insurance brokers, and small business owners. The education sector is particularly well represented in the families of senior *xiha* artists—Teacher Lin and Shortee of the Tripoets, Chang Jui-chuan, RPG, Dwagie, Mr. Brown of Da Ximen, and PoeTek all have at least one parent who is or was an academic. They also identify, for the most part, as Han, which affords them social and economic privileges that are withheld from Taiwan's Indigenous peoples.[18] Born mostly between 1975 and 2000, they crested the wave of the Taiwan Economic Miracle (台灣經濟奇蹟) and were the beneficiaries of both unprecedented parental investment and an expansive, island-wide university system that flourished in Taiwan's post-authoritarian speech environment.

The growth of Taiwan's middle class is a recent development, the consequence of major transformations in the island's economy in the latter half of the twentieth century that both emerged from and drove investment in education. The years immediately following the Second World War were characterized by economic and political turmoil as Taiwan transitioned from Japanese colony to seat of the Republic of China, a period marked by hyperinflation and widespread civil unrest. By the 1950s, however, the KMT had consolidated its power through the imposition of martial law, which created the requisite stability for the island to rebuild and re-form its fragile economy. In this endeavor, Chiang Kai-shek received significant financial and political support from the United States, which commenced its strategic partnership with Taiwan following China's entry into the Korean War. With essentially unchecked power and an injection of cash, the KMT instituted land, industrial, and educational reforms at an unprecedented scale to accelerate economic development.

The early 1960s saw a transition from agrarian to industrial economy as the island began to export non-agricultural goods to other countries. Exponential export-led growth ensued in the following years as the KMT opened Taiwan's economy to international competition, adjusted tax laws, decreased regulation, encouraged foreign investment, and developed the island's infrastructure and heavy industries. In the 1980s and 1990s, the rate of economic development slowed and the island began a process of de-industrialization, spurred in part by rising labor costs and increasing pressure to move manufacturing offshore to more profitable venues. At the same time, however, Taiwan established itself as a premier source for high-tech electronics, taking a leading role in the global production of semiconductors and computers. The government gradually loosened restrictions on cross-strait business during this period as well, setting the stage for Taiwanese companies to invest directly in China, which was still at a much earlier stage in the process of industrialization and therefore a cheaper source of labor. Standards of living rose and income inequality decreased further, helping to push life expectancy from fifty-nine years in the 1950s to seventy-two years in 1983, and tripling the size of the average living space (Clark and Tan 2012, 25). The transition from agrarian to industrial economy catalyzed a significant migration of the population from rural to urban areas, as more workers sought jobs in non-farming capacities (Williams 1994, 218–19, 245).

In combination with land reforms and shifting economic policies, new initiatives in education dramatically transformed the picture of Taiwanese life between 1950 and 2000. With the institution of compulsory primary education in the 1950s, subsequently lengthened from six to nine years in 1968, literacy rates climbed, supporting the growth of an educated work-force that would bolster Taiwan's global competitiveness (Clark and Tan 2012, 11–12). This same period saw an explosion in the number and ac-cessibility of institutions of higher learning. During the Japanese colonial period, Taihoku Imperial University (now National Taiwan University) was the island's only university. By 1969 students with adequate resources and preparation could choose from among 91 institutions of higher learn-ing, of which 22 were universities or four-year colleges and 69 were junior colleges (Wang 2003, 261–62). These numbers increased dramatically af-ter the lifting of martial law, and by 2000, there were 127 universities and four-year colleges and 23 junior colleges (266) crowded onto a landmass not quite 14,000 square miles in size.[19]

Current participants in the rap scene came of age when some-thing resembling a middle class was already established in Taiwan. Their growing-up experiences bore little resemblance to their parents' and their grandparents', who remember when Taiwan was primarily agrarian, chil-dren were expected to contribute to family businesses, and educational opportunities were circumscribed by the small number of institutions of higher learning on the island. By contrast, artists and audiences I inter-viewed, particularly those born in urban areas in the 1980s and '90s, grew up in a post-agrarian Taiwan, where their primary responsibility during youth was to excel at academics and matriculate to the best possible uni-versities in pursuit of upward mobility. After the end of martial law and the period of democratic consolidation, they gained access to universal health care, highly developed systems of mass rapid transit, and global mass media. In adulthood, however, they face challenges that members of their parents' or grandparents' generations did not: namely, the perils of greater economic integration with the PRC, the unceremonious cool-ing of a once-white-hot economy, and increasing uncertainty about the future of Taiwan sovereignty. They have also been tasked with negotiating the deleterious social, cultural, and political effects of neoliberalization, which accelerated in Taiwan during the immediate post–martial law years when the KMT shifted away from statist strategies of economic develop-ment and began embracing privatization, deregulation, public-private partnership, and financial liberalization (Hsu 2009).

Many members of the rap community were first exposed to *xiha* within the university system. The rates of university attendance in Taiwan as a whole are high—matriculation to institutions of higher education from senior secondary schools stood at nearly 96% in 2017.[20] In 2000 Teacher Lin and an older friend whom Lin and others refer to as "Classmate Su" (蘇同學) established the unofficial extracurricular Hip-Hop Culture

Research Society (HHCRS, 台大嘻哈研究社會) at National Taiwan University (NTU), the island's premier public college. Lin had started the online discussion forum Master U during his high school years, which allowed rap enthusiasts all over the island to network with one another and share information remotely for the first time. HHCRS, which Lin helped to initiate when he began his studies at NTU, was designed to serve as a complement to that online experience, a place where aspiring artists and fans could be physically co-present. Many current performers forged early relationships at HHCRS get-togethers during the early 2000s; the group was the first to organize outings, activities, and lectures on rap-related subjects; and regular meetings provided an early venue for the exchange of recordings that were, at that time, difficult to procure on the island. Membership was not sanctioned officially by NTU, and it was open to students from any university; some members told me that they had traveled from more distant campuses to participate because their own institutions did not offer anything comparable (Danny Wang [王韋翔] personal communication, March 7, 2010).

HHCRS quickly assumed an academic atmosphere once meetings started, as Lin describes: "We would meet weekly. The first year, the senior, Classmate Su, was the president. And he would lecture, he would try to be very academic. We would print out a syllabus, we'd assign readings, articles from the Internet talking about hip-hop culture, and I remember when [Nelson George's 2005 book] *Hip Hop America* was first translated into Chinese and there was a book-publishing event, we as a club attended that event. So, it was very scholarly in a way" (interview, October 18, 2010). Anticipating Kung Fu Entertainment's later tongue-in-cheek reference to Confucius, the HHCRS's first club logo depicted the brilliant early Han Dynasty statesman and military strategist Zhang Liang (張良), known for his dedication to studying the art of war (Lin 2020, 163). It was around this time that Lin, whose full given name is Lin Hao-li and who is now himself an assistant professor of anthropology at National Tsing Hua University, assumed the identity of "Teacher Lin," NTU's resident *xiha* pedagogue:

> I think we were trying to educate, because hip-hop at that time was quite well known as a performative genre, some [Taiwanese people] knew graffiti and stuff, the DJ of course is a very popular image. Rap music, [however], had just started, I mean Taiwanese rap music. Well, even American rap music was just starting to be mainstream in Taiwan. . . . So we were trying to teach people what is hip-hop music. And one of our slogans was "hip-hop is music" as opposed to "hip-hop is just dancing." So, we were coming from a place where a lot of people were ignorant

about what is hip-hop music, what is hip-hop music in general. We would talk about the history, we would trace back to the South Bronx, we would talk about the four elements. Then afterward we would go to the technicalities. (Teacher Lin interview, October 18, 2010)

Noting the absence of hip-hop studies and the paucity of opportunities to undertake formal coursework in contemporary popular music at NTU, Teacher Lin and Classmate Su sought to fill a lacuna. Their earliest lessons, perhaps unsurprisingly, centered hip-hop's origins and the narration of what ethnomusicologist Catherine Appert has called the "mythical litany": the Bronx Moment, the emergence of hip-hop from predominantly Black communities, the development of the original four elements and their political potentialities (2018, 4). Lin and Su initiated themselves into a global community of scholars, fans, and artists who tell this story time and time again (as I did in chapter 1). Today the HHCRS continues to expand its educational mission. Group members invite artists and scholars to lecture on a range of subjects and, now that the history of Taiwan rap is several decades long, turn their attention increasingly to music by local artists.

The scholarly character that Lin described was evident at the first of several HHCRS meetings I attended on a balmy October evening in 2010. I was immediately struck by the deep seriousness and devoted attention of the young members of the club, which surpassed what I observed when I sat in on formal undergraduate classes at NTU and at my home institution in the United States. About twenty young men and a few young women gathered in a classroom on the edges of the leafy green campus of NTU for a lecture by renowned Taipei-based turntablist and record collector DJ Vicar. Vicar sat on a raised platform at the head of the room, where a professor would typically stand (see fig. 4.2). His long hair was tied back and secured with a headband, and his backpack, on the floor by his feet, was stuffed to overflowing with LPs. On the blackboard behind him were reminders that this space was typically used to teach more standard subjects—someone had written in English, presumably as part of a lesson in mechanical drawing: "CAD Modeling: 1) wireframe modeling 2) surface 3) solid." By the time I entered the room, Vicar seemed prepped and ready to go—two turntables and a mixer plugged into the outlet behind the table hummed eagerly with electricity. As a few more attendees filtered in and positioned themselves at desks, Vicar started to spin. The HHCRS president introduced Vicar to the group—a formality since everyone present certainly already knew him from his frequent appearances at Beat Square, a long-running all-vinyl Park Jam hosted by DJ Chicano. Brooklyn-based retro soul and funk artists Sharon Jones and the

F I G . 4.2. Members of the NTU Hip-Hop Culture Research Society gather around for a lesson in the basic tenets of DJing with DJ Vicar, October 29, 2010. Photograph by author.

Dap-Kings' "100 Days, 100 Nights" played quietly as Vicar invited everyone to gather around for a lesson in the basic tenets of DJing. We shuffled up to the desk and watched attentively as he demonstrated basic beat-matching techniques, first pairing Sharon Jones with Michael Jackson, then switching out the Michael Jackson for some Otis Redding. His hand motions were quick and fluid and the seams between recordings were hardly perceptible. As Vicar guided our curious flock, one club member picked up a piece of chalk and started transcribing on the blackboard the English-language terms Vicar was using, alongside the mechanical drawing vocabulary: "1) fade 2) loop 3) stylus." In response, several students (myself included) scribbled down notes in small, tidy ledgers.

The HHCRS has inspired the growth of organizations that nurture similar informal academic environments at other schools, as well. A number of universities, especially in the island's major urban centers, now have *xiha* culture clubs or "Black music societies" (黑人音樂社) that are dedicated to the study of rap and other Black American genres. Although these groups are mostly student-led, they can sometimes capitalize on shared institutional affiliation with experienced artists who are willing and eager to teach and mentor. While a graduate student and adjunct lecturer in

FIG. 4.3. Ill Mo introduces guest lecturer MC Hotdog to members of TKU Beatbox at Tamkang University, December 14, 2016. Photograph by author.

English at Tamkang University, for example, Ill Mo founded and served as an adviser for TKU Beatbox, a *xiha*-focused student organization. In this role, he taught rap skills to student members and also helped them arrange showcases and special presentations, including by such luminaries as MC Hotdog (see fig. 4.3). During this period, the *xiha* clubs at Taipei National University of the Arts and at National Taiwan Normal University also invited him to teach and lecture, sometimes for as long as eighteen weeks at a time (Ill Mo interview, March 14, 2019).

Ill Mo applies his formal academic training for a career in English pedagogy to his *xiha* teaching in the hopes of empowering his students to think analytically about rap and to write and perform their own compositions. To this end, he plans ten or twelve lessons of around two hours each, taking care to first establish his credentials as a core member of the community and qualified instructor, and then leads class participants through close reading and discussion of sample tracks. One of his favorites to share with beginners is Soft Lipa's 2009 song "About a Little Bear" (關於小熊), which he feels communicates the importance of developing individualized, idiosyncratic approaches to storytelling:

> The song itself is not like a breakthrough topic—it's a love story between a man and a woman who spent time together, it's very cliché. What makes

it stand out and be different is the perspective it takes—it's from the perspective of a doll, a teddy bear. So, a lot of times, it's not about what
has been written before, it's your take. I [also share] this in my English
classes and my hip-hop classes. As a writer you have to be creative ... you
have to come up with ways that haven't been done before. The topic
itself, it could be anything. Then after we sit and we listen to the song
and I talk about it for a bit, usually some students have experience and
I'll ask them or give them homework and ask them to bring their work
the next time they come so they try to rap in front of peers. (interview,
March 15, 2019)

During subsequent sessions, Ill Mo leads students through the development of key technical skills, encouraging them to be mindful of their approach to rhythm, rhyme, and vocal delivery. He also stresses the value of
repetition because, as he says: "Most of these students, they're not experienced performers, to the point where they become shaky ... that's an important part of the lesson, to overcome stage fright and to be at ease, and
also to let them know the importance of practicing." It is the very same
principle he stresses in his English classes, he says—improvement requires
discipline. To this end, he often takes videos of his students performing
their original pieces—usually original lyrics set to pre-written beats found
online—and shares them on Instagram, where an online audience can
send feedback and, hopefully, inspire further learning.

Considered alongside his descriptions of *xiha* club and creative collective activities, Ill Mo's statement that Taiwan has so many "PhD rappers"
might be read in two distinct ways: literally, as a claim that the island
boasts numerous MCs with graduate degrees, and, figuratively, as an assertion that accruing and disseminating knowledge (of oneself, of one's
community, of hip-hop, of *xiha*) is important to community members. In
both senses, a desire to propagate the fifth element has empowered them
to claim territory for themselves on university campuses, even from their
relatively weak positions as students, lecturers, and adjunct faculty. Their
tactics call to mind Michel de Certeau's "art of the weak" (1984), which
sociologist Vered Amit summarizes as "the capacity to discern in the slippages and gaps of institutional arrangements opportunities for winning
space, which are then quietly grasped" (Amit 2015, 10). The founders of
the HHCRS discerned and responded to such slippages and gaps at NTU
two decades ago. Although hip-hop studies as an academic discipline has
yet to gain a firm foothold in Taiwan's institutions of higher learning as a
part of formal curricula, the infiltration of rap into classrooms via clubs
confers a sense of legitimacy on the community's activities and a sense
of agency on the community's membership.[21] The small but attentive

audiences for the formidable academic skills of artists like Ill Mo and Teacher Lin are in turn driven to share what they know with others.

Extending Social Associations Online

Knowledge work activities like DJ Vicar's workshops and Ill Mo's classes encourage the formation of social associations and help to sustain them not only in physical places like the Kung Fu Entertainment headquarters and classrooms at NTU and Tamkang University, but also online. The Internet has nurtured the growth of local hip-hop communities across the globe, challenging the hegemony of the corporate music industry and mediating the transnational movement of the music and associated cultural products among artists and audiences.[22] The online sphere wields similar power in Taiwan, where those in search of information, camaraderie, and feedback on their original compositions log countless hours on websites and Bulletin Board Systems (BBS). A BBS is a computer-based communication portal that contains forums for special interest groups. In Europe and the United States, the term "BBS" refers specifically to systems accessed via a terminal program, but in much of East Asia a BBS is simply a public online forum, Web-based or otherwise, wherein users can befriend and chat with other users and circulate information.[23]

Master U, the online discussion forum that Teacher Lin initiated in the late 1990s, was the first venue for Internet-based communication among fans of rap music and aspiring performers on the island. It served as a key "affinity space" (Gee 2004), in which members of the *xiha* community created, contested, and consolidated knowledge, and through which they constituted and codified social relations. In 2001 Lin, then a sophomore at NTU, refocused his efforts on establishing a *xiha* bulletin board with similar functionality on a BBS known as the Professional Technology Temple (PTT; 批踢踢實業坊). PTT was, and still is, a premier information and communication technology for high school and college students in Taiwan. Open-source and not-for-profit, it is an expansive terminal-based Bulletin Board System with more than 1.5 million registered users who publish over forty thousand articles and a million comments each day ("What Is PTT?" n.d.).[24] The largest BBS in the Sinophone world, it also encompasses chat, mail, and game functions, catering to those who are, on average, twenty-five years of age and logged into the system for multiple hours on a daily basis.[25] Users—also called "villagers" (鄉民)—visit boards with a wide variety of themes, among which more than a hundred focus exclusively on popular music.[26] They can read, author, or comment on articles; they can also provide positive or negative feedback on the works of others using the shorthand "push" or "recommend" (推) and "hiss" or "do not recommend" (噓).

The formation and activation of the PTT *Xiha* Bulletin Board (嘻哈看板) coincided with what many rappers remember as a golden age, a time of prodigious activity and creative ferment in the musical underground. They used PTT to seek one another out, disseminate information about upcoming performances, exchange opinions on recordings, and debate the musical ethos and ideological imperatives of an incipient, localized rap style. Like many information and communication technologies, PTT imbricates on- and offline worlds. Although registration for the system is open and the service is free, villagers are required to provide their real names and identifying information to administrators, who are liable to report that information in the event that legal action is brought against a villager for a crime committed on the boards. Indeed, very little of what transpires on PTT is truly anonymous: The *Xiha* Bulletin Board community is essentially isomorphic with the offline rap community in Taiwan; users will often arrange face-to-face meetings, and most do not shy away from providing identifying information in messages. On many occasions, rappers and rap aficionados directed me to other board members by providing their PTT handles, real names, and school or professional affiliations.

The lyrics to the 2008 rap track "PTT.cc" (PTT點cc),[27] written and performed by amateur MC Cyrax, testify humorously to the system's importance in its users' lives, online and offline:

回到故事開頭　那結局非常哀愁
唉呦　反正她不愛我　掰摟
沒關係　反正我還有PTT
上去看看有沒有新的pretty lady
"PTT 從今天起　無限期停機"　我的人生就這樣的跟著失去意義
rest in peace

returning to the start of the story, the ending is very sad
aiya, anyways, she didn't love me
no matter, I still have PTT
I'll go on and see if there are new pretty ladies
"From today PTT is shut down indefinitely"
my life is now meaningless
rest in peace

While it ostensibly tells the story of a relationship gone awry, the song is notable as a melodramatic paean to PTT. Cyrax's lyrics attest to the platform's deep entrenchment in Taiwanese youth culture and its significance to members of the *xiha* community in particular. The farcical track is less engaged with the robust institutional qualities of PTT than with its efficacy as a dating tool, but a link to "PTT.cc" and responses from commenters appraising it as "too cool" (太酷了), "awesome" (讚), and "very funny" (好笑) are preserved for posterity on the Hip-Hop Bulletin Board (posted on December 3, 2008, by a user with the handle "hilagu"), rendering the song itself and the discussion it generated more than a decade ago part of the community's extensive historical record.

This historical record is curated by peer-appointed moderators (版主), who exercise the right to periodically clean up a given board, removing posts that have received more hisses than pushes and sequestering articles they deem especially noteworthy in a separate "Best Of" section called the *jinghuaqu* (精華區).[28] Teacher Lin, who uses the PTT handle "holicane," posted more than 150 articles between 2001 and 2009 that remain in the *jinghuaqu*. Among these are accounts of the development of both American and Taiwan rap styles, ruminations on the spread of global hip-hop, and numerous album reviews. The *jinghuaqu* is also home to some of Lin's more imaginative and incisive pieces, including one he describes as a "comparative study of [African American Vernacular English] and the words that are used in the traditional Chinese novel *The Water Margin* (水滸傳)," the purpose of which was to reimagine a classic of vernacular Chinese literature he studied in school using the language of American-style rap music (interview, October 18, 2010).[29] Other materials in the *jinghuaqu* provide information on foundational hip-hop precepts like sampling, graffiti, and breaking, and a number of "hot threads"—postings that provoked memorable or productive discussion among villagers— are also preserved there. This lends the *jinghuaqu* the aura of an online archive, a robust repository of knowledge accessible to all community members.

Prior to posting new articles, asking questions, or participating in existing conversations, new users are expected to first familiarize themselves with the materials in the *jinghuaqu* and on the board proper, to observe the community's norms of discourse and obtain a sense of its history. As Teacher Lin explained to me, those who pose a question or express an opinion without first gaining some knowledge of what has come before do so at their own peril: "I think... that would be very helpful for newcomers. And it's even becoming a way to attack newcomers, like if they ask some question which is perceived as stupid... people will say 'you didn't look at the [*jinghuaqu*]?'" The threat of public castigation has in the past created a hostile environment, Lin explained to me, such that "people [are sometimes] afraid to post opinions on the *Xiha* Board because... they'll be attacked, [accused of being] ignorant" (interview, October 18, 2010). A sense of trepidation is palpable in the language used in many posts, which reveal a clear pecking order among villagers: new PTT users or those less familiar with hip-hop refer to themselves as "new hands" (新手) and address their inquiries with deference to the board's "great ones" (大大), who have mastered or authored materials in the *jinghuaqu* or otherwise demonstrated depth of knowledge.[30]

Measured against the sophistication of today's social networking sites, terminal-based BBS in many ways resemble technological relics.[31] Run on a Linux system platform, PTT lacks rich media. Its signature look has blocky gray text, a solid black background, and eight-bit graphics. To some degree, PTT looks ancient because it *is* ancient, at least by the warp-speed standards of those accustomed to twenty-first-century computing and Internet-based social networking. But far from having vanished in the wake of the World Wide Web, PTT and similar systems continue to thrive throughout the Sinophone world. Their persistence may at first glance suggest a phenomenon described by Marshall McLuhan as the "reversal of the overheated medium," in which media types that "cross-fertilize" eventually transgress "break boundaries" after which they become overextended and prompt a reversal to more fundamental technologies (1995, 169–74). Within this model, the use of PTT might represent a retreat from "overheated" Web-based social networking sites like Facebook, Instagram, and Twitter. It is more accurate to say, however, that terminal-based BBS simply never went out of style in Taiwan; it has been a constant presence on the island since the 1980s and remains a technology in use alongside Web-based social networking sites. In fact, PTT is now also accessible on the Web in a form that retains the minimalist aesthetic and simple functionality of the original.

The longevity of the system can be understood in terms of several specific advantages it confers upon users, who emphasize its speed, efficiency, and ease of use. As Hong Qingqi (洪欽碁), a computer scientist and previous member of the *Xiha* Board, explained to me, PTT attracts and retains users not in spite of its austerity, but because of it:

> Compared to Web pages, BBS is very simple and plain (without any images or pictures). I think it helps to make readers focus on every word. I know many good writers [who'd rather] write articles on BBS than on a blog. I think good writers sometimes also mean experienced writers. They like old stuff. Maybe that's one of the reasons they stay on BBS.... When this wisdom stays in BBS, I think their followers stay, too. It's kind of like a tradition. (interview, September 24, 2010)

Hong's statement alludes to another quality of PTT that is both a cause and effect of its longevity: that "old stuff" accumulates within the system over time, such that it comes to serve as a storehouse of "wisdom" for current and future users. It is perhaps for this reason more than any other that the *Xiha* Board lends itself to a discussion about places of learning— many of those who make use of the system do so with the objective of expanding their knowledge of rap music, starting out as "new hands," dedicating themselves to studying the *jinghuaqu*, and perhaps emerging as "great ones."

PTT has been a critical resource for my research, but I was surprised to find in May 2010 that my work on the island had earned me a place in the archive of the community. An announcement of a colloquium I was invited to present at Academia Sinica, Taiwan's national academy, appeared on the *Xiha* Board, posted by Fan Chiang (screenname "prisonf") of Kou Chou Ching. The posting translated as follows:

> Perhaps there are on this message board some friends who are engaged similarly in creative work, who have been interviewed by this Harvard graduate student. On 6/1, she'll present her experiences [studying the community] at Academia Sinica's Institute of Ethnology. This young woman is quite diligent, spending much time observing and recording Taiwan's rap scene. I hope everyone can come and cheer her on.

Below, he listed the details of the talk title, time, place, and contact information. I was honored by Fan Chiang's efforts to bring people to Academia Sinica and excited that PTT had generated an opportunity for me to contribute to community discourse and receive feedback from community members. At the event itself, I noticed only a handful of familiar faces in the audience, including Ill Mo and several other individuals I had previously met at performances. Still, it was humbling to see my work represented on the *Xiha* Board—in essence, to be granted admission by the community's gatekeepers to a place reserved for its most committed students.

"Just to Play, Not a Real Job": Earning a Living, Earning Respect

The academic imprimatur of rap is a source of pleasure and social respectability for aspiring artists who covet recognition as "great ones," but it offers little solace to their families, who are sometimes concerned that writing, performing, and teaching rap will distract them from the real business of growing up and finding desirable employment. Fan Chiang, for example, was still a student at Fu Jen Catholic University when he began to contemplate performing professionally with Kou Chou Ching bandmate Fish Lin. He quickly encountered resistance from his parents: "The average Taiwanese person's point of view is you first study, graduate from college, then go to graduate school, then you go to work. And my doing this thing, in their eyes, it was just for fun. Just to play, not a real job" (interview, April 7, 2010). The lack of parental approval must have stung, but Fan Chiang explained that he had never felt particularly close to his mother and father. His paternal grandfather, who was his primary caretaker during childhood, was a more critical source of support. He had for many years encouraged his grandson to connect to his Hakka roots, and he was overjoyed when the young MC expressed an interest in rapping in the Hakka language, sampling from traditional Hakka musics, and advocating for education on Hakka history. After releasing their first full-length album in 2007, *Kou!! It's Coming Out!!!* (拷!出來了), Kou Chou Ching was nominated for a Golden Melody Award. The external validation helped his parents to see their son's potential as a musician, and they began to feel more at ease about Fan Chiang's career prospects. But it took many years and a significant industry recognition to arrive at that point. Other artists have shared similar stories about parental pessimism, and parental disappointment has been a persistent lyrical theme in Taiwan rap songs since "My Life" (2001), in which MC Hotdog proclaims: "I haven't graduated from college because I want to put out a record, dad and mom flew into a rage, but I don't care."

Careers in the arts are scarce and hard to sustain, and rap's historically marginal status, especially relative to Mandopop, does little to assuage parental misgivings in an era of increasing economic precarity. Ill Mo lamented the difficulty of making a living as a rapper, through teaching or performance, shortly after we first met more than a decade ago:

> When I first got into this hip-hop thing, started writing songs and forming a group . . . I had this dream of becoming a rap star that actually supports my living. But very soon the dream was shattered. I learned that there's no way that you can make it. The prime example is MC Hotdog. He's like the biggest rap star you can find in Taiwan, but he's not driving a Cadillac or buying huge houses. He's doing maybe a little bit better than normal people, he's getting paid for what he loves to do, but that's about it. And that's not really a stable living condition. (interview, February 12, 2010)

Ill Mo and his partners in the Tripoets explained that all their earnings came from performances, as their record sales at the time generated virtually no profits. Prior to signing with MC Hotdog's label True Color, they typically commanded NTD3,000–5,000 (approximately USD90–150) for a ten- to fifteen-minute set. Their management eventually took on responsibility for negotiating financial matters for the group, but even so, Ill Mo speculated that their fees did not exceed NTD10,000–15,000 in 2010 (approximately USD300–450), and only a portion of that went to the group after various other expenses were paid. Other artists I interviewed have also spoken of being swindled out of profits by unscrupulous record executives and managers.

They might come from relatively privileged socioeconomic backgrounds, but it's exceedingly difficult to get rich in the Taiwan scene. The vast majority of artists have historically taken on full- or part-time work to make ends meet, and many remain at home with parents because the cost of living in Taiwan's major urban areas puts independence out of reach. In some cases, they are able to find employment in music-related businesses, working as recording engineers and studio assistants. When I first met Taipei-based MC Witness in 2011, he was teaching English through rap at a private enrichment school for children (he has since relocated to the United States to work in the restaurant industry); as discussed, Ill Mo and Teacher Lin were graduate students and are now university professors who integrate *xiha* into their teaching. As they have grown older and taken on more family responsibilities, some artists have developed professional profiles that are more or less independent of their identities as musicians: Shortee has worked for Gogoro, a Taiwanese company that develops electric scooters, e-bikes, and battery-swapping technology; Chang Jui-chuan has worked as an English-language editor, educational consultant, and university lecturer; RPG has worked in music production, the film industry, and for cosmetics and apparel companies; Fan Chiang, who split from Kou Chou Ching in 2014, now works in marketing; and Fish Lin, who left Kou Chou Ching in 2019 but still performs as part of the band Community Service, is employed as a research assistant at the Shihsanhang Museum of Archaeology.

Parental concern is not unfounded given the relatively poor prospects of finding fortune—or, as Ill Mo noted, stability—in *xiha*. Things are admittedly looking up since the 2017 debut of the enormously popular Chinese competition television show *The Rap of China* (中國有嘻哈／ 中國新說唱). Three out of four of the show's judges have roots in Taiwan (MC Hotdog, Chang Chen-yue, and Wilber Pan), and several Taiwanese MCs have competed, which both contributed to the show's success among Taiwanese audiences and dramatically increased MC Hotdog's earning power relative to 2010, when Ill Mo and I first discussed the economics of *xiha*. But Beijing strongly constrains expression in news and entertainment media, making it difficult for participants (especially those with pro-Taiwan politics) to really keep it real. While *The Rap of China* has helped to popularize *xiha* in the Sinophone world, the star power of commercially successful rap artists is still dim compared to transnationally successful Mandopop stars like Wang Leehom and Jay Chou—and those who wish to court Chinese audiences must carefully toe the Party line.

The increased mainstream interest in *xiha* generated by *The Rap of China* has trickled down to both emerging and senior artists like Ill Mo, who released several new singles after completing his doctoral studies in 2019. Ten years after our first conversations, he no longer harbors dreams of rap superstardom and his relationship to commerce seems more pragmatic. With this most recent work, his modest hope was to make enough money by selling records and performing to pay the various producers and beatmakers who had assisted him. This, he felt, would legitimize his efforts, at least among his peers. "You make something official by paying," he told me. "And nowadays, if you try hard enough *you* are a record company" (interview, March 15, 2019). Even if his music fails to net a profit, Ill Mo still concedes that it could be professionally advantageous to build his public profile as an artist. While navigating the tight academic job market, one university expressed interest in his application because, they told him, the out-of-the-box thinking and multidisciplinary talents he demonstrated in his rap-related teaching activities might have practical (i.e., commodifiable) applications in the classroom.

For the most part, however, those who commit time and energy to musical knowledge work do so with an awareness of the economic opportunity cost. This is, in fact, part of *xiha*'s appeal. In *Taiwan Hip-Hop Kids* (嘻哈囝), a 2018 documentary focused on the growth and development of Taiwan's rap scene, KAO!INC. founder Dela (迪拉) reflected on the attraction he felt to *xiha* in a neoliberalizing Taiwan:

> The Confucian education we received when we were young told us to study, to do good deeds, but it didn't tell us to try to earn big money. But there was actually a kind of subtext [to that education], which was: "Ah! So-and-so is becoming a doctor! So-and-so is becoming an accountant! So-and-so went abroad to study." It's a very hypocritical educational system. When I was a college student and about to look for a job, well, that would make anyone anxious—and I'd say, "If I can only have a career, something I'll really enjoy…" And then you see the OGs, and they're not doing this for money. Naturally, it was attractive.

Dela has done well enough for himself, opening a small hip-hop-themed café in Taipei called Beans and Beats (see fig. 4.4) and slowly

FIG. 4.4. View of the interior of Beans and Beats, July 20, 2017.
Photograph by author.

growing KAO!INC. into a formidable incubator for *xiha* talent. But his relationship to financial success seems ambivalent—less something he pursued than something he stumbled on serendipitously. Chafing against what he describes as the "hypocrisy" (虛偽) of an educational system apparently rooted in Confucianism but subordinated to neoliberal "regimes of value" (Appadurai 1986), he turned to *xiha* initially for its promise of a life pursuit unmoored from professional ambition.

Following a parallel path, Professor H, an artist relatively unknown to audiences outside the core *xiha* community, made national headlines in 2017 when he quit his job in Shenzhen at Taiwanese multinational electronics company Foxconn in order to devote his time to *xiha*. Although he worked in the corporate office and was not subjected to the well-documented labor abuses endured by Chinese Foxconn factory floor employees (Pun et al. 2016), Professor H cited as his reasons for quitting a litany of grievances characteristic of modern neoliberal work environments (Bal and Dóci 2018): a brutal schedule that kept him on call twenty-four hours a day, entitled him to only one day off per month, and deprived him of time to eat properly (Xiao 2019). Burned out after two and a half years and in rapidly declining physical and mental health, he walked away from what might have been his dream job—with a reported

NTD1,000,000 per year salary (approximately USD32,000), nearly three times the average for new college graduates in Taiwan—and returned to Taiwan in search of a healthier workplace culture.

An online article describes his parents' response to this choice, which recalled what Fan Chiang shared with me: "Professor H is the eldest son in his family, and this crazy decision of course made his parents anxious, such that they repeatedly encouraged him to take the civil servant examination or to take a bank job. His cute grandfather even wanted him to pursue a doctorate, even though he didn't yet have a master's degree, because no one in the family knew what a rap career looked like" (Xiao 2019). Leaving Foxconn was a bold move for a member of Taiwan's "22K" generation, so-called because the monthly wage for new college graduates like Professor H has hovered around NTD22,000 (approximately USD700) since the 2008 global financial crisis. As comparative literature scholar Chih-Ming Wang has described them, the 22K generation envisions the future in an era of neoliberal globalization as "stagnant, alienating, and precarious. It is not something one looks forward to but what must be resisted if one can" (2017, 185). Undeterred, his first order of business was to begin writing and recording with his old friends at Kung Fu Entertainment, his second was to begin teaching rap classes, and his third was to research and publish a primer: *Study Rap with Professor H: With This Book, Your Rap Won't Go Astray* (來韓老師這裡學饒舌 ： 有了這一本 ， 讓你饒舌不走冤枉路 !) (Han 2019). While these efforts, like Ill Mo's, had the trappings of entrepreneurialism, pursuing them required that Professor H make ends meet with a dramatically reduced income.

By assuming the role of performer and pedagogue, Professor H effected a lateral move from conventional to musical knowledge work and sounded a clear note of rebuke to the exploitative corporate culture he left behind. Companies had been luring talent like Professor H—recipient of an elite education in economics from National Chengchi University—to work in China's industrial centers for some time, stoking fears of a Taiwanese brain drain and increased economic reliance on the PRC. The prospect of economic integration and competition with the PRC is particularly anxiety-inducing to the 22K generation, which perceives the cross-strait economy as rewarding primarily conglomerates (even Taiwanese-owned ones, like Foxconn), highly skilled workers, and political-commercial elites (Wang 2017, 185). For Professor H, the benefits of working at Foxconn did not compensate sufficiently for the costs. His flight from Shenzhen made ripples across the Taiwanese Internet, where numerous soft news items reported with shock and awe on the salary he had left behind and the security he had repudiated. The subtext of these stories was no doubt clear to local readers: Professor H hadn't just abandoned stable employment at Foxconn for an unstable, possibly untenable, future in *xiha*—he had rejected conventional success narratives altogether.

Cultivating Narrative Agency

Poor prospects for building wealth in the rap scene do not necessarily deter artists from trying to build lives in *xiha*. On the contrary, those discussed in this chapter have chosen to strengthen social associations and community separate from, or adjunct to, their professional pursuits. To whatever extent possible, they desire to carve out a meaningful existence within neoliberal capitalism. Even if performing musical knowledge work does not lead inexorably to riches, it can generate something valuable by community standards: narrative agency, or a rapper's capacity to formulate and articulate his own subjectivity in relation to the world. Scholars have ruminated on the meaning and import of narrative agency since antiquity, but political theorist and philosopher Sarah Drews Lucas's recent formulation of the concept is particularly useful in this sociohistorical context: narrative agency expresses "an individual's constant, enduring capacity for meaning-making in the face of the limitations to agency posed by the subject's constitution by norms and elucidating the interconnectedness of individual and collective agency" (2017, 124). Drews Lucas extends and engages political philosopher Seyla Benhabib's conception of narrativity (1986, 1992), in turn built on ideas set out by Hannah Arendt (1958), to describe the processes by which people may make sense of their own identities and experiences of the world. Although narrative agency resides in individuals, its object is not self-actualization or sovereignty. It is, on the contrary, fundamentally relational, conferred on individuals by communities that recognize them as partners in ongoing conversations, as imbricated in common "webs of interlocution" (Drews Lucas 2017, 127) and, potentially, as committed to collective political action (124–25). We might imagine musical knowledge work as the pathway by which some artists in Taiwan—resisting neoliberal work cultures and laboring to connect to others through teaching, mentorship, and participation in social associations—enter into these conversations and weave these webs.

Ideas of "realness" or "authenticity" in Taiwan rap derive their discursive power in part from their associations with narrative agency, thus defined. My friend Danny Wang, an office worker who frequently attended *xiha* club activities in Taipei between his teens and early thirties, once told me that the principal distinctions between rap and *shulaibao*, for example, lie not in their different sounds, but in the intimacy and immediacy of their storytelling: "*Shulaibao* is...mostly funny stuff and it doesn't involve a lot of personal information or thoughts. But I think rap is quite personal.

And the strongest, smartest performers, they keep it real and tell whatever story they want to tell" (interview, March 8, 2010).[32] It is in this telling that such "strong" and "smart" artists identify for themselves and express to others the ways in which they make sense of the world. As Dwagie put it:

> I'm not like other singers who are afraid of talking about politics, always hiding from politics. I write about everything—I'll write about how I'm going to party, I'll write about love between men and women, of course I will. Politics are also a part of my life, so of course I'm going to write about them. Sometimes it's intentional, but sometimes I don't give it much thought, just kind of speak off the cuff, because I think I should talk about the things I want to talk about. (interview, September 26, 2010)

Many describe Dwagie as a "political" artist because his most well-known songs highlight social ills and systemic injustices, but he rejects this simplistic characterization: politics are better described as part of his "narrative identity," which Drews Lucas describes as "the shifting constellation of narratives which make up a particular self" (2017, 125). Because *xiha* is a venue for disclosure of the "real," the ineluctably personal, his music is always by necessity political. By differentiating himself from other artists, he positions himself within a web of interlocutors with varying relationships to the political, thereby making explicit the relational nature of the narrative agency he asserts. "Selves are no more single existences than are atoms and molecules," Michael D. Jackson observes (1998, 6). Intersubjectivity is not merely shared experience between two or more autonomous agents—it is, rather, the way relations and experiences create categories of identity itself.

Rappers sound identities not just in relation to other rappers, but also to other members of Taiwan's body politic with whom they share material resources and discursive space—politicians, teachers, employers. In the 2010 song "I Am Insane" (我是神經病), experienced MC RPG deploys his accrued narrative agency to critique the neoliberal capitalist economy, employer abuse, and the dead end of conventional knowledge work. Available to stream online at Streetvoice.com but never sold, the song describes the frustrations he has experienced as an office worker in Taipei, all the while juggling multiple side jobs and struggling to make ends meet.[33] RPG's experiences are reflected in statistics about living and working in Taiwan: in the years before and after he wrote "I Am Insane," the island's workers logged approximately 2,200 hours annually—some of the longest in the world. As in many other neoliberalizing economies, however, inflation has outpaced the growth of salaries. Between 1997 and 2012, the hourly minimum wage only increased from NTD66 to NTD103 (a difference of approximately USD1) in spite of a 16.35% rise in the consumer price index over the same period.[34] The song is a direct response to elected officials who chastise younger generations' apparent preference for remaining unmarried and childless in this economic climate. In particular, RPG targeted incumbent Health Minister Yaung Chih-liang (楊志良), who angered the island's youth when he made public statements implying a connection between single lifestyles and mental illness.[35] RPG explained to me that "the reason young people don't get married is because the wages are too low. Most people our age are responsible for our own life and our elders.... But the wage right now is too low. What the hell—[how am I] going to marry and have children?" (interview, June 21, 2011).

When we first met in 2011, RPG explained to me that he never imagined while growing up in the comet trail of the Taiwan Economic Miracle that his adult life would be so fraught with struggle. Born in 1985, just two years before the end of martial law, he left his hometown of Tainan to study business administration at National Chengchi University in Taipei at the age of eighteen. He had been something of an academic celebrity in Tainan, enrolled in the most competitive high school and ranked among the top-twenty students in the city. His mother, a junior high school teacher, had high expectations for his academic performance, and RPG credits her with much of his success; his father, who worked for the state-owned electric company Taipower, was "very conservative." Neither was thrilled when RPG started writing and performing rap music, but, he told me, they were "also happy for me to not do drugs and just make a living for myself" (interview, June 21, 2011).

RPG works hard to make a living in Taipei, where he settled after college. His family remains in the south of the island, and when we first met, he was living with two roommates in a small apartment in Zhonghe, southeast of Greater Taipei. When I asked his occupation, he sighed deeply and rattled off the names of multiple workplaces and positions: marketing director for Puff Nation, an apparel company; marketing director for BePretty, a women's cosmetics and accessories retailer; freelance marketing planner for indie hip-hop artists; freelance recording engineer for classical artists (his clients included the National Symphony Orchestra, National Taiwan Symphony Orchestra, National Chinese Orchestra, and National Taipei Orchestra); and freelance film producer for music videos and sometimes advertisements. Prior to all that, he was an account executive for an advertising agency and a marketing planner for EMI Music Publishing. At a recent meeting in Taipei, he told me with some excitement that he now has a record contract with indie label RoBoKatz (基械貓音樂) and is making a go at music full-time (interview, April 13, 2021).

RPG's long and winding path to a record contract began with his musical interests in high school. A tenor in a local chorus, singing, not rapping, was his first passion: "I had a very good singing voice when I was younger. And then I formed an R&B group with my junior high school classmates." They covered American artists like Boyz II Men and Blackstreet, a lot of what he labeled simply "Black music" (黑人音樂). Through MTV and radio—English-language stations like ICRT and a local Tainan outlet called Touch—he gained exposure to American hip-hop. Tupac, Biggie, Diddy, Snoop Dogg, Dr. Dre were all over the airwaves in those days, and the beats and rhymes were infectious. "I thought, 'Wow, this kind of music is, like, very inspiring—and it's perfect for partying.' But we don't party, because I was an honors student, so we don't party!" Before long, however, he was hanging out with local b-boys and learning to dance. Captivated by hip-hop culture, he traced a path backward through time to explore the sounds of Grandmaster Flash and DJ Kool Herc. Master U, the online forum initiated by Teacher Lin, connected him to other rap fans with whom to share his original compositions, discuss new music, and share resources and recordings. He was particularly inspired by the sounds and stories of MC Hotdog, who had graduated from Jianguo High School, the most competitive boys school in Taipei, before finding acclaim as an MC. If Hotdog could do it, he thought, what was to stop him (RPG interview, June 21, 2011)?

Like many artists from Tainan, RPG maintains a close relationship with Dwagie and his creative collective, Kung Fu Entertainment. Dwagie's influence is palpable in RPG's early work: both are similarly passionate about local social and political issues and the interlocking questions of Taiwanese identity, sovereignty, and economic solvency. RPG also frequently serves as a mentor to younger performers and contributes to many of Kung Fu Entertainment's outreach activities. He views *xiha* as a mode of affective-political communication and connects with audiences on the level of shared concerns about not just electoral politics but also wages, work-life balance, and the struggles and joys of everyday living (interview, July 12, 2016).

Back in 2011, RPG spoke of intense feelings of dissatisfaction with Taiwan's economy and with politicians who seem perpetually out of touch with the challenges that young people on the island now face. In "I Am Insane," written around this time, he grapples with the masculinity politics examined in the previous chapter and articulates the impotence he feels as an underling in a neoliberal employment environment. The song is less of a personal memoir than what Imani Perry (2004, 91–92) calls a "being narrative," in which RPG employs a first-person narrative voice in order to personify the overworked, underpaid 22K generation:

這首歌送給我們的衛生署長，楊志良先生

副歌
因為我單身的該死　我單身的該死
我單身的該死　我單身的該死
我單身的該死　我單身的該死
我單身的該死　我單身的該死
從今以後不要叫我RPG　叫我神經病　謝謝！

主歌1
這是偉大的政府　全新的力作
官員腦袋運作　結論我腦袋有洞
我想我真的有病　這絕對沒有錯
長這麼大　真的很沒有用
我沒有錢結婚更不用說養小孩了
女人要穩定可是靠我就垮台了
所以決定努力工作為了未來振作
為了得到尊重　更好的生活
領著微薄的薪水然後工時超長
做不好的時候尊嚴被嚴重的踐踏
大家叫我草莓　我怎麼敢反抗？
因為我菜嘛　不然又能怎樣？
不合理的要求　這叫做磨練
所以加班到半夜當然沒有加班費
在這誠摯邀請各位政府的官員
下班後到企業看看燈有沒有滅

（兩個男生，說:）
1: 你跟你女朋友在一起這麼久，　有沒有要結婚啊？
2: 怎麼可能？我都在加班都要分手了啦！

導歌
我沒有錢我怎麼敢生
羊窒糧他叫我不要單身　快點結婚
不然健保費多繳的時候我別想抽身

副歌
因為我單身的該死（男聲說:）你單身的該死
（女聲說:）我單身的該死（男聲說:）你單身的該死
（RPG說:）我單身的該死（男聲說:）你單身的該死
（女聲說:）我單身的該死（女聲說:）你單身的該死
（RPG說:）我是神經病！

this song is dedicated to our Minister of Health, Mr. Yaung Chih-liang

chorus:
because I'm single I should go to hell, I'm single I should go to hell
I'm single I should go to hell, I'm single I should go to hell
I'm single I should go to hell, I'm single I should go to hell
I'm single I should go to hell, I'm single I should go to hell
from now on do not call me RPG, call me "Insane"—thank you

verse 1:
this is our great government's newest stroke of genius
our officials wracked their brains, conclusion: my brain is full of holes
I think I must really be sick, that must be right
I'm so grown up, but I'm still a loser
I don't have money to marry, let alone raise kids
women who want stability can only depend on me to collapse
I decided to work hard, labor for my future
to gain respect, a better life
earning a meager salary and working very long hours
when I fail my dignity takes a serious beating
everyone calls me Strawberry, but how do I dare argue
because I'm green, what else can I do
unreasonable demands, that's what they call training
working overtime until the middle of the night, of course that doesn't
    mean overtime pay
we sincerely invite you government officials
to go to the corporations after you leave the office and look at whether
    the lights are extinguished
(two other men's voices, spoken:)
1: You've been with your girlfriend a long time. You getting married?
2: How? I'm always working overtime, she's ready to break up!

pre-chorus:
I have no money, how am I supposed to have kids
"Sheep Constipated with Grain" tells me I shouldn't be single, hurry up
    and get married
if NHI raises their rates for singles, I won't be able to escape

chorus:
because I'm single I should go to hell, (man's voice:) I'm single I should
    go to hell

(woman's voice:) I'm single I should go to hell, (man's voice:) I'm single
   I should go to hell
(RPG's voice:) I'm single I should go to hell, (man's voice:) I'm single I
   should go to hell
(woman's voice:) I'm single I should go to hell, (woman's voice:) I'm
   single I should go to hell
(RPG, laughing) I am insane!

He opens with a spoken dedication to Yaung Chih-liang, immediately
positioning the song as a response to the health minister's controversial
comments. He then launches into a first statement of the chorus, obses-
sively repeating the phrase "Because I'm single I should go to hell" in a
dull and listless voice before politely conceding that the listener should
cease referring to him by his MC name and instead, per the minister, call
him "insane." In the first verse, RPG articulates his desire for a comfortable future and his frustration at finding his efforts thwarted as he labors
overtime for insufficient pay and suffers the verbal abuse of his superiors.
The justification for such treatment is that he is "green" (菜, Mandarin
slang, lit. "a vegetable"), an inexperienced, immature junior colleague
with little power or status in the workplace. Implying that government
officials are out of touch with the demands being placed on young workers, RPG invites them to observe that employees in most office buildings remain at work even after bureaucrats clock out of their comfortable
government jobs.

The rapper speaks from his perspective as a young man, and he experiences the criticisms of both his elder colleagues and bureaucrats as a
threat to his masculinity: others call him a "Strawberry" (草莓), a term
with clear gendered overtones that references membership in the so-
called "Strawberry Tribe" (草莓族). Political scientist Shelley Rigger has
noted that to be deemed a Strawberry is "an insult, especially for Taiwanese in their 20s, because in the eyes of many Taiwanese over forty, young
people are, like the fruit, beautiful to look at, but easily damaged—and
quick to rot" (2011, 81). There is a general consensus that Strawberries,
many of whom are too young to have experienced the austerity of life under martial law, are allergic to hard work, overeducated, and self-centered.
As Rigger puts it: "The logic behind the Strawberry Tribe discourse holds
that Taiwanese born after 1970, and especially those born in the 1980s,
have known only wealth and comfort. Their indulgent parents—seeking
to spare them the privations of their own childhoods—showered them
with material things and shielded them from hard work. The result is a
generation of youth who are not only immature and materialistic, but

also take Taiwan's freedom and prosperity for granted" (83). RPG chafes audibly against such accusations of softness and sweetness, not to mention apathy. "I Am Insane" registers reasoned objection to the use of an epithet that elides the social, political, and economic challenges that today's youth must negotiate.

Prior to a second repetition of the chorus, two other voices join RPG's for a brief spoken interlude. The first speaker inquires as to whether the second speaker plans to marry his long-term girlfriend, to which the second speaker replies that, on the contrary, his constant need to work overtime threatens to destroy his relationship. RPG returns to rap the next three lines, asking how he can possibly sustain himself on his current meager earnings. He complains that an unsympathetic Health Minister Yaung—whose name is rendered in the lyrics RPG posted online using the characters for "sheep" (*yang* 羊), "constipated" (*zhi* 窒), and "grain" (*liang* 糧), which pun with the more flattering characters of his actual name, "poplar" (*yang* 楊), "aspiring" (*zhi* 志), and "goodness" (*liang* 良)—has asked him, despite RPG's perilous financial situation, to identify a prospective spouse and hurry to the altar. The rapper laments further that if the National Health Insurance Bureau (NHI) raises their rates on unmarried subscribers, he'll have no choice by law but to pay, in spite of already being strapped for cash. This is another direct reference to Yaung, who advocated for charging single individuals higher insurance rates because, he alleged, they were more likely to be mentally ill and therefore rely to a greater extent on the health care system (Wang 2010). When the second repetition of the chorus arrives, RPG is joined by several additional voices, all repeating with increasing fervor the maxim that they ought to go to hell because they're single. The chorus ends with the sound of RPG laughing maniacally before once again declaring his own insanity.

In the second verse, the rapper describes how he is forced to prostrate himself to his employers, if only for the privilege of earning a pitifully low salary. For this, he directs blame toward the policies of the Council of Labor Affairs, led at the time the song was written by Minister Wang Ruxuan (王如玄), whose name is rendered in the lyrics RPG posted online using the characters for "death" (*wang* 亡), "rotting stench" (*ru* 茹), and "hanging" (*xuan* 懸), which pun with the more flattering characters of her actual name, "king" (*wang* 王), "as" or "into the state of" (*ru* 如), and "mystical" (*xuan* 玄). RPG might be "pissing blood," but he remains willing to exert immense effort and take whatever measures are necessary in order to avoid being fired—a circumstance that, indeed, makes him question his own sanity. Invoking the rhetoric of class struggle and comparing himself to a series of worn-out, exploited things (over-tilled soil, a burst liver, a white lab rat), he laments his inability to take a vacation, afford a home, or have a family. For his "failures," he sarcastically claims remorse and issues facetious apologies that suggest an exaggerated sense of filial piety and obligation to authority figures, society, and the nation:

主歌2
先求有再求好所以領 22K
理所當然非常肚爛亡茹懸
我不敢反抗 因為我有病
血尿剛好而已哪敢爭取什麼福利
說加班就加班 說銷假就銷假
我怕我一說話隔天就準備回家
被鬥臭的階層 被深掘的軟土
被凹爆的肝臟 被利用的白老鼠
要正常休假 我是神經病
我要求加班費用我是神經病
我買不起房子 我是神經病
我不敢成立家庭我是神經病
我對不起爸爸 我對不起媽媽
我對不起公司 我對不起師長
我對不起社會 我對不起國家

verse 2:
gotta start somewhere, so I'll take 22K
it goes without saying, I'm pissed at "Hanging Stench of Death"
I dare not resist, because I'm sick
I might be pissing blood, but they think I deserve it, so how dare I ask
    for welfare?
If they say work overtime, then I work overtime, if they say come back
    from leave, I come on back
I fear that if I say something, the next day I'll have to pack my things and
    leave
my social class attacked and maligned, soft soil dug down to the bottom
a liver worked to bursting, a white rat being used
I want to take a regular vacation, I am insane
I demand overtime pay, I am insane
I can't afford a home, I am insane
I dare not start a family, I am insane
I'm sorry, dad, I'm sorry, mom
I'm sorry, company, I'm sorry, teachers
I'm sorry, society, I'm sorry, country

A melodramatic spoken interlude follows, with RPG apologizing to Health Minister Yaung for having ever been born, to which a sample of Yaung's voice responds with a halfhearted apology that he never should have used the word "insane" because mental illness is a sensitive issue. A final statement of the chorus concludes the song; RPG is once again joined by additional voices, claiming this time that they as a community deserve punishment for the crime of being unmarried.

"I Am Insane" clearly echoes Jutoupi and Blacklist Workshop's madness-themed pieces from an earlier era, which responded to social, political, and economic problems in the immediate post–martial law period. RPG was inspired more directly, however, by American rapper Nas's 1999 "I Want to Talk to You," which decries the US government's unwillingness to address the plight of the urban poor (interview, June 21, 2011). Traces of Nas are evident in the directness of RPG's lyrics as he addresses the government in general and Health Minister Yaung in particular, but the two artists do not otherwise sound much alike. In "I Want to Talk to You," Nas deploys a speech-effusive flow and demonstrates a virtuosic rhythmic flexibility with respect to the underlying beat, diverging from and returning to it fluidly. The result is a declamatory yet naturalistic style resembling oratory that augments the forcefulness of his angry message. RPG, however, adheres strictly to the underlying beat and employs a simple end-rhyming pattern. In the setting of his vituperative lyrics, this flow style produces a striking effect. He seems to use the confines of the meter to hold his seething rage in check; a clipped, precise delivery gives the performance a sardonic tone, much like his interjected laughter and self-lacerating lyrics.

While Nas provides thematic inspiration for RPG, a more aurally evident intertextual reference is present in the song's accompaniment: RPG uses the looped vocals, bass, and percussion track from Jay-Z's 2009 song "On to the Next One," material that producer Swizz Beatz in turn drew from French electro-house duo Justice's 2007 song "D.A.N.C.E." RPG downplayed this artistic choice when I asked him about it, explaining that he had picked out the music quickly in order to record and release the song online as a timely response to the health minister's public comments.[36] Nevertheless, the accompaniment places "I Am Insane," a song decrying the problems of social immobility and career stagnation in Taiwan, in scathing dialogue with "On to the Next One," in which Jay-Z celebrates his rise from poverty to fabulous wealth and boasts of the senses of forward momentum and progress that propel his work. A thundering bass and militant snare and hi-hat lend unexpected gravity and urgency to a track ostensibly about the quotidian challenge of meeting expectations in the office and sustaining meaningful relationships with partners and spouses. These instrumental sounds might be interpreted as incongruous with the mundane subject matter and therefore sardonic, but the problems RPG describes have real and ominous consequences for Taiwan's rapidly graying population.

The use of additional voices other than RPG's also marks "I Am Insane," suggesting that the recording is envisioned as a statement on behalf of the broader community of young people in Taiwan. The Jay-Z instrumental includes a chopped-up fragment of the sung, layered vocals in "D.A.N.C.E."—a chorus of childlike voices singing a fragment of the cryptic phrase "Under the spotlight, neither black nor white, it doesn't matter…"—which sounds again and again behind RPG's vocals throughout "I Am Insane." The lyrics to the original are unintelligible, but it produces the effect of a crowd chanting its support, perhaps simulating the legions of similarly disenchanted young professionals for whom he might speak. Some of these individual voices appear in the chorus, where masculine- and feminine-sounding voices take turns repeating the line "I'm single I should go to hell," in one case rising to a hysterical scream. The inclusion of voices from across the gender spectrum sonifies the structural problems that RPG describes, which affect not just young men like him but also women and nonbinary people. Systemic sexism notwithstanding, people of all genders participate in the workforce and in the raising of families. Women are audible on the track not as lust objects but rather as fellow protesters, differentiating the gender politics of "I Am Insane" from those of, for instance, MC Hotdog's "I Love Taiwan Girls."

What "I Am Insane" does have in common with "I Love Taiwan Girls" is the intercontextual character of its narrative. As Health Minister Yaung went on record lambasting the youth of Taiwan for their apparent inclination to remain single, "I Am Insane" registers in a very public way RPG's strong disagreement with the minister's comments. Insofar as it "[participates] in the wider cultural dialogues through which historical understanding is narrated," RPG's song takes on a narrative function, per Keith Negus's conception of intercontextuality (2012, 368). In both its sonic and lyrical dimensions, the song constitutes an arresting narrative about workplace politics and the vicissitudes of everyday life in Taiwan. It leverages RPG's narrative agency to raise unsettling questions not only about his own existence, but also about the fate of the nation should the current political-economic trajectory stay its course.

Although Taiwan's economy rebounded following both the 2000 dot-com collapse and the 2008 global financial crisis, there is widespread concern about the island's long-term financial outlook. Driving these sentiments are fears that the economy has become "boxed in," too expensive for the lower-end economic sectors, but not quite up to the task of competing with more advanced economies in industries like banking and biotechnology (Clark and Tan 2012, 84). Taiwan's two major political coalitions have proposed different antidotes to the island's economic anxieties that affirm their broader political alignments. The KMT and its allies in the so-called "Pan-Blue" camp, who officially support the "One China" policy, argue that greater economic integration with the PRC and other overseas markets is the most promising avenue for sustained growth. The DPP and its allies in the so-called "Pan-Green" camp, who reject "One China," maintain that investment in the domestic economy, especially local innovation and social welfare protections, represents a more expedient and ethical pathway. Although the KMT and DPP articulate different visions for the island's future, both parties promote prosperity as essential to preserving Taiwan's domestic stability and de facto sovereignty, and neither has proposed or enacted plans that challenge fundamentally the broadly neoliberal orientation of current decision-making. The 22K generation experiences life in this political and economic climate in a maddening double bind, despondent about their personal prospects in a stagnating economy and fearful that further economic growth and globalization will imperil the island's democracy.

Rappers cannot escape this bind entirely, of course, but they can mitigate its effects by opting into another value structure and generating feelings of worth—personal, professional, spiritual—through musical knowledge work. To imbue their pursuits with gravitas and respectability, senior artists like Dwagie, Ill Mo, Teacher Lin, and Professor H appeal to distinguished traditions of scholarship, assuming the mantle of teachers and mentors for aspiring young MCs. They embrace their identities as principals of the "Old School" by creatively appropriating long-standing institutional structures and utilizing online archives like PTT. Their pedagogical initiatives are rarely lucrative, and those who sink time into these activities do so with an awareness of the opportunity cost. The upshot is that rappers can anchor themselves in something other than today's raging neoliberalism and bolster their claims to social roles as, variably, disseminators of the fifth-element concept and venerable scholar-gentlemen. Artists like Fan Chiang, who elides the boundaries of rap and traditional musical narrative performance in his work with Kou Chou Ching, may also declare themselves heritors of and teachers in the *liām-kua* tradition discussed in chapter 2. Across their endeavors, rappers trade on the alternative capital of narrative agency and seek out ways to live meaningful lives despite constraints on their autonomy and power.

S. Craig Watkins has argued that hip-hop in the United States "enables its participants to imagine themselves as part of a larger community; thus, it produces a sense of collective identity and agency" (1998, 65). Rap's in-extricable link to Taiwan's vast academic networks likewise furnishes *xiha* with this capability. Narrative agency, as I employ the term, is relational, conferred on individuals by communities that recognize them as partners in conversation and as collaborators in political activism. Socialized as educators, rappers not only create new knowledge but also identify and make themselves legible to members of such communities. In rap—as a way of life, as a way of thinking—they perform what anthropologist Dorinne Kondo describes as the "alternative visions of cultural possibil-ity" and "utopian wish-images" that necessarily precede social transfor-mation (1997, 257). The artists at the center of chapter 5 suggest that these alternative visions might reveal the world beyond the double bind and set out to transform the way the nation beyond the rap community sees itself, where it has been and where it has yet to go.

5
"WE ARE SO STRONG, WE ARE WRITING HISTORY"

Fan Chiang was still a student at Fu Jen Catholic University when he first began collaborating with Fish Lin, his eventual partner in Kou Chou Ching (Fan Chiang interview, April 7, 2010). They encountered one another in 2003 at Lyricist Park, a weekly event held in a basketball court on Taipei's Shimin Boulevard, where aspiring rappers would assemble to freestyle and battle. Organizers Shortee of the Tripoets and Mr. Brown of rap-rock duo Da Ximen supplied beats via a boombox, which they had to wire to a motorcycle for power because batteries were too expensive (Shortee interview, March 3, 2010). Fish Lin and Fan Chiang connected from the outset over their common interest in local politics and their understanding of rap as an ideal medium for thinking through and educating listeners about socioeconomic and political issues, particularly as they affect different ethnic communities on the island. They both looked up to "conscious" American MCs as well as local artists affiliated with the New Taiwanese Song Movement, like Jutoupi, Blacklist Workshop, and Lim Giong (Fish Lin interview, July 13, 2016). As their partnership developed and Kou Chou Ching conspired to record an album, the pair began to formulate their approach to making "real Taiwan-style *liām-kua*" (正港台灣味唸歌).[1]

Developing enough facility with the island's diverse languages and sonic archive to undertake such a project, they realized, would require no small amount of remedial education. Neither Fan Chiang nor Fish Lin felt like they knew all that much about Taiwan back when Kou Chou Ching was just starting out. Both were born in 1980, and their early schooling transpired in the years immediately preceding the end of martial law and democratic transition. The curricula in place under authoritarianism examined Taiwan's history only insofar as it was articulated to the mission of "recapturing the mainland" (反攻大陸), and students were discouraged from learning about local forms of expressive culture. As a result, Fan Chiang and Fish Lin had both studied Mandarin—rather than Hakka or Hoklo—and took classes that emphasized the primacy of European art music over local music:

> From the time we were young, we never studied any local languages, I never studied my mother tongue. All that was studied in music class was Western music, [sings] *do re mi fa sol la si do!* But Taiwan's music doesn't use that system, it's totally different from Western music. The teachers didn't bring us *koa-á-hì*, *lâm-koán*, or *pak-koán* to listen to, but they'd teach Mozart, Beethoven. So, from youth, we didn't understand...we thought *suona* is the thing you hear when someone dies. It's very noisy, it's the music of death. But the *suona* carries other meanings, and so does the *erhu*, even the *yueqin*. They have many different social significations. But the teachers don't teach it, and you don't know anything about their stories.[2] (Fan Chiang interview, April 7, 2010)

Fan Chiang and Fish Lin committed themselves to learning as college students, not just the history and techniques of American and global hip-hop, but also the local languages and cultures that were proscribed during their childhoods. The *suona* is often played at funerals in Taiwan, and Hakka was a language only Fan Chiang's aging grandfather spoke fluently, but rap provided a framework for redeeming these expressive modes and transporting them back into the realm of the young, the vital, the living. Energized by this mission, the members of Kou Chou Ching—which also came to include DJ JChen and two multi-instrumentalists, Achino (張瀚中, 阿雞) and Yobo (尤智毅, 尤寶)—set about scouring night markets and temple gift shops for recordings to study.[3]

There has always been a strong didactic flavor to the group's compositions, which are a meticulously curated mélange of languages and samples from these found recordings, imbricated with the more familiar sounds of globally circulating hip-hop beats and scratch effects. Kou Chou Ching follows earlier artists like Jutoupi in emphasizing the pluripotency of Taiwan's sonic environment and the particular sense of intense liveliness, or *renao* (熱鬧, lit. "heat noise"), that sound ideally engenders in settings of festivity on the island.[4] The group likewise deploys creatively repurposed excerpts from existing recordings to index and comment strategically on matters of local social and political importance. "Intro," the opening track of the 2007 album *Kou!! It's Coming Out!!!*, exemplifies this approach: it intersperses short clips of pieces from disparate local musical traditions, including Taiwanese opera, Hengchun folk songs, Hoklo pop, and Hakka *bayin*, among others, as well as snippets from political call-in radio shows, advertisements, and news broadcasts. Static knits these together, producing the effect of a radio dial moving back and forth along the spectrum of frequencies. If Blacklist Workshop's "Taxi" described the workaday existence of a taxi driver dutifully navigating the streets of an economically booming Taipei at the end of the 1980s, "Intro" might have provided the imagined soundtrack for his travels.[5] The bricolage aesthetic the piece generates is familiar, both as a hallmark of stylistically omnivorous local musical narrative forms like Taiwanese opera and glove puppet theater *and* of global hip-hop. As the album unfolds, however, its carefully considered logic is revealed: one by one, each constituent part emerges as a sample in a different track, to be recontextualized and juxtaposed with novel signifiers.

Kou Chou Ching's technique of layering diverse sounds and samples from preexisting sources accords with what Catherine Appert (2018, 18) describes in her work on Senegalese hip-hop as a "practice of aural palimpsest memory." As existing sonic materials undergo their transformation into hip-hop, she observes, their past is partially effaced to make space for "new ways of knowing"; the resulting musical form is rendered a site of collective memory. Kou Chou Ching's 2007 track "Good Appetite," discussed in chapter 2, samples to such ends: as Fish Lin and Fan Chiang's lyrics lament the decline of Taiwanese open-air banquet culture, Uncle Qilin's *yueqin* accompaniment from his "Improvisation on the Burning of a Fishnet-Drying Hut" provides fodder for an ostinato figure that repeats for the duration of the piece. The meaning of Uncle Qilin's original narrative about the tragic outcomes of a poor marriage in a rural seaside village is subordinated to Kou Chou Ching's newer narrative, yet the sample serves to remind listeners that outdoor banquets traditionally punctuated lives of privation and struggle in agrarian Taiwan. Although Appert's attention to form methodically stakes out distance from the referential aspects of samples in the Senegalese context—as she notes, "producers often do not intend for musical samples to communicate representational meaning" (183)—songs like "Good Appetite" derive much of their affective power from the representational qualities of their samples. They signify deliberately to local listeners on multiple levels, musical and semantic, and are often clearly identifiable as artifacts of local expressive culture once suppressed under KMT hegemony. In order to ensure that listeners have access to their old and new meanings, Kou Chou Ching provides detailed information about preexisting musical sources in paratextual materials like album liner notes, explicating their origins and outlining their selection criteria.

Just as sampling can be understood as one strategy for "telling the stories" that Fan Chiang's teachers omitted, so, too, can Kou Chou Ching's tactical use of non-Mandarin languages. Fan Chiang became noticeably frustrated in one of our early conversations when he remarked on the linguistic limitations of local listeners, who often entreat him to perform in Mandarin because, they complain, relatively few people speak Hakka (interview, April 7, 2010). This strikes him as odd: "Language shouldn't present a problem in music!" he exclaimed. "When people listen to Japanese or American hip-hop, like Dr. Dre and Eminem, they have to study the lyrics for comprehension—so why not Hakka?" He buried his head in his hands when he spoke of their obliviousness to the lingering effects of martial law–era language policies, but he stopped short of criticizing listeners or blaming them for this state of affairs. Instead, he told me, he understood their desires to dispense with Hakka as confirmation that the Taiwanese school system failed to provide them with a comprehensive education not just in local languages, but also in local history.

Experiences of primary and secondary education were prominent themes in conversations I had with most rappers in Taiwan, who hold teachers in high esteem but are deeply critical of what and how they learned in the course of their formal schooling. Artists of Fan Chiang's generation, especially, have never known a time when school curricula were not the subject of intense public scrutiny, at the nexus of broader political conflicts over national identity and sovereignty. Schools have long been recognized in Taiwan, as elsewhere, not just as agents of socialization, but also as vehicles for the transmission of political ideology. The revision of programs of study in history and geography have provoked arguably the most lively debates in the post–martial law period, but scholars and public commentators have likewise noted the relationship between schooling, identity formation, and nation-building discourses during earlier eras. Writing about Taiwanese experiences of colonial modernity within the Japanese educational system, historian Komagome Takeshi acknowledges the ways in which the "narration of history is a space of power/knowledge contestations" (2006, 145). During Taiwan's tenure as a Japanese territory, colonial authorities understood education and assimilation as closely intertwined projects (Tsurumi 1979, 617) and sought through the establishment of compulsory elementary education to inculcate loyalty to the empire.[6] In her work on the ways in which ethnic identity has been shaped by social experience in Taiwan, anthropologist Melissa Brown strikes a similar note to Komagome in her use of the phrase "narratives of unfolding," which describes the processes whereby governments and "ethnic [community] leaders" "draw heavily on selected historic sociopolitical events to galvanize support around claimed ancestry and/or culture" in an attempt to "shape our understanding of the past for political purposes" (2004, 5–6). The KMT strove to interpellate Taiwan's peoples as part of the work of Sinicization, promoting a historical narrative that bound their pasts—and, by implication, their futures—ineluctably to China's. Accounts that threatened this mandate were for many years considered seditious. Until the end of martial law, non-hegemonic histories—including those of Taiwan's Indigenous peoples—were expunged from the historical record, and therefore from syllabi, by the island's dominant political powers.

Although Fan Chiang and Fish Lin do not lead university *xiha* clubs or teach formal classes like Ill Mo or Professor H, their activities within Kou Chou Ching nevertheless represent a practice of musical knowledge work, one that treats rap as an ideal medium through which to examine these histories. Martial law might now seem temporally distant to the youngest participants in the rap scene, but Old School artists—the generational cohort born between 1975 and 1985 who are the focus of this book—are well attuned to its aftershocks. Many were in middle or high school in 1997 when controversy erupted over the reform of history and geography textbooks to reflect an official shift toward political liberalization and Taiwanization/localization (Corcuff 2005). And many were in graduate school—several obtaining PhDs in education or education-related fields—in 2015 when the Ministry of Education faced accusations by student activists from more than 150 high schools of trying to roll back those reforms and whitewash the activities of the KMT regime following their decampment to Taiwan and through the period of the White Terror (Tsoi 2015). These events, both remote and recent, illustrate the ongoing challenges of historical representation against a backdrop of ongoing, often fractious political transformation. They also revive, repeatedly, questions about who has been, and who should be, entrusted with authority to narrate the past.

Kou Chou Ching keeps company with a contingent of rap artists who tell historical stories in their songs, which together span a long arc of time, from six centuries prior to the arrival of Han peoples from China to the imposition of martial law in the mid-twentieth century and beyond.[7] Fan Chiang draws connections between this work and the imperative to safeguard Taiwan's de facto sovereignty. Echoing anthropologist Ann Anagnost's contention that the nation is "an 'impossible unity' that must be narrated into being in both time and space" (1997, 2) and emphasizing the ongoing denial of de jure recognition for Taiwan, Fan Chiang told me: "If you don't know anything about our culture, history, geography, you have no way of knowing that this country *is* a country" (interview,

April 7, 2010).[8] By engaging historical subjects and using local languages, Kou Chou Ching's members commit themselves symbolically to the task of reconstituting, over and over, the democratic nation that they have come to know, against forces both internal and external that might erode its integrity. Although Kou Chou Ching's emphatic support for Taiwan's sovereignty, dedication to local language revitalization, and insistence on exploring memories of state violence reveal the group's pan-Green political sympathies, Fan Chiang strikes me as neither dogmatic nor doctrinaire when we speak in person. In fact, I cannot help but think each time we meet about how much he reminds me of myself in the college classroom—less a professional activist than a teacher trying to catalyze critical thinking in his students. "We don't write to get everyone to feel the same way we do," he told me, "but we hope that after reading the lyrics that listeners will try to challenge them. Then everyone can study together. Rise up and tell us your opinion" (interview, April 7, 2010).

Having established themselves as pedagogues and laid claim to narrative agency, history-minded rappers like Fan Chiang have looked beyond the scene to intervene in the methods of knowledge production through which history is repeatedly written and rewritten in Taiwan. In this chapter, I consider how this intervention transpires in parallel with, but separate from, formal processes of curricular reform. Dominant narratives of history have certainly shifted since the end of martial law, with successive presidential administrations moving the needle in different directions, often in support of diverging political agendas. But the impulse to reframe stories authored by those in positions of power continues to subtend pieces by artists such as Kou Chou Ching, Chang Jui-chuan, and T-ho Brothers (鐵虎兄弟). Their ambitions exceed the airing of historical grievances, or the pursuit of what Sylvia Li-chun Lin (2007) describes in her work on narrative representations of past atrocities in Taiwan as "closure." In both form and content, they reimagine historical narratives in order to reimagine social relationships—those that bind young audiences to their peers, and to their elders in family, educational, and professional contexts—both at and beyond moments of performance. While these relationships have in the past reflected a more or less unidirectional transmission of knowledge from teacher to student and from older to younger generations, senior rappers enjoin audiences and their juniors in the scene to contribute to knowledge production, as well.

Rap's participatory ethos facilitates precisely this kind of disruption. The extensive socialization required for performers to gain a foothold in the rap community—accomplished by way of contribution to online forums, *xiha* clubs, and creative collectives—marks rap as an unequivocally participatory domain. Participation is also, of course, a key feature of performance practice: from the South Bronx to southern Taiwan, a paradigmatic hip-hop gesture positions the MC onstage, mic tipped out, exhorting audience members to make their voices heard.[9] The heightened social interaction that transpires when performers adjure audiences to raise their fists, dance, or reply to a verbal provocation distinguishes rap from other approaches to historical storytelling—musical and non-musical—on the island. In this way, the work of knowledge production diffuses into multiple hands and incites artists and audiences to imagine together an array of possible futures, not just for the rap community, but for the world beyond it.

Of "Cultural Bombs" and Taiwanese Histories

In an interview with the *Central Daily News* (中央日報) on April 16, 1994, Lee Teng-hui reflected on his experiences of language imperialism under Japanese and KMT hegemony, and the deep sense of anguish that the colonial condition engendered in him, his children, and his political constituents:

> I am more than seventy years old. Having lived under different regimes, from Japanese colonialism to Taiwan's recovery, I have greatly experienced the miseries of the Taiwanese people. In the period of Japanese colonialism, a Taiwanese would be punished by being forced to kneel out in the sun for speaking *Tai-yü*. The situation was the same when Taiwan was recovered [by the KMT]: my son, Hsien-wen, and my daughter-in-law, Yüeh-yün, often wore a dunce board around their necks in the school as punishment for speaking *Tai-yü*. I am very aware of the situation because I often go to the countryside to talk to people. Their lives are influenced by history. I think the most miserable people are Taiwanese, who have always tried in vain to get their heads above the water. This was the Taiwanese situation during the period of Japanese colonialism; it was not any different after Taiwan's recovery. I have deep feeling about this. (quoted in and translated by Hsiau 1997, 302)[10]

Lee's observation that Taiwanese "lives are influenced by history" is two-sided: it discloses both the ways that language imperialism ruptured Taiwanese relationships to the past, and the ways in which collective memories of language imperialism now *constitute* the past for many people. Many of those who can recall or who have heard stories of language-based punishments, especially in educational contexts during their earliest and most impressionable years, carry that memory with them decades after the end of the Mandarin-only policy.

In 1987 Taiwan's Provincial Bureau of Education formally outlawed the practice of using physical punishment and issuing fines to penalize students for speaking Hoklo, Hakka, or Indigenous languages on school grounds (Sandel 2003, 530), and these languages emerged incrementally in the popular and political discourses thereafter (Wei 2006) in step with the development of the Mother Tongue Language Movement (還我母語運動).[11] Since the 2000 election of President Chen Shui-bian (陳水扁) of the DPP, ontologies of Taiwaneseness rooted in multiculturalism and multiethnicity (多元主義) have strongly shaped national identity discourses, extending and expanding Lee's "New Taiwanese" model of the previous decade. Following the establishment of the Council of Aboriginal Affairs in 1996, the government created the Council for Hakka Affairs in 2001 to promote and safeguard Hakka culture and language. In the same year, the Ministry of Education mandated the teaching of local languages in school. Mandarin remained the primary language of instruction, but students began receiving instruction in Hakka, Hoklo, or Indigenous languages from first through sixth grades, with the goal of achieving basic proficiency (Wei 2006, 92). The public embrace of multiculturalism has trickled down into numerous domains of daily life and spurred the proliferation of new media outlets dedicated to the promotion of Indigenous, Hoklo, and Hakka culture and new cultural production in non-Mandarin languages.[12] Even mass transit systems in Taiwan now signal deliberately to members of the island's diverse ethnic communities. In addition to Mandarin, subways and buses in major urban areas also announce stops in Hoklo, Hakka, and English. On the TRA Eastern Trunk Line, which runs along the island's eastern corridor, one can also hear station names and instructions on rider etiquette in the Indigenous 'Amis language (Hatfield 2015).

But old prejudices die hard: particularly in the urban centers of the north, Mandarin continues to index the cosmopolitan, the sophisticated, and the literate, while non-Mandarin languages index the provincial, the uncouth, and the oral. The lack of well-known orthographies for Taiwan's non-Mandarin languages, Hoklo especially, have compounded perceptions of them as less "evolved" than Mandarin (Chiung 2005, 315–54; Scott and Tiun 2007, 66–67). In this environment, emotional trauma from prior experiences of language prejudice persists for many. Fan Chiang and many of his senior colleagues in rap describe Mandarin-only language policies in terms closely resembling Kenyan literary theorist and artist Ngũgĩ wa Thiong'o's (1986) notion of English as a "cultural bomb," whose effect throughout colonized Africa was to wreak havoc on dominated peoples' relationships to history (3). Thiong'o argues that language is "the collective memory bank of a people's experience in history" (15), essentially isomorphic with culture; when local languages are supplanted by colonial languages, so, too, are culture and history.

Blacklist Workshop and Jutoupi challenged dominant linguistic ideologies and persistent threats of cultural erasure during the immediate post–martial law period by performing in non-Mandarin languages. With the exception of just a few Mandarin phrases in the song "Democracy Bumpkin"—such as the symbolically potent Cold War slogan "Recapture the Mainland!"—*Songs of Madness* is almost entirely in Hoklo. Jutoupi employs no fewer than seven languages on his *Funny Rap* albums. Dwagie followed in their footsteps in the early 2000s with the predominantly Hoklo-language *Lotus from the Tongue*. In the last decade, successor acts like 911 and DJ Didilong (李英宏) have made names for themselves as artists with equal facility in Hoklo and Mandarin. As Didilong remarked in an interview with online platform Asian Pop Weekly: "Using one's own language to tell the stories of my home, that is what is most natural" (Koh 2017). Despite growing acceptance of non-Mandarin languages since the end of martial law and the efforts of artists to develop new inroads for these languages in popular culture, however, competency among the general population has continued to decline: a 2010 survey showed that only 26.2% of self-identified Hakka people could speak the Hakka language fluently (Jan, Kuan, and Lomelí 2016); most of the Indigenous Austronesian languages, multiply marginalized across colonial regimes for their status as non-Japonic *and* non-Sinitic, have long been considered endangered (Zeitoun, Yu, and Weng 2003, 218–32).

The picture is certainly less grim for the majority-Hoklo population, but artists and audience members with whom I have spoken over the years, particularly in the north of the island, still remark that there are cultural stigmas attached to the Hoklo language. As Didilong has put it: "Before, like back when I was a student, I felt like speaking Hoklo just wasn't that cool, and that went for singing, too. In the past, maybe, it seemed like Hoklo songs were kind of old-fashioned. It was like, when you'd listen to these songs or play them, there'd always be someone at the side laughing" (Black Buddha 2017). Speaking about the Hengchun folk singer Chen Da, Chang Jui-chuan (see fig. 5.1) admitted feelings of inferiority about his facility with Hoklo compared to previous generations. Although he uses the language regularly in his everyday life, he looked wistful and downcast when explaining that he feels unable to access the language's literary registers: "Chen Da, his lyrics, even though he was more like a bum in his time, most of the words [he uses], I can't use those words anymore. . . . His words are very elegant and graceful. And we are, like, very colloquial. So,

FIG. 5.1. Chang Jui-chuan performs his song "My Language" at a concert commemorating the 1989 Tiananmen Square Protests held in Taipei's Freedom Square (自由廣場), June 4, 2011. Photograph by author.

I wouldn't compare myself to him or, you know—they're just way much better. Just listen to their [Hoklo]. They're just way better" (interview, December 3, 2009). Chang embraces the opportunity to hone his language skills through lyric-writing, although he has expressed doubt to me over the years that composing in Hoklo will impact to any appreciable degree the language competency of his listeners. They do not consider Hoklo as invested with cultural or economic cachet, he thinks, and it is difficult to justify the effort needed to learn in these times of precarity (interview, December 21, 2016).

Perhaps more than any other *xiha* artist past or present, Chang uses his art to reflect on language's inescapable and historic ties to political and socioeconomic power in Taiwan. Born in Changhua in 1977 to a Mandarin teacher mother and a science pedagogy professor father, he was inspired to undertake serious study of the English language after developing a fascination with American popular music during his teen years. He followed this interest through to graduate studies in English rhetoric in the United States, where his coursework created opportunities to reflect on the relationship of language to his identity as a self-described "native Hoklo Taiwanese." In a personal essay entitled "My Language," he describes the implicit and explicit means by which he was socialized into monolingualism as a young child:

People who lived in [my] neighborhood were teachers and their families. Most of them were civilians who followed the Chinese Kuomintang (KMT) when it fled China and retreated to Taiwan after losing a civil war to the Chinese Communists in 1949. The rest were native Hoklo Taiwanese, like my family. When I was little, as I recall, I had difficulty understanding the speech of some of the older people in the neighborhood because they spoke Mandarin Chinese with a different accent. I also realized that when I was at home with my family, I spoke Hoklo Taiwanese and Mandarin Chinese, but when I was out with my playmates chasing grasshoppers and asking grownups for candies, I had better speak Mandarin Chinese to get what I wanted. (2010, 2)

Chang learned early on that he would be rewarded for speaking Mandarin in public, even if Hoklo was permissible in the private domain. This lesson was reinforced at school, where students were reprimanded for lapsing into non-Mandarin languages. In "My Language," he recalls a story one of his classmates told him of punishment she received for transgressing the Mandarin-only policy in elementary school during the 1980s:

Most young students like her had no money, so when they were caught speaking Taiwanese dialects, they had to be wandering on the streets after school looking for cardboard waste and empty metal cans, which could be exchanged for a few cents, and it took many days to reach the amount of the fine. When she was fined for speaking Taiwanese at school, she did not want her parents to know about it because she knew they were saving every penny to take care of [their] kids. They could not have helped anyhow because their daughter's punishment actually resulted from the ruling party's language policy. She knew very well, even when she was then only eight years old, that the last thing people wanted to do was to mess with the KMT. She was full of tears when she was sharing the story with the class, which has been engraved in my heart ever since. (2010, 5)

This narrative recalls Lee Teng-hui's account of public humiliation during the Japanese colonial period and under KMT hegemony, and also marks out an indelible connection between social shaming and financial precarity. Like many other Old School artists, Chang was a child in the final years of martial law and a young teenager during the period of democratic consolidation. His recollection of his classmate's story affirms the lasting psychological effects of Mandarin-only policies, even for those who did not experience shaming directly.

Chang is soft-spoken and mild-mannered, but when we first discussed the politics of language at a Taipei coffee shop in 2009, his tone grew strident and he seemed to transform almost instantaneously into the defiant figure I remembered performing "Fuck tha Police" at the 921.87 Benefit Concert earlier that year. In response to my questions about what languages he chooses to perform in and why, he explained to me that he raps exclusively in Hoklo and English and would never consider performing in Mandarin:

> [Hoklo] is historically and politically appropriate to express messages or feelings of people like us who have been in Taiwan for a long time and suffering with the KMT and all that.... When you rap in Mandarin Chinese, you rap in an oppressor's language. That totally goes against the origin of hip-hop, I would say. People argue about that, but for me personally... it would be torture for me to rap in Mandarin Chinese. (interview, December 3, 2009)

Chang invokes Hoklo as a "resistance vernacular," which "[reterritorializes] not only major Anglophone rules of intelligibility but also those of other 'standard' languages" (Mitchell 2001a, 3–4). To rap in Hoklo is to challenge the primacy of Mandarin and categorically refute its claims of superiority. In this regard, Chang has much in common not only with Blacklist Workshop and Jutoupi, but also with rappers in other global contexts, such as Basque artists Negu Gorriak (Urla 2001) and Maori artists Moana and the Moa Hunters (Mitchell 2001b), who have rejected the use of Castilian Spanish and English, respectively, in Spain and New Zealand.

He also raps in English, even though he recognizes global neoliberal capitalism as a malevolent force and the United States as an imperialist power. English is widely spoken outside Taiwan, he observes, and it has an indisputable communicative currency. While Chang hopes that his Hoklo compositions register with local listeners with a personal investment in Taiwanese culture and politics, his English performances target a broader global audience: "Of course, I don't assume that everyone in the world speaks English, but at least [some] people outside of Taiwan, I want to [try to] approach them as well. I don't want to just speak to my own people all the time. I want people outside of Taiwan to understand Taiwan better. I have a message for them" (interview, December 3, 2009). Although contradicting his moratorium on Mandarin, Chang casts his use of English not as surrender to "linguistic imperialism" (Phillipson 1992) but as an alternative tactic of resistance. In this, he is influenced by the work of Jamaican American novelist and poet Michele Cliff, whom he cites in "My Language": "for me to write who I *really* am means 'mixing in the forms taught us by the oppressor, undermining his language and co-opting his style, and turning it to our purpose'" (2010, 7; citing Cliff

1988, 59). This message resounds in the English chorus to his 2006 mixed English- and Hoklo-language anti-globalization anthem "My Language," for which the aforementioned essay was named:

> I speak your language, don't mean I'm your slave
> I speak your language 'cause I'm about to invade
> your music, your culture, your beliefs, and your fate
> with kung fu, Confucius, Tao, and my name

Chang's multilingual rap reconfigures geopolitical and social relationships in which he—a non-native English speaker who claims Hoklo, rather than Mandarin, as his mother tongue—has historically been doubly subordinate. In this way, he urges listeners to consider how language can be used to empower and disempower individuals and the communities from which they hail.

Chang's references both to Cliff's writings and to enslavement refract his narratives of Taiwanese subjugation through the lens of Afro-Caribbean and African American experience, suggesting affinity (though not equivalency) between those histories of oppression. This is, of course, a widespread practice among performers of global hip-hop, the "strategic deployment of signifiers that affords youth a window into their own situation and what it shares with that of racialized minorities" (Urla 2001, 181).[13] Such references invoke what Halifu Osumare refers to as "hip-hop's connective marginalities," or the "social resonances between black expressive culture within its contextual political history and similar dynamics in other nations" (2001, 172). Appearing on the same album as "My Language," the track "Be an Intelligent Person" includes a 27-second recorded excerpt from a 1963 speech by Malcolm X, in which the revolutionary Black nationalist leader implores his audience to reject a white supremacist establishment and practice self-determination. In the liner notes to the track, Chang writes in English and Mandarin: "For better understanding, the 'white' [as I cite it] here does not necessarily mean 'white-complexioned.' I would rather say it symbolizes 'the oppressor.' 在這裡的「白」不完全代表膚色；對我們來說，應解讀為「壓迫者」。" The lessons Chang seeks to teach by analogy are clear: as Black peoples must resist white supremacy, so Taiwan's peoples must resist those who would attempt to dominate them through linguistic, cultural, and economic imperialism.[14]

While political imperatives drive language choice for artists like Chang, such imperatives intersect with pragmatic and aesthetic concerns, and are naturally delimited by language capabilities. The members of Kou Chou Ching and Community Service, with whom Chang has often collaborated over the years, certainly connect language to power structures on the island and seek to promulgate through their performances a sense of Taiwanese discursive space as multicultural and multiethnic. This includes working with speakers of Indigenous languages, such as Orchid Island rapper Alilis, who performs a Tao-language verse on the 2009 song "Gray Coastlines" (灰色海岸). But Fan Chiang also demonstrates an awareness of the relative prevalence of these different languages, placing in context the expediency of choosing one over another:

> [Mandarin, Hoklo, and Hakka] all play different roles in my life, so I look for ways to have all three appear in different places in my lyrics. For example, if I speak Hakkanese it means I have some things that I want to express that I don't want you to understand quite so quickly. Instead, it should make you want to translate our lyrics or look up some information in order to understand. When I use [Hoklo], it's a little like I don't want absolutely everyone to understand, but I want you to know a little, because not everyone really speaks [Hoklo]. Some people do. I use Mandarin for things that I want to be understood immediately, like quickly after listening to the song, for those things I use Mandarin. So, I use all three of these languages, because when you put these three things in *xiha*, each represents, or expresses, or rather the rhymes and flow that they generate, have different feels. (interview, April 7, 2010)

From a discussion of accessibility, Fan Chiang turns to an assessment of the "different feels," or sonic/aesthetic qualities, inherent in the languages available to him. These differences arise from a variety of features but perhaps most fundamentally from the tonal systems of the Sinitic languages spoken in Taiwan. Of note, tone in these languages is phonemic—that is, changes in tonal articulation give rise to changes in semantic meaning. Mandarin has four main tones and a neutral tone, which has no discernible contour. Five dialects of Hakka are in use on the island, but the majority of speakers are conversant in either Siyen (四縣) or Hoiluk (海陸), which have six and seven tones, respectively. Although Hoklo, which varies slightly from the north to the south, once had eight tones, it retains seven in its present form. Each language abides by different rules of tone sandhi, meaning that the tones of individual syllables change differently in response to the tones of the syllables that come before or after them. Mandarin's tone sandhi is limited, but Hoklo and Hakka have complex patterns of allophonic change.

Remarking on the strong tonality of Hoklo and recalling Wang Chenyi's description of Hoklo's musical quality (see chapter 2), Fish Lin told me: "When you use Hoklo, even if you just speak it, it has melody. In fact, you'll find that many Hoklo songs, you might say that they're sung, but the way Hoklo sounds when sung is not that different from the way it sounds when spoken.... Hoklo inherently sounds smooth" (interview, May 12, 2010). The latent musicality of Hoklo, in Lin's opinion, makes it especially well suited to the chanted or intoned speech quality of rap vocalization. Many others echo Lin's assessment of the language as having a fundamentally musical and "smooth" (順利) sound. To this point, rapper Manchuker made recourse to shape metaphors in his efforts to describe the sounds of Hoklo, Mandarin, and English:

> I think it's beautiful.... [Hoklo] has more tones than Mandarin, so that makes it sound full and good. But I think Mandarin can do it, too, it just takes time to master it. I think for English, English is a round circle shape of language... and for [Mandarin], it's like a square... so you maybe have to make it so that it becomes a circle.... And [Hoklo] is somewhat like English, a more round-shape type of language. (interview, September 21, 2010)

While Manchuker's description of English as having "a round circle shape" might seem somewhat cryptic, I interpret his comment as a response to the fact that tone, while an important feature of prosody, is not phonemic in English. Rather, shifts in intonation can be used to convey grammatical, lexical, and paralinguistic information. A performer of English-language rap is relatively free to vary the pitch and tonal contour of individual words as well as whole phrases for expressive effect without concern that meaning will be lost on the listener. Artists working in Sinitic languages, however, must negotiate additional constraints. They can, like an English speaker, manipulate pitch to vary the prosody of an expression, but they must at the same time strongly articulate the tones of individual words if lyrics—especially complex ones—are to be understood. Rapper Manchuker hears in Mandarin a "square" quality, perhaps attributable to its four tones. An artist using Hoklo must also of course articulate the tones of individual words, but three additional tones provide additional sources of sonic variation.

As Chang and Lin acknowledge, rappers may choose their preferred language(s) of performance for both political and aesthetic reasons, with an ear to the pragmatic considerations of reception and communication. But not all linguistic options are equally available to all people: rappers hail from many different cities and towns from across the island and beyond, with varied upbringings that in most cases dictate their degrees of fluency. Young Indigenous rappers, who received primary instruction at school in Mandarin and were pressured to assimilate linguistically and culturally to Han society, perform in Mandarin more often than they do in Indigenous languages. In an interview with the *Liberty Times*, Rapper BCW expressed sorrow at losing his ability to speak 'Amis and Paiwan languages after his family moved from Pingtung to Taipei during his childhood: "I super regret it, my way at that time was wrong. [And] when I returned to our indigenous community, unable to understand the older generation, my father asked me, 'How will you face your ancestors in the future?' Now I'm trying to make up for it" (Luo 2018). Likewise, in a conversation about his use of Hoklo, Mandarin, and English in his songs, aspiring rapper MC Braindeath of Psycho Piggz told me that he hoped one day—after completing his medical education and hopefully finding stable employment—to return to the mountains in Miaoli to learn the Atayal language his mother's family once spoke fluently (interview, April 12, 2010).[15]

Rappers' language choices are, like their personal backgrounds, imbricated within Taiwan's geographic-linguistic gradients as well as its place within larger circles of both the Sinophone and Indigenous worlds. The Taiwan Economic Miracle did not affect the island or its peoples in a uniform fashion: there are well-recognized socioeconomic inequalities dividing the north from the south and the urban from the rural parts of Taiwan. The north of the island is the seat of government and industry, and therefore where the majority of wealth is concentrated; the cities hold the majority of high-paying jobs and therefore promise greater mobility than more rural, agriculture-focused outposts. Indigenous peoples are often pulled from their communities, especially in rural areas, by the promise of employment in major cities. Geographic variations in educational opportunity and achievement historically overlapped with achievement gaps between the *waisheng* and *bensheng* populations (Wang 2001). Although the wealthier, more economically globalized north is ethnically diverse, it is home to the majority of Taiwan's *waishengren* and is predominantly Mandarin speaking. The population of the southwestern part of the island, however, is dominated by Hoklo people, many of whom speak Hoklo.

It is perhaps unsurprising then that Dwagie and many of his southern colleagues in Kung Fu Entertainment profess greater comfort with Hoklo than their northern counterparts. Dadi, of Tainan-based group Brotherhood, sighed when expressing the deep gratitude he feels to Dwagie for inspiring him and his friends to perform in Hoklo, a language that they are both more fluent in and emotionally connected to than Mandarin (interview, September 26, 2010). For these artists, the choice to rap in Hoklo reflects the language's primacy in their everyday lives and activities. Oppositely configured, the same logic prevails for Taipei-based artists like MC Hotdog, the Tripoets, and Mr. Brown, who are sympathetic to the political mission of artists who use Hoklo, but who have greater fluency in Mandarin. As MC Hotdog told me, with characteristic humility: "I sometimes add some Hoklo to my Mandarin, but ultimately my Hoklo isn't very...I'll just say that I was a kid who grew up in Taipei, and I occasionally go to the south, and I can speak Hoklo, but it's not too smooth. And I'm not going to use it if it's not smooth" (interview, August 12, 2010). Mr. Brown shared similar sentiments when I visited his home studio, also in Taipei: "I can't really write much in Hoklo. Taipei isn't a great place for Hoklo, even though I understand it" (interview, August 27, 2010). Language in these cases is a geographically specific marker, an expression of hometown identification, with attendant distinctions between outsiders and insiders and occasional opportunities to blur the lines.

Though central to Taiwan's internal politics, the north-south divide does not have the same salience for Manchuker, perhaps by virtue of his particular life experiences beyond Taiwan's borders. Born in Taipei, Manchuker struggled in the local school system and moved overseas at the age of sixteen to stay with relatives in affluent Cupertino, California (interview, September 21, 2010). After several years on the West Coast, he traveled across the country first to Jersey City and then to Queens, New York, where, working mostly among other East and Southeast Asian immigrants as a delivery boy for a Chinese restaurant, he discovered a love for hip-hop. Within a few years he began making beats, writing rhymes, and performing as one of the founding members of R&B/hip-hop collective Asian Power. Hoping to develop a career in Asia, he returned to Taipei in 2005 at the age of twenty-eight. It is perhaps owing to his experiences among diverse Sinophone communities in the United States that he identifies as ethnically Chinese and seeks to represent on behalf of diasporic Chinese throughout the world.[16] He cast this project in conspicuously historical terms when we first talked about what motivated him to pursue a career in music: "For Chinese people, it was very hard for us for the past two hundred years. Like people looked at us like we were inferior, and all the war, like opium and you know. So Manchuker is really about that—it's about representing and telling the history, it's really about letting our own people know what's going on. We are not going to hold this as a grudge against other races, but it's just a fact, it's history how others treated us back then when we were poor, when we were insufficient" (interview, September 21, 2010). His references to the humiliations of the opium wars and the struggles of the "past two hundred years" express clear identification with China's painful decline in the nineteenth century, during which numerous rebellions, natural disasters, and clashes with foreign imperial powers led inexorably to the fall of the Qing Dynasty in 1912. To this point, the name "Manchuker" (滿人, lit. "Manchurian") is not an indication of Manchurian ancestry but a tribute to the Qing.

Balancing his aspirations to communicate with and represent on behalf of his "own people," Manchuker understands his multilingual music as a broadly anti-colonial tool for bridging a divide among the Mandarin-speaking East and the English-speaking West:

> I think it's because of my background, but I always want to relate back to New York, to Cali, to Taiwan, to China.... I want to relate to everybody. I want to speak a common language, and the [reason] I use a lot of mixed English and Chinese is because I also want to get English listeners into Chinese hip-hop, because it's more interesting [...] and especially nowadays a lot of people want to learn Chinese. And my thinking is that my music is good for people to listen to learn Chinese [...] just like how we started to learn English. We always find lyrics and look it up, see what they really mean. I think Chinese hip-hop has the same function. (interview, September 21, 2010)

Manchuker hopes to attract a broad constituency, including English speakers whose interests in studying Mandarin are motivated primarily by the PRC's rise. He sees rap as not just a source of entertainment, but also as a potential medium for communication with these audiences, a means of speaking back—this time on equal terms—to a West that once again seeks to exploit Chinese prosperity.

To be sure, Manchuker's tactics are not unlike Kou Chou Ching's or Chang Jui-chuan's, as all three deliberately use multiple languages and demand that listeners take personal initiative to fill in the gaps in what they can comprehend aurally. The ideological valences of their gestures, however, could not be more different: whereas Chang Jui-chuan deploys English to challenge the discursive and material legacies of American cultural imperialism in Taiwan, and the members of Kou Chou Ching mix languages as, among other things, a means of directing their messages to specific language communities, Manchuker posits his Mandarin-English alloy as a "common language" with the potential to unite not disparate groups in Taiwan, but the more expansive "East" and "West." He does not seek to assert difference as the others do, but turns to multilingual rap to illuminate that which he believes is shared across boundaries.

History, Pedagogy, and Concentric Circles Narratives

The contrasting examples of Chang Jui-chuan and Manchuker demonstrate that there is ample space within the *xiha* world for diverging visions of individual identity and, hence, for diverging relationships to historical narrative. And, as Michel-Rolph Trouillot writes: "Each historical narrative renews a claim to truth" ([1995] 2015, 6). Chang centers Tai-wan's internal history of interethnic strife and positions his artistic choices within a framework of historical injustices suffered under KMT hege-mony. Manchuker centers the historic victimization of China by European imperialist forces and promulgates a mode of pan-Chinese identification that encompasses the broader Sinophone world, beyond Taiwan's shores. These conceptions have obvious dissonances, of course, as the notion of pan-Chineseness is often instrumentalized to support irredentist claims to Taiwan. They also echo competing historiographies—"China-centered" versus "Taiwan-centered"—at the heart of debates over curricular reform since the immediate post–martial law period.

This reform was a natural outgrowth of Taiwan's democratization and liberalization in the 1990s. It reflected growing desires among progres-sives to dispense with the Sinocentric historiography espoused by the KMT, for whom both national education and military conscription had served as efficacious tools of political socialization under authoritarianism (Corcuff 2005, 133–34).[17] Taiwanization catalyzed far-reaching projects of cultural and educational amelioration, beginning in earnest during Lee Teng-hui's presidency (1988–2000). Initial efforts to amend the na-tional curriculum, which commenced in 1995, focused on redefining the way geography, history, and social studies were taught at the junior high school level.[18] Calls for the revision of school textbooks led to the 1997 publication of *Knowing Taiwan* (認識台灣), a trio of manuals that broke dramatically with state-produced primers (134). The authors distanced themselves from the "Great Han" ideology (大漢注意) that characterized previous books, which emphasized Chinese civilizational achievements and relegated discussion of Taiwanese history to a scant few chapters on the post-1945 period (142).

Knowing Taiwan was informed instead by the so-called "concentric circles" (同心圓) pedagogical framework developed by historian and politician Tu Cheng-sheng (杜正勝), which recommended that students commence their work in history, geography, and social studies by attend-ing first to the peoples, places, and things closest to them and steadily moving outward.[19] The first "circle" proposed by Tu was Taiwan, the sec-ond was continental China (中國大陸), and the third was the wider world (Corcuff 2005, 141). By centering Taiwan, *Knowing Taiwan* "[presented], for the first time, a constitutive dimension of Taiwan's identity and an issue at the core of the national identity debate: the plurality (*duoyuan hua*) of the island's ethnic structure and historical experience" (140). The text generated a firestorm of controversy, with anti-reformists arguing that the "concentric circles" approach tacitly endorsed pro-independence perspectives (Stolojan 2017, 107). Hard-liners also alleged that *Knowing*

Taiwan was insufficiently critical of the Japanese. The controversy dragged on in the public arena for several months, but *Knowing Taiwan* ultimately gained traction with moderates and became widely adopted for use at the junior high level.

High school curricula, however, continued to hew closely to the narratives promulgated under authoritarianism (Stolojan 2017, 105). Although some textbooks increased the number of chapters dedicated to Taiwan and emended references to the island as a "model province" (模範省), the island's past was still contextualized within the grand narrative of Chinese history (Schneider 2008, 171). The Chen Shui-bian presidential administration (2000–2008) launched a more comprehensive process of reform in 2002 to extend the "concentric circles" approach for students at the high school level and continue the process of educational de-Sinicization. Over the next several years, however, successive versions of a new curriculum were thwarted by conservative members of the KMT, who took exception to many of the proposed changes, including characterizations of the two Chiang regimes (Chiang Kai-shek's and Chiang Ching-kuo's) as authoritarian and of postwar events such as the 2-28 Incident as examples of "bad governance of the Nationalist government" (Stolojan 2017, 108). Debates raged for several years as working groups banded and disbanded, their members tried not just in the legislative chambers of government but also in the court of public opinion. Some of those associated with the new curricula, including historian Chang Yuan (張元) and Tu Cheng-sheng, were accused by anti-reformists of pushing pro-independence agendas and "insidiously eroding the historical conscience of the youth" (默默地侵蝕青少年的歷史意識) (109). Although a revised curriculum was passed by the legislature in 2008, the Chen administration was by then in its final months and mired in serious allegations of corruption. The curriculum was never implemented.

Ma Ying-jeou's election to the presidency in 2008 heralded the KMT's return to power and the beginning of yet another phase of curricular reform that tempered some of the changes proposed under DPP leadership and reversed others entirely. Anti-reformists advocated for the redemption of China-centered perspectives and reinstatement of key nomenclature: "occupation" (日治) to describe the Japanese colonial period, and "recovery" (光復) to describe Taiwan's liberation from Japanese rule by the ROC. Historian and academic Wang Chung-fu (王仲孚) argued that changes that had been made to the curriculum under Chen Shui-bian were unconstitutional (Stolojan 2017, 110). By 2012 Ma announced that he had come to the same conclusion, that previous reforms violated the mandate that "education and culture shall foster a Chinese identity (in the terms defined by the government) within the national community" and that "the history of China and Taiwan should be merged within a single unit entitled 'National History'" (本國史) (113).

Following Ma's reelection in 2012, another working group was convened by the KMT to review and rewrite a number of programs, including those in history, civics, and social science.[20] This group's work transpired quickly, mostly behind closed doors, and was led by non-specialists in the academic fields under consideration. Controversy flared again in early 2014, when more than 130 historians signed a petition that denounced the revised curriculum this working group produced, which signatories saw as a brazen attempt to realign pedagogy with KMT ideology. Calling back to the historic 1947 civil uprising known as the 2-28 Incident (discussion of which was reduced under the proposed new guidelines), teachers gathered at the Ministry of Education to voice their opposition on February 28; several went on a hunger strike (Loa 2014). While the specific contents of the revised curriculum were concerning to those assembled, they also condemned the "black box" (黑箱)—that is, non-transparent, non-democratic—policy-making process the Ministry of Education had employed to implement the changes.

The same critiques would be made by youth protesters active in the Sunflower Student Movement (太陽花學運), which erupted several weeks later. Anchored by massive demonstrations in front of the federal government offices in Taipei, the Sunflower Student Movement's focal point was the occupation of Parliament by several hundred student demonstrators for twenty-three days. Protesters objected to a breach of procedure in the KMT's passage of the Cross-Strait Service Trade Agreement (CSSTA), a major piece of legislation intended to liberalize trade between the service industries of the PRC and the ROC. KMT legislators reneged on a previous agreement to undertake a clause-by-clause review of the CSSTA and attempted instead to fast-track ratification in a plenary session. Protesters characterized the secret negotiations that took place around the CSSTA as an exemplar of "black box" politics and a grave threat to the integrity of the island's democratic institutions.

The curriculum debates and the Sunflower Student Movement intertwined around anti–black box sentiment. Indeed, during the period of protest, the most prominent topic on PTT's largest discussion board was curriculum reform (Hsiao 2017, 35). Taking its cue from Sunflower, the Anti–Black Box Curriculum Movement (反黑箱課綱運動) that raged into the summer of 2015 was led primarily by students. In late July, after diligent organizing and a series of smaller demonstrations, they descended on the Ministry of Education. Authorities were swift and unyielding in their response: thirty-three people were arrested, twenty-four of whom were high school students (Stolojan 2017, 117). Several days prior to the scheduled August 1 implementation of the revised curriculum, one of those arrested, twenty-year-old activist Lin Kuanhua (林冠華), committed suicide. Among his widely publicized final words on social media were: "I only have one wish: Minister, please withdraw the curriculum" (我只有一個願望：部長，把課綱退回吧) (Kyodo 2015).

Lin's untimely passing provoked an outcry from the public, in response to which the Ministry of Education proposed a compromise: moving forward, teachers could select teaching materials based on the curriculum of their choice. The ministry refused, however, to cancel outright the revised curriculum to which the protesters had so strenuously objected. It was not until the presidency transferred back to the DPP in 2016 that the newly formed government under Tsai Ing-wen nullified the proposed revisions. Several years later, educational reform remains a deeply divisive issue, with advocates on both sides of the political spectrum arguing forcefully for the legitimacy of their perspectives (Lin, Shih, and Chung 2018).

Hip-Hop Historiography of Taiwan: A Rap Syllabus

The corpus of songs that rappers write about the past represents a parallel process of curricular reform, one that intervenes in the formal processes of knowledge construction brought under scrutiny before and during the Anti–Black Box Curriculum Movement. Drawing on a robust tradition of post–martial law student activism that evolved alongside rap—in all its guises as *xiha*, *raoshe*, and *liām-kua*—artists raise questions about how knowledge is produced and whose knowledge is affirmed. Keeping their pedagogical aspirations in mind, we might listen to this corpus less as a playlist than as a syllabus. Doing so permits us to better hear the modes in which rappers organize and conceptualize their performances of this repertoire as teaching moments. It also compels recognition that, just as a syllabus is necessarily dialogic and anticipates student response, so, too, is musical repertoire composed and performed in collaboration with others.

What kind of "class" does this imaginary syllabus describe? What catalyzes its pedagogy? The liner notes to Kou Chou Ching's *Kou!! It's Coming Out!!!* (2007) raise some possibilities. Outlining their motivations for composing the song "Civil Revolt, Part 1" (see fig. 5.2)—discussed briefly in the prologue to this book in the context of the 921.87 Benefit Concert—they write:

> Perhaps you've often heard people say, "Taiwanese people should know about Taiwanese history." That's right, we all have a place in Taiwanese history, but how much do you really know about Taiwan? From elementary school onwards, people of our generation have studied Chinese

FIG. 5.2. Members of Kou Chou Ching—Fish Lin (*left*), DJ JChen (*center*), and Fan Chiang (*right*)—perform "Civil Revolt, Part 1" in Vancouver, Canada, September 6, 2010. Photograph by author.

history and world history, but how much did we study Taiwanese history? You might be able to able to recite the histories of each and every empire in China; you might be able to tell me when each important event happened in the West. But how much do you understand about Taiwan, this place where you grew up? Because we have such questions, we have started to put together a series of stories about Taiwan. In this first part, we want to talk about Taiwan during the Ching Dynasty (1636–1912).... If we use the past as a mirror for the present, won't we see that if Taiwanese people work together, we won't repeat the tragedies of the past?[21]

Kou Chou Ching critiques approaches to teaching history that privilege the concentric circles represented by China and the West, and offers a "series of stories"—of which "Civil Revolt, Part 1" is the first—to listeners who wish to know more about "this place where [they] grew up." The lessons the group proffers are not merely intended to provide educational enrichment for listeners, but to argue that reckoning with the past is a necessary prerequisite for a more just and humane future.

Composed and performed in collaboration with Chang Jui-chuan, "Civil Revolt, Part 1" implores listeners to break free from centuries-long cycles of interethnic conflict, to remain attentive to failures of government,

and to protest when warranted. Although "Civil Revolt, Part 1" was released the year the KMT commenced its efforts to roll back curricular reforms made during the Lee and Chen administrations, Fish Lin told to me
that the song took nearly three years of intermittent work for the group to
complete. During that period, Kou Chou Ching's members grappled with
lacunae in their own educations and deepened their knowledge through
extensive reading (interview, July 13, 2016). Refusing to submerge their
politics beneath layers of metaphor or to wear a false veneer of journalistic
reportage, they aspired with "Civil Revolt, Part 1" to an ideological trans-
parency and emotional immediacy that was absent from the history textbooks they had encountered in their schooling. The song's rich historical
detailing and intricate sonic construction merit especially close reading.

The track opens with the sound of a *guzheng*, or plucked zither, playing a
rapidly ascending and descending pentatonic scale that is evocative of flow-
ing water, a sonic effect for which the instrument is traditionally prized.
In the introductory text that Kou Chou Ching provides for the piece, the
group notes that this gesture is intended to illustrate the motion not of flow-
ing water, but of "flying banners on battlements of old." The figure is the
first of many instances of text painting in "Civil Revolt, Part 1," in which an
instrumental or environmental sonority creates a backdrop against which
vocal performances unfold. Beyond this opening, the *guzheng* is the source
of multiple motifs, which recur throughout the song's twelve verses. It features prominently in a rising two-note tremolo figure that underpins each
verse and provides a counterpoint to a *suona* melody introduced in the
chorus. The vocals do not enter right at the top of the track; there is initially
no indication of an underlying rhythm and the *guzheng* plays freely.

Seconds later, the metallic clash of swords propels the listener into a
first statement of the chorus and the muscular, low-end beat that underlies
the remainder of the recording. This chorus, a once-repeated rhyming
couplet delivered by Fan Chiang and Fish Lin, issues a rousing call for Taiwanese rebellion against government corruption in Hoklo and Mandarin.
It is followed immediately by Chang Jui-chuan's first two verses, in Hoklo:

副歌 (Fish Lin, 范姜)
政府刁難 人民起度爛
推翻腐敗 台灣人造反

主歌1 (張睿銓)
聖經創世記有講 古早只有一種語言
也無南北東西不同的口音
你和我也攏是兄弟姊妹
無誤會 無怨仇 無戰爭

主歌2
世間人過得太爽驕傲靠勢 挑戰上帝
起一個巴別城 起一個巴別塔
塔頂愈起愈高 凶凶就要遇到天
耶和華生氣 空氣變冷支支

chorus (Fish Lin, Fan Chiang)
the government fucks with the people, the people get pissed off[22]
overthrow corruption, Taiwanese people rebel

verse 1 (Chang Jui-chuan)
in Genesis it says that in the beginning there was only one language
there were no different accents from south, north, east, and west
you and I were brother and sister
there was no misunderstanding, no hatred, no war

verse 2
but the people of the world lived too indulgently and pridefully, challenging God
created the city of Babylon, erected a tower of Babel
the tower got higher and higher, almost reaching heaven
Jehovah was angered, the air turned cold

Chang—who is a Taiwanese Presbyterian—invokes the story of the Tower of Babel from the book of Genesis as an allegory for present-day multilingual, multiethnic Taiwan. Although he laments that people in Taiwan struggle to comprehend one another, he expresses hope in subsequent verses that they will find ways to "understand our different languages, cultures, opinions, and voices." The object of his critique is not multiculturalism, per se, but the feelings of linguistic and ethnic difference that have historically factored in conflicts among disparate groups in Taiwan. As Fan Chiang and Fish Lin will propose, the governments that have controlled the island over the years sometimes fomented and profited from this sense of difference, impeding the development of a unified "Taiwanese" subjectivity that might have served as a basis for resistance to corrupt regimes.

Following Chang's four verses and another statement of the chorus, Fish Lin enters with a fifth verse, also in Hoklo, which transports the listener from biblical time-space to the end of the seventeenth century, when the Qing Emperor Kangxi annexed Taiwan:

主歌5 (Fish Lin)
綁著頭鬃尾仔 咱兮皇帝住北京

大清帝國彼呢大　台灣歸去放乎爛
人講做官若清廉　食飯就愛澆鹽
貪污嘛無啥　只是提濟提少爾爾

verse 5 (Fish Lin)
hair tied in a queue, our emperor lives in Beijing
the Qing empire is so big, Taiwan is left to rot
it is said that if the officials were clean, they'd just eat rice with salt
they're all corrupt, only some steal more and some steal less

Prior to 1683, thousands of Taiwan's Han settlers were Ming loyal-
ists, fighting the Dutch East India Company for control and resisting the
Manchu-ruled Qing. After defeating the Ming loyalist movement, the
Qing incorporated Taiwan into Fujian Province and did relatively little
thereafter to govern the island. The lyrics in this verse ask listeners to
imagine themselves as newly minted Qing subjects who must surrender
to the so-called "tonsure decree," shaving off their hair at the front of their
heads and braiding the rest into a long queue in deference to the Kangxi
emperor. Although the tonsure decree was enforced by authorities, Taiwan was otherwise "just left to rot" and chaos reigned: the island was
rife with coastal piracy, dissident activities, and ongoing disputes with
Indigenous peoples over land and natural resources. This disorder exacerbated existing conflicts within the heterogeneous Han group—members
of various Hakka and Hoklo communities tended to cluster together in
kinship and surname groups, and the bloody feuds that arose frequently
between them were "an appropriate form of conflict for rival communities contending in an insecure environment plagued by disorder and weak
government" (Lamley 1981, 315). In the sixth verse, Fish Lin describes the
corruption of Qing authorities, alleging that they overtaxed and "conspired with the rich to defraud honest people." The seventh and eighth
verses refer to increasing frustration at this corruption on the part of the
Hoklo and Hakka, who, Lin cries, ought to have rebelled against the representatives exploiting them.

Following a third repetition of the chorus, Fan Chiang enters with verses
nine through twelve, which alternate between Mandarin and Hakka languages. The ninth verse restates the argument that the Qing government
did little to govern the island effectively but instead "pushed the people into
chaos, giving rise to a time of unrest." Fan Chiang then invokes the names
of three individuals—Zhu Yigui (朱一貴), Lin Shuangwen (林爽文),
and Dai Chaochun (戴潮春)—who led three major popular rebellions
against the Qing. The tenth and eleventh verses, in Hakka and Mandarin,
suggest that it was the Qing government's desire not merely to govern

lackadaisically and ineffectively, but to encourage feuding among Hoklo and Hakka groups. Fan Chiang decries this division and asserts that "the brave people of Taiwan turned their guns in the wrong direction"—that is, at one another—ultimately assisting Qing efforts to subjugate them. The twelfth and final verse takes listeners back to the present, asking how many remember historical figures like Zhu, Lin, and Dai. Fan Chiang ends the piece by suggesting that interethnic conflict remains a problem on the island and encourages Taiwan's peoples to look past their differences because, "united together, only then will [they] have a future." Following Fan Chiang's final verse, the chorus returns several more times, followed by the voice of an uncredited female vocalist, who sings the title phrase "civil revolt, civil revolt" over and over again atop further repetitions of the chorus performed by Fish Lin and Fan Chiang.

There is chaos at the heart of the story unfolding in "Civil Revolt, Part 1," but the vocal performances of all three MCs sound surprisingly orderly. What Adam Krims refers to as a sung rhythmic flow—that is, the approach to rhythm and rhyme typical of old-school American hip-hop, character-ized by "repetition, on-beat accents (especially strong-beat ones), regular, on-beat pauses," and couplet groupings with end rhymes that fall consis-tently on the fourth beat (2000, 50)—predominates throughout twelve verses of the song. Although there are moments of spillage beyond the established metrical unit and places where syntactic units become dis-sociated from the meter, for the most part the performers deliver their lyrics in a manner that is rhythmically constant and organized into cou-plet units that emphasize end rhyme over internal rhyme. The use of sung rhythmic flows expands and enriches the song's engagement with history through subtle suggestion of a relationship with old-school hip-hop, the feeling of returning to a bygone era not only in Taiwan's history, but also in rap's. It also facilitates audience participation in live settings: Kou Chou Ching strongly encourages audience members at shows to raise their fists and pump them along to the beat, and then to punctu-ate the end of each line of the chorus with the rousing off-beat vocable "ho! ho! ho! ho!"

The piece is thickly textured, including the different voices of the three MCs working in three different languages, environmental and other non-musical sonorities, live instruments, samples of traditional music, and vi-nyl scratch sounds. Each of these elements not only supports the anthemic qualities of the song, but also punctuates and illustrates the progress of the narrative. Like the *guzheng*, the *suona* has a storytelling role to play, as Kou Chou Ching explains in the liner notes that its melody represents "the calls to rebellion among Taiwan's inhabitants." Each time that Fish Lin and Fan Chiang repeat the chorus, the *suona* wails beneath them like a siren, augmenting the voice of dissent and creating a sense of emergency. The presence of the *suona*, with its characteristically strident, penetrating sound, marks "Civil Revolt" as distinctly local: used in a variety of Taiwanese religious rituals and musico-theatrical forms, the instrument is an integral part of Taiwan's soundscape. Its timbre contrasts with the sound of a third traditional instrument heard once in a momentary pause that immediately follows Chang Jui-chuan's verses, the transverse bamboo flute *dizi* (笛子). The *dizi* strikes a different tone at this juncture—its mellow and melancholy sound begs for a moment of contemplation at the end of Chang's sage proclamation that "without justice, there can be no real peace, without real mercy, there can be no good conscience."

Kou Chou Ching employs a variety of sampled, live, and synthesized instrumental sounds, but "Civil Revolt, Part 1" is also rich with environmental and other non-musical sonorities. These vivify key moments in the narrative, particularly at the start of the piece: The metallic clash of swords and sounds of wind gusting accompany the flapping of flags in the breeze suggested by the *guzheng*'s rapidly ascending and descending pentatonic scale; the chopped-up and scratched sample of a man crying out in pain punctuates the moments before the initial statement of the chorus; a horse neighs at the ready as Chang Jui-chuan begins his first verse and Kou Chou Ching perform their final choruses; and the sound of a single waterdrop falling interrupts the silence after Chang's fourth verse as the beat drops out and the *dizi* fades. These non-musical sounds not only heighten the sense of drama present in the lyrical text but also lend it a graphic representational quality—so vivid are these representations that "Civil Revolt, Part 1" sometimes feels less like music from an epic film than it does an epic film itself.

Kou Chou Ching notes in the introductory text to the song that this is the first in a "series of stories about Taiwan." The second, "Civil Revolt, Part 2," was released in 2012 on the album *What's Happening?* (發生了什麼事). That piece addresses the Tapani Incident (噍吧哖事件), a major 1915 Han and Indigenous rebellion against Japanese colonial authorities. A third installment in the series, examining civil uprising under KMT hegemony, is planned for a future album. The arc of this trilogy communicates that the group's objective is not merely to fill gaps in the shared historical knowledge of listeners, but also to trace a direct line through these disparate examples of popular uprising to the social movements of the present day. Kou Chou Ching proposes that there is a lesser-known narrative underpinning Taiwan's history, based not on successive states of subjugation, but rather on stubborn recurrences of popular revolt. The specific political contexts they describe perhaps matter less than the cumulative argument: that there is precedent for active, even disruptive political engagement, to which listeners can refer—for inspiration, justification, and solidarity.

A narrative emphasis on uprising also characterizes Chang Jui-chuan's "Hey Kid" (囝仔) (2007), part of a small but powerful cohort of rap songs about the 2-28 Incident and the period of White Terror. Chang's English-language liner notes claim that "Hey Kid" was "the first rap (and might be the first musical composition) ever that explicitly depicts" this history.[23] The rapper's use of the word "explicitly" is noteworthy: discussing the 2-28 Incident was taboo throughout the period of martial law. As Sylvia Li-chun Lin argues, "One of the most pernicious effects of the White Terror was the fear instilled in the citizenry and the self-censorship that the people of Taiwan learned to practice in response to the omnipresence of the Garrison Command's surveillance apparatus" (2007, 5). Fragmented narration, nonlinear time progressions, and other tactics of strategic ambiguity characterize works by those who endeavored to address state violence (61–62). Chang explained to me that he wrote "Hey Kid," a gift to his brother's firstborn son, with this legacy of strategic ambiguity in mind: "Just imagine this kid sitting next to you and you want to tell them a story. What would you say to him?... Why not do something about this land, this country, telling a little bit of history? I think for me it also is about time for stuff like that to come out. This is a time that we don't have to speak metaphorically anymore. Of course, I'm not denying the beauty of speaking metaphorically, but for 'Hey Kid' I wanted to tell the story honestly. I don't have to be afraid anymore" (interview, December 3, 2009). Chang's account of the 2-28 Incident and decades of political repression that followed eschews figurative language in favor of more direct modes of address. Not only does he stage a blow-by-blow of the history in question, but he also clearly identifies the listeners to whom this history should matter—namely, the next generation, whose responsibility it will be to safeguard democratic principles and processes.

Although Chang frequently samples historically significant musics and incorporates sound clips from political speeches into his other songs, "Hey Kid" is distinguished from much of his output by its attempts to "tell the story honestly" with clarity and sparseness. The track is sound worlds apart from "Civil Revolt, Part 1"—its instrumental does not obviously illustrate the text, and its texture is much thinner: a slow beat, a simple ascending three-note synthesizer riff, and a brief, scalar ascending and descending synthesizer melody loop over and over again. Soft static clicks sound alternately like crackles and pops from an old vinyl record, or like sparks coming up from a hearth fire. One can imagine Chang taking his nephew aside

and sitting him down for a heart-to-heart "about this land, this country."
His flow is measured and deliberate, his tone even, his dynamics consistent. His lyrics suggest urgency as he reminds the titular kid to remember
the sacrifices of those who came before, but his voice is calm—he does not
sound desperate, but hopeful that those receiving his narrative will "change
society in the future" and "fight injustice and oppression." Chang and the
members of Kou Chou Ching hold a common belief that one must know
the past in order to have a hand in building the future, and that rap—as a
participatory art that makes possible the affective communication of emotionally and intellectually complex ideas—can help facilitate that process.

As in "Civil Revolt, Part 1," historical details take center stage in "Hey
Kid." The second verse of the song, which Chang himself translated from
Hoklo into English for the liner notes, underscores the particular impor-
tance of knowing and speaking the names of White Terror victims and
pro-democracy activists who were omitted from history books when
Chang was a student:

維來戒嚴三十八年白色恐怖
管你外省本省客家福佬抑是原住民
黨看你袂爽，你著馬上無去
林義雄老母兩个查某囝全部刣死
雷震批評蔣介石hông關十年
殷海光寫冊hông監視逼死
蔣經國全面禁止台語節目
連布袋戲歌仔戲嘛愛講北京話
勇敢的台灣人拍拚追求民主自由
政治改革的美麗島，農民抗爭的五二〇
關的關死的死
鄭南榕為言論自由點起來彼支火猶未燒了
囝仔，你著愛會記
恁的流血流汗艱苦犧牲予你自由的空氣
毋通袂記，民主革命才開始
無經過寒冬的風雪，看袂著春天的花蕊

What ensued was 38 years of the martial law era called "White Terror"
Doesn't matter if you're Mainlander, Formosan, Hakka, Holo, or
    Aborigine
If you mess with the Party, you'll vanish in no time
Or be butchered like the mother and two daughters of Lin Yi-hsiung
Lei Jhen was imprisoned for ten years for criticizing Chiang Kai-shek
Yin Hai-guang was under surveillance for his political articles until
    he died

Chiang Ching-kuo banned all the Taiwanese TV shows
Even puppet shows and Taiwanese operas must be aired in Chinese
Brave Taiwanese souls fought and struggled for democracy and freedom
Beautiful Island Incident for political reform, 520 Farmer Protest
Jail after jail, kill after kill
Cheng Nan-jung burst into flames that'll last forever for free speech
Hey kid, you must remember
Their blood and sweat, torment and sacrifice, gave you the air you're
    breathing
Don't forget the revolution for democracy has just begun
You won't see the spring buds if you don't go through the winter snow

For the most part, this verse exchanges figurative language for "surrogation" (Roach 1996), a practice of presencing recollections of the persecuted that Benjamin Tausig (2019) describes in the context of his work on sound and protest as "an unyielding type of repetition, a mode of dissensus." Addressing the use of this tactic in Black Lives Matter demonstrations in the United States, Tausig notes that one of the effects of surrogation "has been an insistence that those unjustly killed will not be fully laid to rest without reparations for their deaths."[24] By naming specific victims of state violence and reproducing collective social memories of state violence, Chang likewise implores the listener both to learn who these figures were and to seek redress on their behalf.

Chang's injunction predated by eleven years the establishment of the independent Transitional Justice Commission by the Tsai Ing-wen administration on May 31, 2018, which has focused on exonerating those convicted of political crimes during the White Terror, declassifying martial law–era government documents, and removing symbols of authoritarianism from public spaces.[25] In May 2020, the commission announced that it would begin including lessons on transitional justice in primary and secondary school curricula (Y. Chen 2020). Chang, who now works at a Waldorf School in Changhua County, is encouraged by these reforms but "pessimistic about their actual effects," primarily because college entrance exams to the best of his knowledge remain unchanged:

The exams overwhelmingly dominate students' learning, teachers' teaching, and parents' expectations of test scores. The history exam consists of 72 multiple-choice questions, with no essay questions, or those that allow reasoning or argument. I don't think it's the meaning of history learning to look for one standard answer to a question about history events . . . but the way they test the students determines how they learn and what they should pay attention to—memorizing names and dates and believing everything the textbook tells you. It could also be quite ironic when you realize that many people were killed or persecuted in the past because they didn't give the answers [their] oppressors wanted to hear. (personal communication, August 22, 2020)

It is perhaps for this reason that Chang has continued to perform "Hey Kid" regularly in concert settings. He has released two music videos for two of the song's many remixes in 2008 and 2014 and shares the latter on social media each year on the anniversary of the 2-28 Incident. His continued resurrections of "Hey Kid" as remix, live performance, and video are themselves a kind of surrogation—a continued endeavor both to teach and "disturb the complacency" of the living (Roach 1996, 2).[26]

Although Chang takes care to note that Taiwanese people of all ethnicities were vulnerable to persecution during the White Terror, the pieces I have thus far discussed leave intact for the most part settler-colonial frameworks for thinking and feeling about history. Figuring Hoklo and Hakka peoples as "native," the Taiwanization/localization movement failed to reckon meaningfully with the role those groups played in subjugating Taiwan's original inhabitants. Moreover, legislative proposals for transitional justice have, for the most part, elided the specific claims of Indigenous peoples (Caldwell 2018, 453).[27] As Katsuya Hirano, Lorenzo Verancini, and Toulouse-Antonin Roy assert: "Uncovering Taiwan's long history of settler-colonial formation has significant consequences for the way the island is located in space and time. Is it within China? Is it post-colonial? … A perspective formed through historical orthodoxies, whether representing the KMT or DPP position, has defined the contours of the debate" (2018, 213). In other words, whether based on "great Han" or "concentric circles" perspectives, history curricula have continued to marginalize Indigenous experience. Hirano, Verancini, and Roy argue that excavating Taiwan's settler-colonial history is necessary in order to expose the island as "an intersectional node where different regimes of domination worked against each other for the expropriation of Indigenous people's land and means of sustenance" (197). The T-ho Brothers' 2003 track "KMT 1947" undertakes precisely this kind of excavation, disrupting historical orthodoxies by centering the experiences of Indigenous peoples in the postwar period. As pedagogical measures, the group's methods are distinct from settler (i.e., Han) efforts to incorporate indigeneity into Taiwanese multicultural education, which have served primarily to underscore claims to difference from China rather than to restore Indigenous autonomy.[28]

The T-ho Brothers did not coalesce from *xiha*'s typical social networks but came together in an ad hoc fashion at the urging of Zhang Yiping

(張議平, aka "43 Zhang" 張四十三), president of indie label Taiwan Colors Music (角頭音樂, TCM). The group's membership modeled a diverse coalitional politics: Jeff, a rapper of Tao heritage, grew up on Orchid Island; Red-i, a reggae singer, rapper, and guitarist of Paiwan heritage, grew up in Canada and Central America before returning to Taiwan as an adult; and Ty (鈦), a drum 'n' bass DJ and self-described "Han Taiwanese," was born and raised in Taipei (interview, January 26, 2010). They performed alongside guest vocalists Samingad (紀曉君) and sister Jia Jia (紀家盈), who have Puyuma and Bunun heritage. For "KMT 1947," the trio enlisted the further assistance of singers Lin Hsiu-chin (林秀金), who is 'Amis, and Lu Hao-ming (陸浩明), who is Puyuma. The majority of the group's songs—including "Orchid Island Protest" (核能牌丁字褲), "Conquer" (我的那根), and "Formosa 2003"—reflect on socioeconomic and political concerns that span the island's Indigenous communities.

As in "Hey Kid," the lyrics to "KMT 1947" dispense with metaphor, rebuking state violence directly. If Chang's vocals are characterized by their quiet intensity, however, Red-i's and Jeff's sound as furious pleas for long-deferred recognition of Indigenous protest. A jagged instrumental begins with short bursts of a yelp siren staggered against a midtempo breakbeat and syncopated, dirty bassline.[29] The first verse, performed forcefully by Red-i in English, decries the KMT's crimes against Indigenous peoples:

> let's begin with then and now
> KMT enslaved my people, they killed Mr. Gao
> drug lords from China took over my motherland
> no love for my people, wickedness in their game plan
> upon their arrival Taiwan struggling for survival
> no chance, killed all the rivals
> no chance for my culture, fed off my people like vultures

The enslavement to which Red-i alludes is not chattel slavery, but a complex of laws and systems that were designed to bring about the slow erasure of Indigenous peoples. These included—but have by no means been limited to—practices of sex trafficking (sexual slavery), which have disproportionately victimized Indigenous women and girls, and extreme economic exploitation linked to land expropriation. Red-i condemns the KMT's illicit activities before and after Chiang Kai-shek's retreat to Taiwan; his reference to "drug lords from China" calls out the Party's participation in the opium trade, which it leveraged to fund its military operations between the 1920s and 1970s.

Tactics of surrogation respond in this verse to the murder of "Mr. Gao," or Kao Yi-sheng (高一生), also known by his Indigenous Tsou name

Uyongu Yatauyungana. An accomplished educator, composer, and advocate for Indigenous autonomy, Gao was executed by the KMT in 1954, along with five other prominent Indigenous activists. Despite the participation of these and other Indigenous peoples in the 2-28 uprising and in organized resistance throughout the White Terror years, their involvement was marginalized or ignored entirely in early writings (Smith 2012, 211). Much to the chagrin of activists, Gao's name and story still did not appear in Taiwanese history textbooks well into the period of textbook reform (Wang 2016). "KMT 1947" cites Gao not just in name but also in sound: the piece interpolates his composition "Hunting Song" (打獵歌) as a chorus sung by Lin Hsiu-chin in the Tsou and Japanese languages. Steeped in reverberation, Lin's lilting voice calls out: "Come! Come! Let us all go deer hunting! Come! Come! Over the mountains and across the hills..." The strains of "Hunting Song" recall not only the importance of subsistence hunting in Indigenous life, but also the central role of the deer trade in Taiwan's incorporation into regimes of capitalist accumulation under Dutch, Spanish, Zheng, Qing, and Japanese rule.[30] Although the title of "KMT 1947" declaims the song's focus on the postwar period, Lin's voice—channeling Gao's—summons the ghostly victims of conflicts and massacres that predate Chiang Kai-shek's arrival on the island.

Gao's presence in "KMT 1947" takes on added significance when we consider that the song was released three years into the Chen Shui-bian administration. The DPP mobilized the 2-28 Incident at key moments throughout Chen's tenure as "a symbol of autonomous Taiwanese nationhood and statehood" (Hwang 2014, 300). During this period, Indigenous culture producers, working within the constraints of political discourse, sought to intervene in a rapidly intensifying national conversation about Taiwanese identity and sovereignty. As Craig A. Smith notes, they labored to "transform and destabilize [Han-centric historical] narratives with the introduction of subnarratives that problematize the perceived unity of the nation and conflict with romantic tropes of nationalism" (2012, 210). In "Taiwan Ti-ho" (台灣鐵虎) another track on the eponymous *T-ho Brothers* album, Red-i extols the power of narrative agency in this regard. He sings, in a voice both joyful and imperious: "We are so strong, we are writing history!" Songs like "KMT 1947" invoke that strength to force reconsideration of the 2-28 Incident and White Terror as solely, or even primarily, conflicts between "native Taiwanese" (i.e., Hoklo and Hakka) and postwar migrants from China. Sounding instead the specter of Indigenous suffering, they affirm Indigenous personhood and historical knowledge as central to the imagination of a just and humane future for all the island's peoples—including, at last, the descendants of its original inhabitants.

This hip-hop historiography of Taiwan testifies to an ongoing desire among musicians and their larger social networks to consolidate collective memories of state violence under the KMT, as well as to limn the connections between recent history and the more distant past. Although such works by no means constitute the mainstream of Taiwan *xiha*, the selections I have discussed here are not the only ones of their kind and do not represent the only historical milieus interrogated. Kung Fu Entertainment artist Ma Xun's (馬訓) 2008 song "His Story" (他的故事), for example, interweaves a looped sample of a plaintive minor-key melody with recorded excerpts of an interview that Ma conducted with his elderly father, a Chinese Civil War veteran, and rapped verses that chronicle the hardships endured by KMT soldiers as they fled China. Through lyrics that highlight the sadness of prolonged separation from relatives across the strait and the trauma of physical injury incurred in the line of duty, "His Story" asks listeners to empathize with the struggles of KMT servicemen who have often played the role of historical villains in post–martial law narratives of Taiwan's unfolding. Hakka MC Dai Shiyao and Playa Club (戴士堯 & 玩樂俱樂部) released "Fate Is in Our Hands" (命印在手) on their eponymous 2010 album, which lionizes the achievements of Hakka soldiers who resisted Japanese aggression in the First and Second Sino-Japanese Wars. Kou Chou Ching's 2010 "The History of Taipei City" (北城講古) surveys the development of Taipei from its earliest Indigenous inhabitants to the present. It urges listeners to remember the city's many places of historical significance and cautions against forgetting the stories of the past. Other artists record songs that document and interpret contemporary events, in hope or expectation that their chronicles of the present will one day constitute the historical record.

The present discussion of history brings this book full circle. We began by tracing three distinct but overlapping Taiwanese histories of rap, and we conclude by pondering three rap histories of Taiwan. The affective power of the latter works—and their ability to channel qualities of "honesty" and "realness," specifically—is bound up with the masculine identities of their composer-performers who, notably, enlist female accomplices only in sung choruses. It is also intertwined with their social respectability and claims to moral-intellectual authority as shored up by their status as musical knowledge workers. Even those who do not claim membership in a *xiha* club or creative collective benefit from the close ties between rap, knowledge production, and male associational life on the island. Such life constitutes a public sphere in which rap community members not only assess collectively their epistemic and ethical commitments, but also undertake the transformation of social discourse into civic action.

EPILOGUE
Then, the Sunflowers

When the Sunflower student protesters stormed the Taiwan legislature on March 18, 2014, I was not in Taipei but in Cambridge, Massachusetts. More precisely, I was preparing to lead a discussion about rap and historical narrative in Taiwan for a small cohort of undergraduates in a Sinophone popular musics course I was teaching at MIT. Social media–savvy activists set up livestreamed video to provide a window on the occupation of the assembly chambers for those not present. We paused our discussion that day to gather around and watch, shoulders tense and mouths gaping, fearful for the safety of everyone involved. The scenes playing out through the small rectangular portal of our classroom computer screen were nothing less than remarkable. Dozens of young people packed tightly together sat on the floor, holding signs and holding hands, while dozens of others tended dutifully to logistics. A large portrait of Sun Yat-sen set against an even larger ROC flag was flanked by two doors that had been barricaded with chairs. It was surreal to be so far away, yet to be granted such intimate access to what was occurring. Protest organizers carried on broadcasting for the duration of the occupation, distrustful of traditional media and demanding visibility for their cause on their own terms. As the days wore on and we continued checking in with the livestream during class, my students and I observed the walls surrounding the portrait and flag becoming progressively more embellished with hand-printed posters and banners bearing movement slogans. One in particular seemed to capture both the idealism and sonic intensity of the moment. It read: "Hear the sound of freedom" (聽見自由的聲音).

From nearly eight thousand miles away, we listened closely. Sunflower was sound-saturated, not just in the assembly chambers but also directly south of the legislature on Qingdao East Road, where hundreds of thousands of demonstrators rallied in front of the federal government offices, and on Jinan Road one block farther south, where a heterogenous community of activists coalesced in a raucous "democracy night market" atmosphere (Rowen 2015, 14). In addition to sounds of festivity, sounds of conflict—shouts, screams, police whistles, sirens, exploding high-pressure water cannons—proliferated across traditional and social media channels. Makeshift stages with massive speakers were erected for orations and performances. Public service announcements and proclamations issued from megaphones and portable sound systems. Clutching their hopeful, heliotropic sunflowers, protesters broke into chants: *Review the trade pact! Proper oversight! Review the trade pact! Proper oversight!*

Those who gathered also sang, both contrafactum and newly composed tunes. Among the more popular local adaptations of existing music was "Do You Hear the People Sing?" from the stage musical *Les Misérables*. The defiant spirit of that piece was clearly audible in its sound and translated Hoklo text, especially for those aware of the musical's setting in the French Revolutionary period. It also linked Sunflower to anti-military protests that had taken place in Taiwan the year prior, when it was first sung in response to the death of a young army conscript.[1] Sunflower's official anthem, the resolutely optimistic "Island's Sunrise" (島嶼天光), was written for the protests by Sam Yang (楊大正) of Kaohsiung-based rock quartet Fire EX (滅火器) in collaboration with students from National Taipei University of Fine Arts (Hioe 2017), and recorded inside the assembly chambers (Wang 2017, 182). A soaring, guitar-driven pop-punk hymn, the piece affirmed a need to remain courageous in the face of adversity.[2] The members of Fire EX were joined at the protests by a number of musicians with long-standing connections to activism in Taiwan, including Chen Ming-chang (formerly of Blacklist Workshop), and indie singer-songwriters Deserts Chang (張懸) and Crowd Lu (盧廣仲).

The Sunflower Movement was largely overlooked by the international news media, and journalists who did report on the protests tended to frame them somewhat one-dimensionally as expressions of opposition to greater economic integration with the PRC.[3] For those more closely acquainted with the vicissitudes of Taiwanese history and politics, however, the events that unfolded in Zhongzheng District told a more complex story, as much about growing anti-neoliberalist sentiment and support for continued democratic consolidation as about naked Taiwanese Sinophobia.[4] They also testified to the emergence of an anti–free trade, left-wing political subjectivity among those born after the end of martial law. As many of the artists with whom I had spoken over the years shared key identity characteristics with student leaders—including elite educational backgrounds, middle-class upbringings, and male gender identities[5]—I was not entirely surprised by this turn of events. Sunflower represented precisely the kind of grassroots, youth-led civic activism anchored in civil disobedience that artists at the 921.87 Rap Benefit Concert had extolled in Tainan five years earlier. Student leaders' grievances recapitulated complaints articulated by RPG and peers, in songs and other public utterances, against increasing and seemingly inescapable stagnation and precarity.

The occupation of the legislature was the culmination of months of planning and coalition-building that drew on the talents of local musicians, including several whose stories have unfolded in this book. Fish Lin and DJ JChen of Kou Chou Ching, for example, took part in meetings with student organizers for over a year prior to the occupation. Attendance was always fewer than a hundred people at these gatherings, Lin remembered when we met for coffee in Taipei in 2016, but grew steadily as student leader Wei Yang (魏揚) requested that they bring more trustworthy people along (interview, August 19, 2016).[6] With other members of Kou Chou Ching and offshoot band Community Service, as well as Chang Jui-chuan, Lin performed at earlier protests against black-box trade-agreement activities (反黑箱服貿協議活動), nuclear power proliferation, and government land expropriation. Inside the assembly chambers some ten days into the occupation, he and bandmates performed "Civil Revolt, Part 1" (as they had at the 921.87 Benefit Concert) and "Civil Revolt, Part 2." The group also took the stage outside the legislature for protesters, the numbers of which peaked around 500,000. Many in the crowd carried black towels with bilingual text reading "Civil Revolt 官逼民反" and outfitted themselves in black T-shirts bearing the bilingual slogan "Fuck the Government 自己國家自己救" in white text. These now-iconic designs were originally produced by streetwear label Radicalization (激進工作室), founded in 2011 by members of Kou Chou Ching.[7]

Dwagie's presence was likewise felt in multiple dimensions at the scene of Sunflower, as he both performed for and circulated among the crowds of protesters, shaking hands and thanking those present for their efforts. One week after the occupation began, on March 25, he shared a message on Facebook informing fans that he was pausing promotional activities for his newest album to devote his full attention to writing a song in tribute to Sunflower. Fully embracing the democratic and social-communal spirit of the moment, he asked his numerous followers to leave messages describing the ideas they felt the track ought to express. He followed this up several days later with a call for fans to contribute photos and film clips to use in a video for the song—anything, he said, that they felt was representative of the moment: "I need touching… angry… desperate… hopeful…" Finally, just a day before the song's April 3 release, he offered for public comment the complete lyrics to the composition that had emerged from this collaborative process, which he titled simply "Sunflower" (太陽花).

Recalling the corpus of songs about history discussed in chapter 5, "Sunflower" employs a third-person omniscient perspective that favors plain language over more florid or figurative modes of expression. In the first of three verses and a chorus performed by featured vocalist J. Wu, Dwagie describes a clash between protesters and police attempting to eject them from the scene of the occupation:

(大支)
救護車的聲響伴隨隨著學生入睡
然後被大陣仗警察驚醒在午夜
糾察隊內疚心痛 說無法保護群眾
然後跪著向英勇 向留下的學生鞠躬
記者問女學生等等驅離怕不怕呢
女學生說很怕但她第一天就準備好了
然後學生們舉起雙手表示不抵抗
接著該在胸腔的熱血撒在地上
警察沒得休息 爸媽打不通孩子手機
老師為了學生被攻擊倒地抽蓄
噴水車從歷史課本裡出現幫你溫習
滿頭鮮血學生喊著不是警察的問題
受傷學生哭著應答說爸爸也是警察
人民被逼到廝殺對立不斷激化
這是時代悲歌 這回合我們沒轍
接著早上了 但台灣天空是黑的

(J. Wu)
我們受盡了命運巨棒的揮打
我的頭在流血但不曾垂下
我們爬過那佈滿鐵絲的拒馬
放上一朵照亮陰暗角落的太陽花

(Dwagie)
the ambulance siren accompanies the students to sleep
just to be awakened by throngs of police at midnight
volunteer guards feel guilt and heartbreak, saying they cannot protect
    the crowds
and they kneel down and bow to the courageous students that stay
a journalist asks a female student if she's afraid of being driven away
the female student says yes but that she's been preparing since the
    first day
and then the students put their hands up, showing no resistance
only to see the hot blood from their chests spill on the ground

the police have no time to rest, fathers and mothers cannot reach their
  children's cellphones
a teacher takes a hit for the students, falls to the ground convulsing
water cannon trucks appear as if from history textbooks, I'll help you
  recall
students with bloodied heads shout that it's not the cops' fault
injured students cry out that their fathers are also cops
the people are forced to fight and the opposition continues to intensify
this is the threnody of our era, in this round we are helpless
and then it is morning, but the sky in Taiwan is still dark

(J. Wu)
we are beaten by a club of fate
my head bleeds but does not hang down
we climb across barbed wire and barricades
to place a sunflower where it can light up the darkest of corners

Dwagie's narration in the first verse makes no pretense to political
neutrality—his sympathies lie clearly with the "courageous" (英勇) student protesters. But he observes that this brutal encounter is one that
activists and authorities alike are compelled to play out by larger and more
powerful forces, which he goes on to delineate in the second verse as "busi-
nessmen whose values have broken and collapsed" (商人價值觀崩壞掉)
and "a government of wolves" (狼一般政府). Even if it is not impar-
tial, his commentary assumes an aesthetic of reportage: Lyrics are
packed densely with detail and long phrases leave little space for breath.
Dwagie's flow, characterized by fine rhythmic subdivisions over a plod-
ding beat in 4/4 time, is insistent and charged with quiet momentum.
J. Wu's singing at the chorus, faint and sinuous, sounds the exhaustion of
protesters persisting in nonviolent resistance.

Dwagie explained to me in an interview several months after the occupation that he understood "Sunflower" as fulfilling a separate mission
from Fire EX's "Island's Sunrise": "They released [that] song during the
movement. But for me, I wanted to write a song, to make everything into
a story, those events. So, what I decided was, I'm going to write its history,
for when the movement is finished" (interview, October 25, 2014). These
diverging goals gave each piece a distinctive shape. "Island's Sunrise" has
an inspirational tenor, intended to encourage those in the midst of protest to persevere and prepare for the dawn of a new day. "Sunflower," by
contrast, does not take sunrise as a foregone conclusion. Rapping at the
end of the first verse that "the sky in Taiwan is still dark," Dwagie inti-
mates that even if the protests are successful, there will still be work to do.

Activists can celebrate their participation in the movement, but maintaining the integrity of Taiwan's democratic institutions will require ceaseless, strenuous civic engagement. If "Island's Sunrise" aspires to a moment of transcendent victory, "Sunflower" embodies a wearying march, under crushing pressures, toward elusive change. Steering sharply clear of descent into melancholia at the chorus, Dwagie calls the listener's attention to a silver lining: protesters need not sit in passive expectation of daylight. As long as they're willing to fight the good fight, they can be their own sources of illumination.

The senior artists at the center of this book came of age just as martial law ended and Taiwan entered a prolonged process of democratic consolidation. Responding to the vicissitudes of their times, some sought to "change Taiwan" through bold acts of language revitalization and historical revisionism. Others more quietly affirmed their humanity through rap, giving voice to their own subjective experiences of the world. Whatever their preferred style of engagement, they recognized, as so many Taiwanese musicians have, that their works are immanent in politics. They attested, sometimes with enthusiasm and sometimes with ambivalence, to the fundamentally relational character of storytelling and what Hannah Arendt (1958) observed as its capacity to function as a bridge between the private and public realms.

As I have argued, the affordances of rap as both local and global praxis have galvanized its mostly male public not just to imagine, but also to engender new forms of post-authoritarian sociality. From its inception in the immediate post–martial law period, rap has been imbricated with complex processes of community (re)building. These processes have constituted themselves through rappers' performances of musical knowledge work and have anchored their claims to narrative agency. More recently, they have also positioned artists on the front lines of conversations about precarity. When the Sunflower Movement is described as "an affective response to the uncertainties of the future released by neoliberalism" (Wang 2017, 179), its critics might just as well be describing the rap scene writ large. "Future" is an operative term here, and the one that perhaps most clearly distinguishes Taiwanese anxieties from anxieties expressed by those living in other neoliberalizing societies: What, indeed, does the future hold for Taiwan given its particular experience of unrelenting existential uncertainty? Even if rap cannot revoke such uncertainty, can it at least mitigate uncertainty's effects?

The latter question preoccupied me when I caught up with Ill Mo over FaceTime in September 2020, as I was composing this epilogue. It was late in Taipei; Mo's two daughters were asleep, and his wife, Kay, tended to her own work in the background as we chatted. In the midst of rising tensions with the PRC and economic contraction in the wake of the COVID-19 pandemic, he and Kay had established a creative venture called "Knowledge Collective" (哪裡聚).[8] Through this venture, they were able to apply as a business for government money to upgrade their recording equipment. The Ministry of Culture funds projects it believes will help to increase the global visibility (or, in this case, audibility) of Taiwan. Kung Fu Entertainment, KAO!INC., and numerous indie bands have applied in the past several years to support special projects, overseas tours, and equipment purchases. We discussed ongoing, at times heated debates within the rap community regarding relationships between artists and the government, and the impact of such relationships on political expression and perceptions of artistic integrity. Nevertheless, Mo recognized and welcomed the opportunity: By leveraging grant-writing skills acquired in the course of his academic career, he could amass the resources necessary to up his game as a performer, an impressive feat in these challenging times (interview, September 25, 2020).

Even as he expressed hope for the future, Mo cited his ongoing personal struggles, transformed but not erased by age, as the impetus for his newest single, the stoutheartedly titled "Not Afraid" (不害怕). A trap-style track with dreamy synths and crisp, rapid-fire hi-hats, its lyrics articulate feelings of inadequacy and describe the tensions between Mo's desire to be an artist and his obligation to support his family. He explained to me that he tried to express something in "Not Afraid" of his anxiety about missing opportunities in life and of failing to reach his full potential as either an artist *or* as a husband and father. Although the story that Mo tells is a personal one, listeners on a variety of online platforms have, in their comments, identified with the experience it describes—a moment of self-questioning, a hunt for inner strength. Moreover, many of them attest to a widespread effect: by listening to a story about Mo's personal fears, they find their own fears assuaged. One YouTube commenter asks, "Teacher is already so brave, what do we have to be afraid of?"

ACKNOWLEDGMENTS

In this book, I examine how a community of musicians pushes against the limits of language to tell its own stories. As I compose these acknowledgments, I find myself wrestling with the same challenge, searching for a way to narrate my experience of the twelve years this project encompassed. If I am being honest, words fail me; the years were, and my heart feels, too full. There was so much joy—the birth of my daughter, the passing of milestones, the warmth of a close circle of friends and family. But also hardship and grief—a complicated pregnancy, years of long-distance commuting and caregiving, a pandemic, and the wrenching loss of both my parents less than a year apart. The totality of this experience overwhelms me. Life seems bigger than language, at least the language I am capable of. I can only vouch for the sincerity and depth of my gratitude to the people named here. Without their love and support, this book would not exist.

My scholarship and personhood have been shaped indelibly by so many extraordinary teachers. First and foremost, I am forever indebted to Kay Kaufman Shelemay, who advised with the greatest care and compassion my earliest work on this project at Harvard University. Ingrid Monson and Richard Wolf were transformative presences in both the classroom and on my dissertation committee. I would also like to highlight the special impact of Virginia Danielson, Tomie Hahn, Christopher Hasty, Michael D. Jackson, Shigehisa Kuriyama, Marcyliena Morgan, Carol Oja, Michael Puett, Alexander Rehding, Barbara Retzko, Jason Stanyek, Xiaofei Tian, and Margaret Wan. Eileen Chow and Shiamin Kwa shared with me not only their knowledge but also their powerful love of stories. With warmth and wisdom, Sindhumathi Revuluri helped me chart a course through key moments of personal and professional transition that have led directly to this point. I lucked into the most convivial graduate cohort, and our ceaseless banter empowered me to embrace joy in this work: Sofía Becerra-Licha,

Andrea Bohlman, Louis Epstein, Johanna Frymoyer, Glenda Goodman, Michael Heller, Frank Lehman, Tom Lin, Danny Mekonnen, Rowland Moseley, Matthew Mugmon, Torbjorn Ottersen, and Sasha Siem.

In Taiwan, a core group of senior artists in the rap scene—the ones whose work inspired *Renegade Rhymes*—have been my most critical guides and most cherished interlocutors. I remain astounded and humbled by the generosity with which they welcomed me into their worlds and allowed me to stay for so long. I owe a special debt of friendship to Chang Jui-chuan, Dwagie, Fish Lin, Ill Mo, RPG, Shortee, and Teacher Lin for their indefatigable support and innumerable hours of illuminating conversation. I hope that they recognize in this book the fulfillment of some of their greatest ambitions, and that they find it useful in their continued efforts to teach others. Applause is overdue to Kay Wu, whose work holding down the home front made it possible for me and Mo to prattle on as much as we have. Danny Wang, Lans Hung, and Tiff Chou shared their big-hearted enthusiasm for rap and years of personal experience in the scene. Sophia Su, who arranged my earliest meetings with Dwagie and other Kung Fu Entertainment artists, modeled the hospitality for which Tainan is famous. Catherine Shu was a magnificent travel companion to the Mosaic Music Festival in Singapore, where she memorably persevered through weather that can only be described as "boiling hot rain." Anna Fodde-Reguer and Brigid Vance accompanied me to shows and danced by my side. It was a true pleasure to study language with Lin Chiufang at National Taiwan University, and I continually return to notes from our lessons for insights into Hoklo poetics. I thank Teri Silvio and Tasaw Lu at Academia Sinica, as well Tsai Hsin-hsin at National Chengchi University, both for their kindness and for inviting me to concerts and lectures that left deep impressions. Ma Shih-fang and Chang Tieh-chih have helped me to think both broadly and deeply about rap's place in Taiwanese musical and political history. I was overjoyed to meet translator and amateur dancer Kathy Kao at the very end of the revisions process and am so thankful for her feedback on my translations of song lyrics.

Research for this book was undertaken with the support of a number of funding agencies and institutions, including a Fulbright-Hays Fellowship from the US Department of Education, an Asian Cultural Council Grant, a Mrs. Giles Whiting Foundation Fellowship, and a Harvard Fairbank Center Grant. A Mellon Postdoctoral Fellowship in the Humanities at the Massachusetts Institute of Technology enabled me to begin retheorizing and expanding the dissertation into a completely different book. A Chiu Scholarly Exchange Program for Taiwan Studies Fellowship from Oregon State University supported additional fieldwork in Taiwan. I completed the manuscript with critical assistance from an Emory University

Research Committee Award and am grateful to the Emory College of Arts and Sciences for a generous publication subvention. I benefited immeasurably from the input of faculty at the Graduate Institute of Musicology at National Taiwan University, who were the most gracious of hosts during my initial fieldwork trips. Years later, I remain inspired by the work of Chen Jen-yen, Chen Szu-wei, Shen Tung, Tsai Chen-gia, Wang Ying-fen, Wang Yuh-wen, Yamauchi Fumitaka, and Yang Chien-chang. I was incredibly fortunate to join the dynamic intellectual community in Music and Theater Arts at MIT, where I had energizing conversations about this work with Ian Condry, Rebecca Dirksen, Kurt Fendt, Peter McMurray, Emily Richmond-Pollock, Lara Pellegrinelli, Charles Shadle, Patty Tang, Emma Teng, and Lamine Touré. When in the middle of my postdoc I had to move my family to New York and begin supporting my father through his cancer treatment, my uncle Scott and aunt Julie Handorff welcomed me into their home in Holbrook on the days I had to be at MIT to teach; both Patty and Lamine and Emily and Andy Pollock offered me their spare rooms on the nights I was too worn out to travel out to Holbrook—their kindness and help made it possible for me to continue this work at a challenging time.

I am extraordinarily thankful to have found a home at Emory University among so many wonderful colleagues. Kevin Karnes has been an exceptional faculty mentor, and I am deeply appreciative of his close engagement with my ideas. Dwight Andrews, Lynn Bertrand, Melissa Cox, Stephen Crist, and Kristin Wendland offered wise counsel that helped me strategize completion even amid the upheaval of a pandemic. Jia-Chen (Wendy) Fu and Jenny Wang Medina have been sources of levity and gravity. I am thankful to Maria Sibau for welcoming me so warmly to the East Asian Studies program when I arrived at Emory in 2015. Much gratitude to Dion Liverpool for amplifying the sounds and stories of hip-hop at Emory. Finally, I am so glad to have been in the junior faculty trenches with Laura Emmery, Adam Mirza, Heidi Senungetuk, and Katherine Young, who have been essential sources of solidarity and good cheer.

Staff from across so many institutions were indispensable to the processes of researching, writing, and publishing *Renegade Rhymes*. Special thanks are due to Peter Shirts at the Marian K. Heilbrun Music and Media Library, Guo-hua Wang at the Woodruff Library, and Liza Vick and Kerry Masteller at the Loeb Music Library. The incredible staff of the Emory Music Department, Harvard Music Department, and MIT Music and Theater Arts draw from a seemingly inexhaustible well of administrative prowess and good humor as they go about their daily tasks. I extend sincere gratitude to Cynthia Verba for the tough love she gave my earliest grant proposals. At the Taipei Asian Cultural Council office, Rita Chang and Leona Yu helped me add new links to my academic and artistic circles. Because life and work happen simultaneously and because so much of this book was written at my parents' bedsides, I offer heartfelt thanks to the hospital cafeteria workers, nurses, custodial staff, social workers, and doctors who watched over for my family day after day for the better part of three years. Likewise, my deepest gratitude to the friends who loved and helped care for my daughter while I commuted between New York and Cambridge, and then between New York and Atlanta, especially the heroic Annie Silva-Austin and Lauren Rich.

I was honored to present my materials to astute cross-disciplinary audiences at Emory University, as well as at the Duke University Department of Music, Department of Ethnic Relations and Cultures at National Dong Hwa University, Graduate Institute of Musicology at National Taiwan University, Institute of Ethnology at Academia Sinica, Trinity College International Hip-Hop Festival, UCLA Center for Chinese Studies and International Institute, MIT Women and Gender Studies Intellectual Forum and Comparative Media Studies Colloquium, and SOAS University of London Taiwan Studies Summer School. I shared work and received vital suggestions from colleagues at conferences at the University of North Carolina at Chapel Hill ("Communities of Song: Performing Sung Poetry in the Modern World") and Northeastern University ("Discourse in Music"), and on numerous panels at annual meetings of the Society for Ethnomusicology, Association for Asian Studies, Conference on Chinese Oral and Performing Literatures (CHINOPERL), European Foundation for Chinese Music Research (CHIME), North American Taiwan Studies Association, and the International Association for the Study of Popular Music.

Outside of such formal settings, I am thankful to colleagues and friends who shared their scarce time and abundant expertise. Among those who provided feedback on key pieces of my text or shaped my approach through productive conversation are Marié Abe, Catherine Appert, Shalini Ayyagari, Corinna Campbell, William Cheng, Eileen Chow, Laurence Coderre, Brigid Cohen, Ian Condry, Elizabeth Craft, Dafydd Fell, Anna Fodde-Reguer, Jia-chen (Wendy) Fu, Eleanor Goodman, Deonte Harris, DJ Hatfield, Christina Huang, Umi Hsu, Andrew Jones, Sheryl Kaskowitz, Adam Kielman, Krystal Klingenberg, Ellen Koskoff, Shiamin Kwa, Donna Kwon, Clara Latham, Fred Lau, Dion Liverpool, Katherine In-Young Lee, Louise Meintjes, Ever Meister, Adam Mirza, Lei Ouyang, Matt Pereira, Ian Power, Rumya Putcha, Helen Rees, Chérie Rivers Ndaliko, David Rolston, Kendra Salois, Maria Sibau, Matthew Sussman, Patty Tang, Brigid Vance, Margaret Wan, David Der-wei Wang, Yun Emily Wang, Chuen-Fung Wong, Wang Ying-fen, and Biyu Zhang. I am enormously grateful to Bonnie Gordon for uplifting me and helping me to navigate faculty life with a vision disorder. Nancy Guy has been a critical sounding board and unwavering source of encouragement as this project has moved through all its stages of development. Andrea Bohlman always seemed to understand what I meant before I did, and shared with the utmost benevolence her borderless knowledge. Glenda Goodman galvanized me to think ambitiously and to ask big questions about the relationship between past and present. Chanda Prescod-Weinstein offered profound wit, wisdom, and perspective—she has transformed my thinking across so many domains.

It has been a great privilege to work with Elizabeth Branch Dyson at the University of Chicago Press. When we first met in 2013, I was clutching a new baby in one hand and a new dissertation in the other—and I wasn't entirely sure how to usher either into their next stages of development. The parenting piece would ultimately be up to me, but Elizabeth's probing questions about my project yielded precious clarity. I am endlessly grateful for her exhortations to trust my instincts and to keep moving forward. My deepest appreciation to series editors Philip Bohlman and Timothy Rommen, for their advocacy and for understanding what I aspired to achieve with this book. Thanks to Mollie McFee, Dylan Montanari, and Erin DeWitt, who have personified diligence and solicitousness through the production process. The two anonymous peer reviewers helped me see what was working and what wasn't—their suggestions, big and small, helped give rise to a stronger and more lucid *Renegade Rhymes*.

Part of chapter 1 is adapted from an article that appeared in *CHINOPERL* 33, no. 1 (2014). An earlier version of chapter 3 appeared in *Ethnomusicology* 60, no. 3 (2016). My thanks to University of Hawai'i Press and the Society for Ethnomusicology for granting me permission to incorporate these texts into this book.

I count among the greatest blessings of my life that I have friends who are like family, and family among my dearest friends. Their collective care in Taiwan and the United States across so many years made this book possible. To Jon, Ally, Jenn, Brian, Eric, and Irene, I am so grateful that we get to walk through life together. To Jensen and Yu-an, thank you for making a true home for me in Taiwan. To Andrea and Glenda, thank you for your steadfast friendship and for so many astonishing acts of kindness. To my extraordinary husband, Andres, thank you for being our North Star. And to my brilliant daughter, June, who has never known a time when I wasn't at work on this project, thank you for your patience—I can't wait to write the next chapter with you.

NOTES

Prologue

1. For more on the 921 Earthquake, see Ding (2007).

2. In a 1999 English-language article for *Foreign Affairs*, Lee Teng-hui (李登輝), Taiwan's first popularly elected president, used this terminology. Recently, there have been calls in the English-language media to dispense with its use. See, for example, Fish (2016).

3. Sinitic languages have proven particularly fertile ground for research on music performance in tonal languages. Linguist Yuen Ren Chao (1956) and ethnomusicologists Bell Yung (1975, 1983, 1989, 1991) and Francesca Sborgi Lawson (2011) have published substantial English-language scholarship on this topic.

4. The Austronesian languages spoken by Taiwan's Indigenous peoples are nontonal, but no rappers performed in Indigenous languages at this event.

5. Scholars studying a wide variety of past and present world musical traditions have long been interested in the affinities between music and language, from ethnomusicologist George List's early inquiries into "The Boundaries of Speech and Song" (1963) to Kofi Agawu's more recent forays into "Music as Language" (2009). Among the other formative works exploring this topic are Frisbie (1980), Seeger (1986), and Feld (1990).

6. Nancy Guy has considered how musical performance in Taiwan "[reconnects] the past and the future to the present in a meaningful way" (2008, 77). Guy explores how the Hoklo popular song "Flower in the Rainy Night" (雨夜花) has accumulated meaning in multiple contexts as a metaphor for Taiwanese history, and how "through this key symbol, potentially disparate experiences or phenomena are interconnected and viewed as related" (70).

7. "Fuck tha Police" has been broadly influential to politically oriented rap artists in many places. For accounts, see, for example, Urla (2001) and Osumare (2007).

8. The sample's vocalist, who is unidentified, sings the phrase *"naluwan haiyang"* set to a pentatonic melody. For discussions of *"naluwan haiyang"* songs and the ways they circulate within and beyond Indigenous societies in Taiwan, see Chen (2012).

Introduction

1. My language here recalls Sari Hanafi's characterization of post-authoritarianism in the Arab world as "a political project concerned with reconstructing and reorienting local knowledge, ethics and power structures" (2018, 81).

2. The term *shuochang* is used to describe rap more frequently in the PRC than in Taiwan.

3. For more on rap's antecedents in various African and Afro-descendent musical storytelling traditions, see Keyes (2002, 17–25). Hip-hop has also been generative of new forms of narrative. In addition to "hip-hop theater" and "hip-hop cinema," for example, there is the genre known as "hip-hop fiction," which Eve Dunbar has argued is notable as "a productive literary genre for black women writers and readers" (2013, 93). Rap also infuses works of literary fiction by scholars like Regina Bradley (2017a), who channels its emotional immediacy and candor in short stories about "the hip-hop South."

4. Almost since rap's inception, these stories have sometimes been distorted in order to maximize their profitability under white supremacist capitalist patriarchy. This distortion has also impacted the creation of other hip-hop narrative media. Writing about hip-hop cinema, for example, Bradley has noted that as hip-hop's influence on American popular culture grew in the 1980s and '90s, it "needed to simultaneously amplify its beginnings in urban working-class black and brown communities while making room to present a narrative that was alluring and profitable to a mainstream white audience" (2017b, 141).

5. For example, Paul Ricoeur (1990) argues that narrative is a critical means by which human beings make sense of temporal existence. Hannah Arendt's notion of storytelling takes a variety of different shapes in her writings but can be understood partially as, in philosopher Annabel Herzog's words, "the only way to represent the fragmentary nature of individual life, which fights and collapses between past and future, and later reappears crystallized" (2000, 9). Arendt outlines her views of storytelling most extensively in *The Human Condition* (1958).

6. In the first half of the seventeenth century, at least fourteen distinct groups inhabited the western and northern coastal areas, and an additional nine groups resided in the Central Mountain Range and along the southeastern coast (Knapp 2007, 11). The government currently recognizes sixteen distinct groups ('Amis, Atayal, Bunun, Hla'alua, Kanakanavu, Kavalan, Paiwan, Puyuma, Rukai, Saisiyat, Sakizaya, Sediq, Tao, Thao, Truku, and Tsou); several others have also petitioned for official status.

7. Settlers from China began arriving in Taiwan no later than the thirteenth century, however, and many likely came much earlier, as well. For more on early migration, colonialism, and settler-colonialism, see Andrade (2007).

8. Within the Hoklo group, there was further subdivision among those with origins in Zhangzhou and Quanzhou Prefectures.

9. Estimates of the number of civilian deaths following the 2-28 Incident are wide-ranging. In her work on literary and cinematic representations of 2-28, Sylvia Li-chun Lin shares the widely held view that the exact number will never be

determined because of government suppression of information about the event (2007, 3).

10. The precise number of troops and civilians who decamped to Taiwan is the subject of scholarly debate. For more, see T. Lin (2009, 323–36).

11. The term *benshengren* refers generally to those whose presence in Taiwan precedes the arrival of the KMT in 1945. Some consider Taiwan's Indigenous peoples *benshengren* while others reserve this appellation for the descendants of Hoklo and Hakka settlers. Although this term is sometimes disfavored by those who reject the notion of Taiwan as province, it has long been common parlance in Taiwan.

12. See Brown (2004) for discussion of the process by which some Indigenous peoples who inhabited Taiwan's western plains regions gradually assumed Hoklo identities.

13. For more on the Chinese Cultural Renaissance Movement, see Lin (2005) and Chun (2017, 15–38). For more on cultural policy relating specifically to music during this period, see Guy (2005, 66–74).

14. The KMT employed a variety of techniques to enforce its policies of monolingualism, most notably fines for speaking non-Mandarin languages in school. For more on Mandarin-only policies in educational settings, see chapter 5.

15. For more on the 1976 Radio and Television Broadcasting Law that regulated program and advertising content, see Zhang (1997, 1–23) and Fell (2018, 25).

16. According to the State Department, the United States now "[enjoys] a robust unofficial relationship" with Taiwan, "in line with the U.S. desire to further peace and stability in Asia" (Bureau of East Asian and Pacific Affairs 2018). (The question of whether actual US foreign policy aligns with these aspirations is, of course, a subject of ongoing debate.)

17. A series of upsets in international diplomacy for the ROC transpired in the 1970s, including its expulsion from the United Nations in 1971.

18. The island's population of 23 million is typically described in news and magazine articles as comprising approximately 70% Hoklo, 15% Hakka, 13% Mainlander, and 2% Indigenous peoples, although the Ministry of the Interior does not publish census data regarding ethnicity, except in the case of the Indigenous population.

19. In its attention to historical narrative, my project resonates with the work of Regina Bradley, whose theorization of "the hip-hop South" considers the ways that Black southerners "use hip-hop culture to buffer themselves from the historical narrative and expectations of civil rights movement era blacks and their predecessors" (2021, 6).

20. Ya-Chung Chuang likewise notes the suspenseful character of this time period in his ethnography of Taiwanese democracy: "The transition . . . to the post-martial law democratization invoked a pervasive sense of urgency trying to come to terms with what had actually happened and would happen" (2013, 2).

21. Several other elements of hip-hop have been proposed, including but not limited to beatboxing, fashion, and language.

22. The notion of "knowledge" as an element of hip-hop is closely associated with artist-philosopher Afrika Bambaataa. A hip-hop progenitor and one of the founders

of the Universal Zulu Nation, Bambaataa stepped down from his role as leader of that organization in 2016 following multiple allegations that he sexually abused underage boys (Golding 2016). It is important to emphasize, however, that the so-called "fifth element" derives from cultural currents larger than Bambaataa's individual circle of influence. As Travis Gosa characterizes it, "knowledge" or "knowledge of self" emerges from an "Afro-diasporic mix of spiritual and political consciousness designed to empower members of oppressed groups" (2015, 57). This consciousness both predates Bambaataa and has retained its potency far beyond the limits of his legacy.

23. Keith Negus notes that while scholars have acknowledged the importance of narrative in media from written fiction to ritual spectacle, "the popular song—one of the most pervasive narrative forms that people encounter in their daily lives—has been almost entirely ignored in the vast literature on narrative" (2012, 368). A field of study with deep roots in literary studies, narratology has seemed more or less oblivious to the complexities that musical sounds, and those of popular song in particular, might introduce to its theoretical formations. Likewise, "whereas narratological methods have often featured in the interpretation of Western art music and film music, and literary approaches to lyrics have sometimes emphasized a poetics of storytelling, theories of narrative have rarely been foregrounded in the study of popular songs" (368). Scholarship by musicologist Carolyn Abbate (1991), composer Martin Boykan (2004), and music theorist Byron Almén (2008), for example, is concerned not with "popular" but with "art" musics.

24. Music theorist Jocelyn Neal (2007) has also written about the importance of narrative in country songwriting practices and audience interpretation.

25. I paraphrase here Shlomith Rimmon-Kenan's discussion of the etymology of "narrative" and its quotidian identity as a "mode of knowledge" and "cognitive scheme" (2006, 14). Rimmon-Kenan in turn draws from Martin Kreiswirth (2000, 304).

26. The passage of United Nations General Assembly Resolution 2758 on October 25, 1971, recognized the PRC as the legitimate representative of China to the United Nations.

27. Although I speak Mandarin, I am not fluent in Hoklo, Hakka, or any of Taiwan's Indigenous languages. I have translated non-Mandarin Sinitic and Austronesian-language lyrics in this book with the aid of printed lyrics and, where noted, in collaboration with the songwriters themselves.

Chapter One

1. Contestations about the origins of local hip-hop practice are common and strongly shape engagements with hip-hop in contexts outside the United States. Scholarship on Senegalese rap (see, e.g., Tang 2012, Appert 2018) has perhaps most closely scrutinized such debates. Narrations of history are of course contingent and variable in musical worlds beyond hip-hop, as well. See, for example, Christopher Waterman's accounts of "alternative levels of explanation" of the development of Nigerian jùjú (1991, 49–50).

2. My use of the term "unfolding" here is inspired by Melissa Brown, who refers to "narratives of Taiwan's unfolding" in her work on identity change in Taiwan (2004, 19). Brown's use of this phrase draws on Steven Harrell (1996, 4), who in turn invokes Homi Bhabha (1990, 1).

3. I follow Tony Mitchell and Alastair Pennycook's assertion that "the global locatedness of Hip Hop demands that we rethink time and space" and that "Global Hip Hops" can have "multiple, copresent, global origins" (2009, 40).

4. Bakhtin was writing about Dostoevsky's novels, which feature a "plurality of independent and unmerged voices and consciousnesses, a genuine polyphony of fully valid voices" (1984, 6).

5. Catherine Appert (2018) critically interrogates the notion of "origin myths" in her work on Senegalese hip-hop. As she observes (201n3), a narrative similar to the one I recount here also anchors works by Rose (1994), Perkins (1996), Keyes (2002), Forman (2002), and Perry (2004). Rappers in Taiwan have also received and retransmitted this narrative to younger participants in the scene.

6. This community was primarily composed of African Americans, Puerto Ricans, Dominicans, Jamaicans, and people from other parts of the West Indies.

7. For a discussion of how hip-hop's widespread adoption and global diffusion builds on a longer tradition of African American cultural circulation, see Bennett and Morgan (2011).

8. For additional accounts of *Wild Style*'s global circulation, see Condry (2006).

9. For more on mass media under martial law, see Huang (2009, 3–5).

10. Of course, sowing confusion and/or unevenly distributing meaning to different listenerships is often an artist's intention. As Henry Louis Gates notes, hip-hop lyrical content frequently "complicates or even rejects literal interpretation" and "demands fluency in the recondite codes of African American speech" (2010, xxv). Imani Perry has also observed "the self-conscious incomprehensibility of hip hop lyricism" and the ways in which "[difficulty] is a strategy in hip hop, both in terms of words, which are fast and hard to understand if you are not privy to the hip hop community, and of demands for an authentic personal connection to hip hop and its geography, the hood" (2004, 50–51).

11. Perry likewise notes such "attention to the ancestors, to the history behind the music" in hip-hop, observing that popular music of the 1960s, '70s, and '80s has often furnished hip-hop with raw material for its samples and hooks (2004, 54–57).

12. "Bopomofo," known more formally as *zhuyin fuhao* (注音符號), is a phonetic system widely used in Taiwan, especially among schoolchildren, to represent the sounds of Chinese logograms.

13. On indexical reference, phonetic strategies, pragmatic strategies, and code-switching in Jutoupi's work, see Chen (1998).

14. Shortly after the government legalized multi-channel cable and satellite television, local music channels began to spring up. Channel V, owned by STAR TV and Fox International Channels, initiated broadcasting in Taiwan in 1994. MTV Taiwan followed in 1995.

15. The Spring Scream Festival was started in 1995 by Americans Jimi Moe and Wade Davis. According to Moe, a frenzy erupted when MC Hotdog and Dwagie took the stage for the first time at the event in 2000 (Jimi Moe personal communication, October 12, 2010).

16. Chang Chen-yue is sometimes known as A-Yue (阿嶽). Of Indigenous heritage, he also uses his 'Amis name, Ayal Komod.

17. For further discussion of "Korean Wave Invasion," see chapter 3.

18. The title and chorus of "Taiwan Song" exemplify the clever cross-linguistic wordplay that characterizes much Taiwan rap: the English "song" puns the Mandarin song 頌 ("ode") and the Hoklo *sóng* 爽 ("cool" or "awesome"), such that the phrase "Taiwan song" can be heard as meaning "song of Taiwan," "ode to Taiwan," and "Taiwan's where it's at."

19. The group's English name does not directly translate from the Chinese, which means, literally, "everyone has a [martial arts] practice." The Chinese name is a tongue-in-cheek reference to Hong Kong comedian Stephen Chow's (周星馳) 1994 film *King of Destruction* (破壞之王, also known by the English name *Love on Delivery*), in which a con artist swindles Chow's character out of money by posing as a martial arts teacher who promises to teach him. The con artist carries a collection box that reads "everyone has a [martial arts] practice," or, more colloquially, "martial arts for everyone."

20. Nativist literature (鄉土文學) first emerged in Taiwan during the 1920s and experienced a resurgence in the 1970s that coincided with the rise of localization discourses. As Sung-sheng Yvonne Chang describes it, literary nativism was a broadly anti-hegemonic movement that sought to "destroy the political myth of the mainlander-controlled Nationalist government, to denounce bourgeois capitalist social values, and to combat Western cultural imperialism, which was thought to be exemplified by the Modernist literary movement" of the late 1950s and 1960s (Chang 1993, 2). June Yip (2004) has noted the anti-Western bent of the literary nativists, whose use of the Hoklo language, preference for realist narratives, and valorization of rural lifeways opposed the modernists' invocation of American and European forms and techniques, deployment of abstract symbolism, and interest in individual psychology. For an overview of nativist literature, including its symbolic vocabulary, see Lai (2008).

21. For more on Iron Bamboo, see chap. 4, n. 11.

Chapter Two

1. The polyphonic history rendered in this chapter accords with the goals of what Andrew F. Jones has termed "circuit listening," wherein we attend to "the particular circuits of media and migration in which [all local musics] are embedded" in order to disrupt or dislodge assumptions of unidirectional influence and to discern the multiple circuits a given music (or musician) might activate through performance" (2016, 73).

2. Taiwanese artists are in good company here, as Tony Mitchell and Alastair Pennycook note that "in the case of indigenous cultures such as New Zealand Maori, Indigenous Australians, and Somalian Africans, not to mention Native Americans,

entrenched oral traditions of storytelling and poetry stretching back thousands of years have incorporated Hip Hop into their cultures rather than the other way around" (2009, 30).

3. For more on music during this historical period, see Lü (2003, 132–34).

4. For more on the development of and use of Western instruments in Shanghai-style Mandarin popular songs and Japanese *ryūkōka*, see Jones (2001) and Yano (2003), respectively.

5. For additional discussion regarding Taiwan's popular music industry during the Second Sino-Japanese War, see Zhuang (2009, 30–32).

6. For example, Sylvia Li-chun Lin (2003, 88) cites Zhuang's use of this term.

7. For a brief discussion of the production and consumption of *haipai* songs in Taiwan, see Wong (2001, 226–31). For more on the musical characteristics of *haipai* songs, see Chen (2005).

8. Andrew F. Jones (2016) has further argued that the musical cinema of Hong Kong and Taiwan was an important node in the global circulation of Afro-Caribbean vernacularized musical forms during this period.

9. The First Taiwan Strait Crisis began in 1954, when the PRC began shelling and bombing the ROC-controlled Jinmen, Mazu, and Dachen islands in response to KMT attempts to fortify and increase troop counts there. The PRC hoped to gain control of Jinmen and Mazu, both to take advantage of their strategic location in the Taiwan Strait and to counter the anti-Communist military alliance between the United States and the ROC that developed following the outbreak of the Korean War. The conflict prompted the United States to sign the 1954 Mutual Defense Treaty with the ROC, which promised support in the instance of military conflict between the ROC and PRC (although it excluded Jinmen and Mazu from protection). This was followed in 1955 by the US Congress's passage of the Formosa Resolution, which authorized President Eisenhower to deploy American forces to defend the ROC from armed attack on Taiwan and its offshore areas by the PRC. Following the crisis, the United States Taiwan Defense Command (USTDC) was founded in Taipei in 1955, and the United States stationed troops on the island until it broke relations with the ROC in 1979.

10. For a complete history of AFNT/ICRT, see Chun (2011).

11. I use the English term "Mandopop" in this book to describe the Mandarin-language popular music—distinct from *haipai* popular songs—that began developing in Taiwan in the mid-1950s and gained traction in the late 1960s. In Taiwan, however, the terms "Sinitic-language popular songs" (華語流行歌曲) and "national-language popular songs" (國語流行歌曲) are often used instead. These do not necessarily imply a distinction from *haipai* popular songs.

12. In recent years, the standard two-year period of conscription has gradually been reduced and new forms of "alternative service" have been introduced. The Ministry of the Interior has announced plans to shift to a volunteer force, but it has repeatedly moved back the timetable for implementing this policy change.

13. For an example of one such performance, see Yu's *Ha Century Live Show* (2002).

14. The government's guidelines for censorship were highly subjective and mutable. For more, see Lin (2010).

15. The term "Taiwanese" here refers to the Hoklo language. For more on the genesis of the New Taiwanese Song Movement and its relationship to both political nativism and the commercial music industry, see Ho (2020, 33–36), and Jian, Ho, and Tsai (2020, 235–36).

16. I excerpt here Sylvia Li-chun Lin's excellent translation of these lyrics as they appear in her article "Toward a New Identity: Nativism and Popular Music in Taiwan" (2003, 91–92).

17. For more on the domination of the Legislative Yuan and National Assembly by legislators elected in 1940s China, see Clark and Tan (2012, 113–15).

18. The term "rap" is rendered in English in the original text.

19. Jay Chou and Fang Wenshan are often credited with popularizing the "China Wind" (中國風) style of pop music, which Yiu Fai Chow and Jeroen de Kloet describe as "defined musically by its juxtaposition of classical Chinese melody and/or instruments with trendy global pop styles, particularly R&B and hip-hop. It can also be defined lyrically by its mobilization of 'traditional' Chinese cultural elements such as legends, classics and language, implicitly or explicitly in contemporary contexts" (2013, 60). Much of Wang Leehom's "Mandohop" could also be described as China Wind.

20. "Descendants of the Dragon" was recorded and popularized in 1980 by Wang Leehom's elder cousin, singer Lee Chien-Fu (李建復).

21. For more on the complex politics of the "chinked-out" style, see Wang (2015).

22. The subjects of *liām-kua* narratives tend to fall into one of three main categories, as delineated in the *Encyclopedia of Taiwan Music* (台灣音樂百科辭書): (1) songs of exhortation and enlightenment (勸世教化性的), (2) tales (故事性的), and (3) other (其他). The first category encompasses songs intended to persuade audience members to behave as responsible, ethical individuals. Examples include "Exhortation to Quit Gambling Song" (勸戒賭博歌), "Exhortation to Quit Prostitution Song" (勸善戒淫歌), and "Exhortation to Quit Drinking Song" (勸戒酒歌). The second category encompasses folktales, local color stories, and historical stories about both China and Taiwan. Examples include "Koxinga Opens Taiwan" (鄭成功開台灣), "Treasure Island New Taiwan" (寶島新台灣), and "The Legend of White Snake" (白蛇傳). The final category is a catch-all, encompassing a wide variety of songs about weddings, products an itinerant singer might be hawking, place-names, and current events. Examples of these include "Song of Flies and Mosquitoes" (胡蠅蚊仔歌), "Song of Talking Mice" (貓鼠相告歌), and "Call and Response by a Hundred Plants" (百草對答). Moving between these categories sometimes in the space of a single performance, *liām-kua* artists are constituted not merely as entertainers but as keepers of historical and folkloric knowledge, promoters of moral and ethical responsibility, and bearers of information about current events (Chen 2008, 350–52).

23. For a survey of songbook types and history of the trade, see the National Museum of Taiwan Literature's *Koa-á Booklets Database*: http://koaachheh.nmtl.gov.tw/bang-cham/.

24. On Hengchun folk songs, see Lü (2003, 451–56).

25. This project was known as the Folksong Collection Movement (民歌採集運動).

26. For a complete discussion of the Modern Folk Song Movement, see Chang (2003).

27. Such compositions fall under the rubric of what Chao (1956) would have called "tonal style."

28. There is a range of opinions regarding the extent to which speakers of Sinitic languages preserve speech tone in popular song performance. Psychologists Randy L. Dielh and Patrick C. M. Wong maintain that pop artists working in Cantonese languages during the 1990s did try to maintain some semblance of the tonal contours of what they were singing (2002, 202–9). Studies of Hoklo speech tone in music have not approached the question of comprehensibility but have nevertheless found a relatively weak relationship between melodic and tonal shapes at the syllabic level (Wang 2008).

29. It is possible that the word translated as "storytelling" was actually *liām-kua*.

30. This interview was conducted in Mandarin, but terms rendered here in quotes were given by Zhu in English.

31. By "Taiwanese Mandarin," I refer to the localized Hoklo-, Hakka-, Japanese-, and Indigenous language-inflected Mandarin that is commonly spoken on the island.

32. For additional perspectives on Jutoupi's "Taiwan Language Battle," vis-à-vis "language anxieties" on the island, see Hatfield (2002). Nancy Guy (2018) has also written about language play in Jutoupi's music.

33. This phrase often appears in their promotional materials. Tainan-based duo Punker Brothers (胖克兄弟) and MC Dami collaborated on a 2017 song called "Liām-kua" (English title "Rap") with celebrated *liām-kua* artist Yang Hsiu-ching. In addition to featuring Yang's narrative singing about the art of *liām-kua*, the song also refers to rap as "real Taiwan-style *liām-kua*" (正港台灣味唸歌) and encourages young Taiwanese fans of *xiha* to learn about *liām-kua*.

34. This interview was conducted in Mandarin, but terms rendered here in quotes were given by Fan Chiang in English.

35. *Beiguan*, referred to in Hoklo as *pak-koán* and glossed in English as "northern pipes," is a genre of traditional ensemble music that dates to eighteenth-century Fujian but achieved great popularity in Taiwan. It is difficult to characterize stylistically, having both loud and strident qualities (as in *beiguan* percussion and wind ensembles) and quieter, more dulcet qualities (as in *beiguan* silk and bamboo ensembles). *Beiguan* is performed at a wide variety of outdoor events in Taiwan, including funerals, weddings, and temple festivals. As a theatrical music, it also features in performances of Taiwanese opera (歌仔戲) and glove puppet theater (布袋戲).

Chapter Three

1. As discussed in the introduction to this book, the Democratic Progressive Party (DPP) is one of two major political parties in Taiwan. The DPP coalesced

in the 1970s in opposition to the KMT, at that time under the leadership of Chiang Kai-shek. The DPP has historically been associated with the Taiwan independence movement, environmentalism, multiculturalism, and democratic pluralism. Dwagie has in the past campaigned for DPP political candidates.

2. *Gong* (功) is also the first syllable of *gongfu* (功夫), from which the English-language moniker "Kung Fu Entertainment" is derived.

3. Those I refer to in this chapter as "men" identify, for the most part, as cisgender. This does not preclude the possibility, however, of participation in the scene by those with different gender identities who present as masculine.

4. A 2010 study indicates cigarette smoking is far more common among Taiwanese men (55–60%) than among women (3–4%) (Wu et al. 2010, 1). Likewise, a 2004 study indicated 69.53% of high school–age males play video games on a regular basis, compared to 30.47% of females (Chou and Tsai 2007, 816).

5. Several of these campaigns have traditionally been associated with the DPP. Throughout my fieldwork, however, I found that many artists and fans characterized themselves as political independents, aligned loosely with the so-called Pan-Green Coalition (an informal alliance that includes the DPP, Taiwan Solidarity Union, Taiwan Independence Party, and Taiwan Constitution Association) or with the smaller social justice–oriented "third force" parties, such as the Social Democratic Party and New Power Party.

6. It is important to note, however, that a number of prominent rap artists spoke out in support of LGBT marriage equality in Taiwan, which was signed into law in 2019.

7. Noodles identifies publicly as a lesbian, one who might be identified by others as a "T," or "tomboy," as opposed to either a "P," or *po* (婆, "matron" or "woman"), or someone who is *bufen* (不分, "undifferentiated"), meaning androgynous or genderqueer, according to the social categorizations of Taiwan's lesbian community (see Pai 2017). These categorizations of course transcend the club environments in which Noodles and her colleagues work, but it is nevertheless interesting to note that the term "T" in Taiwan has probable roots in the American-style restaurants, bars, and clubs that opened in major port cities during the 1960s, when Taiwan was a prime R & R destination for American soldiers in the Vietnam War (Chao 2000, 378–79). During the course of our interview, several other male club DJs present in the room referred to Noodles in English as "just like a man" when opining on how she had found success in *xiha*. Although Noodles neither acknowledged nor refuted this portrayal, her colleagues' suggestions of hip-hopness as tantamount to maleness accorded with Dwagie's reading of *xiha* gender dynamics—that women *can* perform *xiha*, but that doing so requires conformity to norms of expression coded (in Taiwan's majority-ethnic communities, see n. 8) as male/masculine. For more on the sociology of queer and trans identities in Taiwan, see Brainer (2019).

8. Bringing into focus the intersectional (Crenshaw 1989) relationship between gender and ethnicity, Emma Jinhua Teng observes: "Taking Confucian gender ideology as the norm, Qing travelers interpreted unfamiliar gender roles as an index of people's 'otherness.' The subsequent adoption of Chinese gender roles by colonized

peoples such as the Taiwan indigenes was taken by Chinese observers as a sign of their becoming 'civilized'" (Teng 2001, 256). Although traditionally matrifocal peoples such as the 'Amis, the largest Indigenous group on the island, might no longer take matrinames or maintain uxorilocal residence, they have redefined matrifocality in the present day to describe, among other things, "the way that women remain the agents of house building" (Hatfield n.d.). For more on the traditional social organization of the 'Amis, see Yeh (2013).

9. For more information about organizations advocating on behalf of women's interests, see the webpage of the National Alliance of Taiwan Women's Associations (台灣婦女團體全國聯合會), www.natwa.org.tw.

10. The National Statistics Bureau of the Republic of China (Taiwan) publishes data on the makeup of the labor force, earnings and productivity, population and housing, public safety, and national wealth statistics, among other metrics of social and economic significance. This data is generally updated on at least an annual basis at https://eng.stat.gov.tw/ (accessed April 20, 2021).

11. In his study of gender in Mandopop, Marc Moskowitz likewise notes "conceptions of innate male and female characteristics" (2010, 71).

12. My research associates' frequent references to power bring to mind the importance of the aesthetic principle of *isigqi* among Zulu *ngoma* singers and dancers, which Louise Meintjes observes can be used to describe "strong sound or gesture" as well as "that magic moment when a groove absolutely works because its components are tightly co-ordinated" (2004, 174–75). Extending this parallel, *ngoma* can likewise be understood as "an expression of masculinity" and a "process of obtaining forms of political power" (175). Diverging from rap as it is performed in Taiwan by artists like Dwagie and MC Hotdog, however, *ngoma* dancers also invoke "sweetness," which "in its multiple guises heightens the drama of the dense, fast and powerful move it precedes. It is a preparatory rhetorical device that by means of contrast hardens the hit" (174). This complicates the idea of masculinity in the context of Zulu *ngoma* as solely or primarily a function of its performers' strength or power.

13. In her work on *sajiao*, communication studies scholar Hsin-I Sydney Yueh notes that while classical Chinese texts do not cast *sajiao* women in positive terms—they are seen as lacking Confucian moral discipline and as "vulgar and despicable"—"*sajiao* became a preferred form of femininity" in post–martial law Taiwan (2017, 53). Yueh argues that the redemption of *sajiao* and its connections to feminine attractiveness in Taiwan have much to do with the importation of *kawaii* (cute) culture from Japan in the 1980s. For more on the history of *kawaii* and its exportation from Japan to other parts of the world, see Yano (2013).

14. Drawing on fieldwork conducted in the early 2000s, Lisa Gilman and John Fenn (2006) observed a similar phenomenon at work in the rap and ragga scenes in Malawi, where women have historically participated more frequently as dancers than as rappers. Writing on American gangsta rap from around the same time, Leonhard Kreuzer (2009) writes that the "question could be raised whether or not, within the production and reception conventions of (gangsta) rap music, rap is coded male and singing female" (210). Kreuzer notes that there are, of course, many

female rappers but wonders "how far these re-appropriate or subvert a male-coded practice" (210n8).

15. This interview was conducted in Mandarin, but terms rendered here in quotes were given by DJ Mr. Gin in English.

16. The form is characterized by alternating six- and seven-character lines that conclude with the same linguistic tone and rhyme on the final syllable.

17. Kao and Bih identify school, the military, and work as the three pillars of masculine identity in Taiwan (2014, 179). For an ethnographic exploration of how the experiences of military service, marriage, and child-rearing configure masculine-becoming across ethnic, age, and socioeconomic strata in Taiwan, see Cheng (2011).

18. These include the songs "Refuse to Listen" (不聽) with Nas (2014), "Endless Cycle" (無盡輪迴) with Talib Kweli (2015), and "Words to Trump" (給川普) with Raekwon (2017).

19. It is important to acknowledge that what Miles White calls "performatives of blackness" easily veer into racism when non-Black performers fail to "advance progressive or anti-racist agendas" (2011, 129) in their work. To this point, I have found that senior artists are sometimes dubious that their more commercially oriented colleagues share their appreciation for rap music either as craft or as a tool of political resistance.

20. Masculine icons such as Bruce Lee and practices such as kung fu assert themselves in scholarly works that probe the powerful influence of East Asian cultural ideas and products on African American popular culture (e.g., Ongiri 2002; Mullen 2004; Hisama 2005; Cha-Jua 2008; Wilkins 2008; Rollefson 2018).

21. "The General's Orders" is a Chinese folk song that has over time become associated with the Huang Feihong films.

22. For more on the notion of *wenrou* in Mandopop, see Moskowitz (2010).

23. The *wenrou* male has deep roots in Taiwan's musico-theatrical forms. Ethnomusicologist Nancy Guy argues that, far from being a modern phenomenon, "sensitive" male roles (typically performed by female actors) are among the most popular in Taiwanese opera (2011, 193).

24. I have located no peer-reviewed scholarship that definitively identifies the origins of the "oriental riff," sometimes referred to as the "Asian riff" or "Asian jingle." There are, however, several Internet sources that trace the figure to the 1935 Betty Boop cartoon *Making Stars* and locate possible proto-forms in earlier cartoon music and popular tunes such as the Jean Schwartz and William Jerome 1910 classic "Chinatown, My Chinatown." For more, see Nilsson (n.d.) and Micic (2008). Ethnomusicologist Thomas Solomon (2014) has written about the riff's presence in American cartoons. Variations on the "oriental riff" have been featured in many cultural products available to members of the Taiwan rap community, ranging from Carl Douglas's 1974 international disco hit "Kung Fu Fighting" to the 1989 Nintendo video game *Super Mario Land*.

25. Taiwanese American rapper Shawn Sung (宋岳庭), whose watershed 2003 album *Life's a Struggle* was released after his tragic death from bone cancer at twenty-three, likewise critiqued mainstream Taiwanese pop music on the track

"Taiwan Pop Sucks 2000." While his lyrics were similarly bumptious and boastful, however, they were more or less free from the misogynistic and homophobic sentiments that mark "Korean Wave Invasion." Of note, Teacher Lin remarks on the importance of "Taiwan Pop Sucks 2000" as the first song to contain multisyllabic Mandarin rhymes, which would later become a hallmark of so-called "academic rap" (2020, 163). For more on academic rap and its relationship to masculine identities, see chapter 4.

26. In her study of African American musical influences on K-pop, Crystal S. Anderson notes a similar phenomenon in mainstream Korean hip-hop videos, which "cite limiting and liberating hip-hop tropes": "Male hip-hop artist Jay Park," she writes, "invokes both a playful male swagger as well as reductive images of women" (2020, xxii).

27. Dwagie previously employed the English-language moniker "Dog G."

28. A useful example of such a performance is the 2018 track "Peace?" (和平), which features Dwagie, MC Hotdog, PoeTek, BR, Professor H, and Xiao Ren. Recalling "Korean Wave Invasion," the song brings together multiple artists in the service of an ideological agenda. Graphic descriptions of abject violence delivered with rapid-fire flows seem to likewise index hard-core masculinity. In this case, however, the performers direct their ire at those who commit or are complicit with cruelty toward animals—including men who wear fur or leather, who "massacre to achieve handsomeness" (殺戮成就帥氣).

29. There are, naturally, exceptions to this generalization. Solo artist Witness and the group MJ116, for example, have recorded a number of songs that reference relationships with women, ranging from benign romantic narratives to narratives that rehearse familiar sexual and sometimes misogynist tropes. More recently, younger artists, particularly those who identify with the trap subgenre, have also turned increasingly to romantic and sexual themes.

30. See, for example, the character of Pao in Peter Chan's 1996 film *Comrades: Almost a Love Story* (甜蜜蜜), or Boss Geta in Doze Niu's 2010 film *Monga* (艋舺).

31. The term *shui* (睡), which I translate here as "sex," puns with the word *shui* (稅), meaning "tax." "Betel nut" (檳榔) is a slang term for "breast." Therefore, this line can also be heard as "two betel nuts for $100 is expensive, does that include tax?" or "two breasts for $100 is expensive, does that include sex?"

32. It is also possible to hear this reference to "Chinese girls" (*zhongguo xiaojie* 中國小姐) as a reference to a national beauty pageant known in Taiwan as "Miss China" (*zhongguo xiaojie* 中國小姐) between 1960 and 1990. This interpretation underscores MC Hotdog's distaste for the refinement that pageant queens presumably represent, and his preference for local, lower-class charms. I thank Kathy Kao for bringing this reading to my attention.

33. Kao and Bih (2014) also discuss Taiwanese men as doubly castrated—racially desexualized by Western colonial-imperial powers and deprived of national recognition.

34. A number of community members described Soft Lipa's work in terms of its poeticism and effortlessness, but Manchuker, in English, was the only one who

used the term "delicate": "I like his stuff very much, he would be my favorite rap artist in Taiwan. Because he's so delicate, his stuff is delicate.... And he rarely uses any English, so that is very special. For Chinese[-language] rappers to be this type of scale, like using all Chinese, and being delicate.... His stuff is artsy, poetic, masterful" (interview, September 21, 2010).

35. Early Confucian texts delineated five relationships, the preservation of which were necessary to maintaining social harmony. They include ruler to ruled, father to son, husband to wife, elder brother to younger brother, and friend to friend. The term "fictive brothers" here refers to those bonded by friendship (友). Scholars have diverged in their understandings of friendship, with some speculating that this relationship threatens the social order because it is outside the realm of state and family and potentially non-hierarchical. Friends, like those constituted through common participation in the Taiwan rap scene, will often use kinship terms to refer to one another, acknowledging a hierarchy between elder and younger. For more, see Weller (1999, 24).

36. For more on Taiwan's fertility transition, see Freedman et al. (1994). For past and present fertility rate statistics, see https://eng.stat.gov.tw/ and https://www.ris.gov.tw/app/en.

37. Yang used the English term "chill" in the interview. The term I translate here as "fly" is "帥氣" (lit. "handsome") in the original Mandarin-language source. Yang's use of this word, which is often invoked to describe masculine attractiveness, reflects her awareness of the rap community's gendered sensibilities. I thank Kathy Kao for suggesting "fly" as a possible translation in order to communicate the influence of African American Vernacular English on the ways that rappers think and talk about their craft.

38. For more on the compatibility of Confucian ideologies and liberal democracy, see Fetzer and Soper (2013).

Chapter Four

1. This hand sign likely signifies and originates from the city of Houston, Texas, which has a thriving rap scene. It closely resembles other signs, however, including the "hook 'em horns" associated with University of Texas at Austin football, and the "devil's horns" associated with rock and metal music. The gesture, decontextualized here to suggest a general hip-hop ethos, also puns visually with the *karana mudra* hand position common in Buddhist iconography.

2. The *wen-wu* framework, as it was first articulated by Kam Louie and Louise Edwards (1994), has been widely influential in musicological studies of the Sinophone world. See, for example, Baranovitch (2003) and Wong (2011).

3. To wit, *Taiwan Hip-Hop Kids* (嘻哈囝 ：台灣饒舌故事) (2018)—a chronicle of the rap scene published by KAO!INC. as a companion to a film of the same name that is discussed later in this chapter—imagines the rap community as a "martial arts world" (武林世界) divided into four main schools (四大門派) represented by four local *xiha* labels.

4. Although some aspiring artists also learn to compose and produce instrumentals, the vast majority use beats they find online for these purposes.

5. BR, who now tours with Dwagie, was a reticent college student when I first encountered him on the set of the video shoot discussed in chapter 3; PoeTek, a 2016 Golden Melody Award nominee for Best New Artist, was barely twenty years old when he gathered around DJ Vicar's turntable at the meeting of the National Taiwan University Hip-Hop Culture Research Society pictured in fig. 4.2. Eagle-eyed observers will identify him as the young man with glasses, second from the right, with hands tucked into the front pocket of a hooded sweatshirt.

6. For more on the notion of hip-hop knowledge, see Chang (2005) and Gosa (2015).

7. Other scholars have defined "knowledge work" in different ways over the years. For more on the term's shifting usage, see McKercher and Mosco (2007). I also wish to underscore that my deployment of "musical knowledge work" should be distinguished from terms that theorize music *as* labor, like anthropologist Marina Peterson's "sound work" (2013).

8. A small number of *xiha* performers on the island have been financially successful, including MC Hotdog and the groups 911 and MJ116. These artists have not only sold millions of records but can also fill large-capacity performance venues like the Taipei Arena (台北小巨蛋).

9. I am grateful to Louise Meintjes and Deonte Harris for asking questions that generated this observation in an early discussion of this chapter at the Duke University Ethnomusicology Lecture Series.

10. This state of affairs is not peculiar to rap, of course, as the music industry's business models have shifted in recent years in Taiwan and elsewhere. Artists with some degree of notoriety outside of rap's community of dedicated listeners attempt to generate capital by partnering with brands, applying for government grants, and monetizing online content.

11. The failure of Iron Bamboo to connect with mass audiences during the early 2000s, discussed in chapter 1, discouraged future investment in rap music for at least the next decade. As Ill Mo told me, "Their sales flopped . . . and it scared the shit out of all these major labels and they were like 'no more hip-hop for us,' basically. That's their mentality, because they put out two million, three million, five million, just to make it happen. . . . All this huge money put into promotion and nothing happened, they never made it actually. So [the record companies] decided to let go for a while" (interview, November 5, 2010).

12. Mandopop artists have of course also received their share of censure. Most famously, singer A-Mei was banned from traveling to the PRC for three years following her performance of the ROC national anthem at the presidential inauguration ceremony of Chen Shui-bian in 2000. For a full account of this incident, see Guy (2002).

13. Ill Mo's financial arrangement with Xue Xue provided NTD9,000 for an enrollment of thirteen or fewer students; if more than thirteen enrolled, his pay would increase to 50% of the total tuition paid.

14. See Tsai (2001) for a complete overview of Taiwan's neoliberal transition until the early 2000s.

15. See, for example, Spence (2011).

16. What defines an "academic rapper," according to Ill Mo, is simply that they are "deeply obsessed with hip-hop, to the point that they want to know everything about it" (personal communication, March 15, 2017). Although the most prominent academic rappers have been the recipients of elite educations, he rejects the notion that this *must* be the case: "It's not about that. Rhyme techniques are so well-developed these days, and nowadays it's all on YouTube, everything you need to learn: the most difficult ways of producing rhymes, so that even if you're not a college graduate, you can still be an outstanding MC. E.so from MJ116—he's respected not only because he's successful, but because he's killer at rapping. Most of the time, his verses will stand out. You can expect him to come out with something that's unexpected. That's characteristic of academic rap."

17. Eric Charry observes that while rap has now taken root in a wide variety of communities on the African continent, it was "initially only an elite Westernized segment of African youth that embraced rap" (2012, 3).

18. Subject to systemic and institutional racism and less able than their non-Indigenous counterparts to access post-secondary education, many Indigenous Taiwanese lack means of entry to the rap community's social networks. Moreover, those who migrate to urban centers from rural areas often do so under economic duress and may not have the leisure time or disposable income to pursue interests in rap. For information on educational inequality in Taiwan's Indigenous communities during the formative years of *xiha*, see Cai (2004).

19. There are currently 165 institutions of higher education in Taiwan. The 1994 University Law, which "[reduced] the power of the central government by granting more academic autonomy, institutional flexibility, and self-reliance to universities," played a key role in stimulating growth and privatization in Taiwanese higher education (Chou 2008).

20. A full range of statistics is available in English and Chinese from the Taiwan Ministry of Education website at www.edu.tw.

21. In 2018 Teacher Lin won a small victory at National Tsing Hua University, where, now on the faculty, he was invited to teach an undergraduate course in *xiha* for the first time (Teacher Lin personal communication, August 25, 2018).

22. For more on hip-hop and virtual communities, see Richardson and Lewis (1999), Yasser (2003), and Clark (2014).

23. For a brief history of the Taiwanese Internet, see Li, Lin, and Huang (2017).

24. PTT was developed by a student from the Computer Science Department at NTU as a personal project, but an organization called the NTU Electronic BBS Research Society (台灣大學電子佈告欄系統研究社) currently manages the system using NTU's facilities and technology infrastructure.

25. User statistics—from average user age to average user astrological sign—are available in the "Announce" section on PTT.

26. The term "villager" is a reference to Stephen Chow's 1994 film *Hail the Judge* (九品芝麻官) and refers to characters in the film who habitually follow others or exhibit a mob mentality.

27. Although originally posted at http://tw.beta.streetvoice.com/music/Cyrax /song/62370/, the recording of "PTT.cc" is unfortunately no longer available online.

28. My research associates referred to the *jinghuaqu* in English as the "historical archive" and the "juicy section." The term translates more directly as the "essential area."

29. This novel, also known by the English names *All Men Are Brothers* and *Outlaws of the Marsh*, is regarded as one of the four classic novels of Chinese literature alongside *Romance of the Three Kingdoms* (三國演義), *Journey to the West* (西遊記), and *Dream of the Red Chamber* (紅樓夢). Lin was not the last to give the story a "hip-hop" treatment—Taiwanese actor and director Wu Hsing-kuo (吳興國) merged hip-hop, rock and roll, and Peking opera aesthetics in the Contemporary Legend Theatre's *108 Heroes of Water Margin I* (2007) and *108 Heroes of Water Margin II* (2011). For more on these productions, see I. Chang (2018).

30. This terminology is not specific to the *Xiha* Bulletin Board but is in use on other boards as well.

31. In spite of some common features, BBS are distinct from the social networking sites that have become popular globally over the last decade. Key differences include that social networking sites are Web-based and place users at their center, while BBS were historically terminal-based and cohere around discussion topics (see Boyd and Ellison 2007).

32. Danny reiterated this same point to me, almost verbatim, when we met for another conversation in July 2016.

33. "I Am Insane" is no longer featured on RPG's social media pages or websites, but it appeared originally at http://tw.streetvoice.com/music/Rapguy /song/109804/.

34. For these and other data on work hours and salaries, see statistics given by the Council of Labor Affairs, http://statdb.mol.gov.tw/ (accessed January 21, 2019). For more on cost of living, see statistics given by the Directorate General of Budget, Accounting, and Statistics, Executive Yuan, R.O.C. (Taiwan), https://eng.dgbas .gov.tw/ (accessed January 21, 2019). For more on the phenomenon of overwork-related death, see Lin, Chien, and Kawachi (2018).

35. For the media's response to Yaung's comments, see Wang (2010).

36. Joseph Schloss notes that the ethical codes of American hip-hop discourage sampling from other rap recordings (2004, 114–19), but the practice does not seem to carry the same stigma in Taiwan, at least where sampling from non-Taiwanese artists is concerned. Although many consider quotation a cornerstone of their art and are painstaking in their choice of music to sample or interpolate, others take a more pragmatic, even casual, approach to appropriating existing materials. Kung Fu Entertainment's current social media accounts (and erstwhile website) sometimes features songs responding to current events that lift the beats from other rap

recordings. These kinds of tracks are not intended for placement on albums but are designed to be streamed and consumed quickly, before the public has forgotten the current event in question. When I chatted online with RPG regarding the use of Jay-Z's work, he explained that the choice was a purely pragmatic one: "I gotta be in time, so I just grab whatever beat n wrote it...when [the song's] related to News, we won't spend too much time on perfecting our own works on the music side, [but] on the lyric side. Cuz the consumer's behavior in Taiwan...short-sighted, easy to forget...so our songs need to come out fast...but when it comes to making an album, we will definitely put a lot of effort on [the beat]" (personal communication, July 1, 2012).

Chapter Five

1. For discussion of Kou Chou Ching's notion of "real Taiwan-style *liām-kua*," see chapter 2.

2. For more on music education in Taiwan from the Japanese colonial period through the immediate post–martial law period, including the central role of European art music traditions, see Kou (2001).

3. MC Jason Shu performed with the group during the early days but left Kou Chou Ching before they recorded their first album. Since Fan Chiang's 2014 departure, MC Chu Pi (朱皮) has served as the group's resident "Hakka MC." Collaborating with other musicians and some members of Kou Chou Ching, Fish Lin has also formed a second group called Community Service (勞動服務), which according to its Facebook page, likewise samples from old records and combines "Western" (西洋) and "Han" (漢式) musics, including rap/*liām-kua*, in order to produce a "post-colonial" (後殖民) sound (Community Service, n.d.).

4. For more on the concept of *renao*, see Hatfield (2010, 23–46).

5. For more on "Taxi," see Schweig (2013, 251–53).

6. The elementary education established through the so-called "common school" system (公學校, Japanese: *kogakko*) "offered a core of Japanese language and arithmetic, some basic sciences, a considerable amount of classical literature to attract gentry parents, and singing and physical educational exercises to win the children" (Tsurumi 1979, 619). Wai-Chung Ho notes in her study of the relationship between national identity discourses and music education in Taiwan that "song texts were intended to help students in learning Japanese" and that "Taiwanese students were also educated about the supposed divine origin of Japan's imperial rulers and the superiority of the Japanese race" (2016, 61). Likewise, Leo T. S. Ching highlights how policies of "imperialization through education" compelled Indigenous peoples to serve as members of the Takasago Volunteer Army during the Second World War (2001, 170).

7. Rap artists have not undertaken this work alone. Sylvia Li-chun Lin notes that since the lifting of martial law, "literary, scholarly, historical, personal, and cinematic accounts of the past have mushroomed" (2007, 6). Although music is conspicuously absent from Lin's list of media, composers working in a number

of idioms have been eager participants in the project of representing Taiwanese history, from Tyzen Hsiao's (蕭泰然) neo-Romantic vocal and orchestral works *1947 Overture* (1947 序曲) and *Ilha Formosa: Requiem for Formosa's Martyrs* (「啊！福爾摩沙」 為殉難者的鎮魂曲, 蕭泰然), to black metal band Chthonic's (閃靈) albums *Seediq Bale* (賽德克巴萊), *Mirror of Retribution* (十殿), and *Takasago Army* (高砂軍). Sociologist A-chin Hsiau (2005) has written about how these kinds of historical narratives have, through the medium of literature, "typically played a major role in identity construction and collective action based on ethnicity and nationalism" on the island. Notably, Hsiau also invokes narrative theory, including the ideas of Ricoeur and Barthes, in the formation of a theoretical approach he terms "narrative identity."

8. Anagnost's reference to the nation as an "impossible unity" quotes Homi Bhabha (1990, 1).

9. Practices such as call-and-response—which Samuel Floyd has called "the master trope" of African American music (1995, 95) and Cheryl Keyes "the life force of black communication" (2002, 26)—are fundamental to live rap performance, contributing to a sense of this music as participatory in its numerous global configurations.

10. *Tai-yü* (lit. "Taiwanese language") here refers to Hoklo.

11. For a complete discussion of language politics in Taiwan during this period, see Ang (1992).

12. For example, there are now television channels directed at the island's diverse ethnic communities, including Taiwan Indigenous TV (http://web.pts.org.tw/titv /about.htm) and Hakka TV (http://www.hakkatv.org.tw/). The 1993 revision of the Broadcast Bill made the creation of such media outlets possible.

13. In his study of hip-hop and globalization in Japan, for example, Ian Condry likewise argues that Japanese MCs perform a "new cultural politics of 'affiliation' that draws inspiration from African American struggles while generating distinctive approaches to race and protest in Japan" (2006, 29).

14. For an exploration of resonances between the Black Lives Matter movement and Taiwanese struggles for civil and human rights that acknowledges the contributions of activist-rappers, see Prescod-Weinstein (2016).

15. Teacher Lin has noted that while many Indigenous rap artists—such as Hip-Hop Bunch ('Amis), GrowZen ('Amis), and Atayal Hood (Atayal) perform in Mandarin—others, including Tayal Squad (Atayal and Seediq), Kasiwa (Paiwan), and Drunkey (Paiwan), have also performed in Austronesian languages (2020, 162).

16. Manchuker referred to himself using the English word "Chinese."

17. For a detailed account of constructions of "national history" prior to 1949 and comparisons of approaches to post-1949 historiography in the PRC and ROC, see Schneider (2008).

18. In 1995 primary school students began receiving lessons that encouraged them to pay attention to their immediate surroundings, focused on learning about local ethnic groups, religious practices, cultural traditions, and languages (Jones 2013, 180).

19. Tu's "concentric circles" idea closely resembles Chinese sociologist and anthropologist's Fei Xiaotong's (費孝通) earlier notion of *chaxuegeju* (差序格局, lit.

"differential mode of association"). As it appears in his landmark 1947 work *From the Soil* (鄉土中國), *chaxuegeju* describes Chinese social organization as like the concentric circles that radiate out when a stone is tossed into water. I thank Jia-Chen Fu for bringing this similarity to my attention.

20. This coincided with controversy surrounding the proposal of a new "Moral and National Education" curriculum in Hong Kong in 2012. In collaboration with Hong Kong's MC Ren, Dwagie released a song called "Brainwashed Education" (洗腦教育) denouncing the curriculum.

21. Notably, this text echoes questions about the listener's familiarity with Taiwan's history and culture in the liner notes for Blacklist Workshop's *Songs of Madness*, released almost two decades earlier.

22. The Hoklo term "度爛" resists easy translation, but it originally described the piercing or puncturing of a man's scrotum. In common parlance, it is used to express extreme dissatisfaction.

23. There are many versions. The one to which I refer here was produced by Adia (阿弟仔) and South African composer-producer Jean Marais (aka "MoShang" 莫尚) and appears on *Exodus*, a 2009 compilation album.

24. Tausig's reference to "surrogation" in the context of the Black Lives Matter protests builds on the prior work of Daphne A. Brooks (2008) and Vanessa K. Valdés (2016).

25. For more on transitional justice legislation in Taiwan, see Caldwell (2018).

26. In his study of 2-28 fiction, Michael Berry likewise notes an insistence on telling the story of the 2-28 Incident over and over again (2008, 233).

27. Although the pace of change is slow and the end goal uncertain, there have recently been some positive developments in this regard. For example, Tsai Ing-wen established the Presidential Indigenous Historical Justice and Transitional Justice Committee in 2019.

28. P. Kerim Friedman argues, furthermore, that "Indigenous people were never intended to be the primary beneficiaries of" multicultural education policies. Rather, "the embrace of multiculturalism by Taiwan's elites was in fact…a strategic move aimed at heading off the threat posed by the rise of Taiwanese nationalism" (2018, 79–90).

29. Basslines with gritty timbres are sometimes referred to by hip-hop and drum 'n' bass DJs as "dirty."

30. The deer trade became a point of contention beginning in the Dutch colonial period, as the spread of both Dutch and Han commercial activities encroached on Indigenous hunting lands. The Japanese later crowded Indigenous peoples onto mountain reservations and sought to disrupt their hunting activities in order to subsume them into the economy of the empire.

Epilogue

1. "Do You Hear the People Sing?" continued to resonate across mass demonstrations in the region for the next several years, including Hong Kong's 2014 Umbrella Revolution and South Korea's 2016–17 Candlelight Revolution.

2. Student leaders commissioned "Island's Sunrise" after members of iconic Taiwanese band Mayday (五月天) declined to associate their 2009 song "Rise Up" (起來) with the demonstrations, presumably for fear of retribution from Chinese fans and government authorities (Mack 2014). Mayday's dependence on the PRC market seemed to discourage them from explicitly supporting the Sunflower protesters.

3. See, for example, Ramzy (2014).

4. For recent exploration of "Sinophobia" in the pre- and post-Sunflower Taiwan context, see Lee, Tzeng, Ho, and Clarke (2018).

5. For discussion of gender dynamics in the Sunflower Movement and its "distinctively male nature of leadership," see Hioe and Liu (2014).

6. Along with Wei Yang, Chen Wei-ting (陳為廷) and Lin Fei-fan (林飛帆) are recognized as the leaders of the Sunflower Movement. They were later charged, along with nineteen other defendants, with "inciting others to commit a crime, obstruction of police officers in the discharge of their duties and other crimes" (Pan 2017). All were acquitted based on the principle of civil disobedience.

7. Radicalization donates its profits to NGOs. Their missions, as articulated on their website (radicalonline.net), are to "use music to change the world" and to "take action! Change Taiwan!"

8. The Mandarin name of the business means literally "where to gather?" but the characters are pronounced *nali ju*, which sounds like the English "knowledge." Mo credits Kay for coming up with this clever play on words (interview, September 25, 2020).

REFERENCES

Abbate, Carolyn. 1991. *Unsung Voices: Opera and Musical Narrative in the Nineteenth Century*. Princeton: Princeton University Press.

Agawu, V. Kofi. 2009. "Music as Language." In *Music as Discourse: Semiotic Adventures in Romantic Music*. Oxford: Oxford University Press.

Almén, Byron. 2008. *A Theory of Musical Narrative*. Bloomington: Indiana University Press.

Amit, Vered, ed. 2015. *Thinking through Sociality: An Anthropological Interrogation of Key Concepts*. Oxford: Berghahn Books.

Anagnost, Ann. 1997. *National Past-Times: Narrative, Representation, and Power in Modern China*. Durham: Duke University Press.

Anderson, Crystal S. 2020. *Soul in Seoul: African American Popular Music and K-Pop*. Jackson: University of Mississippi Press.

Andrade, Tonio. 2007. *How Taiwan Became Chinese: Dutch, Spanish, and Han Colonization in the Seventeenth Century*. New York: Columbia University Press. ACLS Humanities E-Book edition.

Ang, Uijin 洪惟仁. 1992. *Taiwan yuyan weiji* 台灣語言危機 [Taiwan language crisis]. Taipei: Qianwei.

Appadurai, Arjun. 1986. Introduction to *The Social Life of Things*, edited by Arjun Appadurai, 3–63. Cambridge: Cambridge University Press.

Appert, Catherine. 2018. *In Hip Hop Time: Music, Memory, and Social Change in Urban Senegal*. New York: Oxford University Press.

Arendt, Hannah. 1958. *The Human Condition*. Chicago: University of Chicago Press.

Austin, Joe. 1998. "Knowing Their Place: Local Knowledge, Social Prestige, and the Writing Formation in New York City." In *Generations of Youth: Youth Cultures and History in Twentieth Century America*, edited by Joe Austin and Michael N. Willard, 240–52. New York: New York University Press.

Bakhtin, Mikhail. 1981. *The Dialogic Imagination: Four Essays*. Austin: University of Texas Press.

Bakhtin, Mikhail. 1984. *Problems of Dostoevsky's Poetics*. Edited and translated by Caryl Emerson. Minneapolis: University of Minnesota Press.

Bal, P. Matthijs and Edina Dóci. 2018. "Neoliberal Ideology in Work and Organizational Psychology." *European Journal of Work and Organizational Psychology* 27, no. 5 (March): 536–48.

Baranovitch, Nimrod. 2003. *China's New Voices: Popular Music, Ethnicity, Gender, and Politics, 1978–1997*. Berkeley: University of California Press.

Barthes, Roland. 1975. "An Introduction to the Structural Analysis of Narrative." *New Literary History* 6, no. 2 (Winter): 237–72.

Benesch, Oleg. 2011. "National Consciousness and the Evolution of the Civil/Military Binary in East Asia." *Taiwan Journal of East Asian Studies* 8, no. 1: 133–37.

Benhabib, Seyla. 1986. *Critique, Norm, and Utopia: A Study of the Foundations of Critical Theory*. New York: Columbia University Press.

Benhabib, Seyla. 1992. *Situating the Self: Gender, Community and Postmodernism in Contemporary Ethics*. London: Polity Press.

Bennett, Dionne, and Marcyliena Morgan. 2011. "Hip-Hop and the Global Imprint of a Black Cultural Form." *Daedalus: Journal of the American Academy of Arts and Sciences* 140, no. 2 (Spring): 176–96.

Berry, Michael. 2008. *A History of Pain: Trauma in Modern Chinese Literature and Film*. New York: Columbia University Press.

Bhabha, Homi. 1990. Introduction to *Nation and Narration*, edited by Homi Bhabha, 1–7. London: Routledge.

Black Buddha. 2017. "Shengyin" 聲音 [Voices]. Video, 4:35. https://zh-hant.black-buddha.com/voices/dj-didilong.

Blacklist Workshop 黑名單工作室. 1989. Liner notes. *Zhuakuang ge* 抓狂歌 [Songs of madness]. Rock Records, compact disc.

Bo, Zhiyue. 2009. "Cross-Strait Relations: Typhoon Morakot and the Dalai Lama." *East Asian Institute Bulletin of the National University of Singapore* 11, no. 2.

Boretz, Avron. 2004. "Carousing and Masculinity: The Cultural Production of Gender in Taiwan." In *Women in the New Taiwan: Gender Roles and Gender Consciousness in a Changing Society*, edited by Catherine S. P. Farris, Anru Lee, and Murray Rubinstein, 171–98. Armonk, NY: M. E. Sharpe.

Boyd, Danah M., and Nicole B. Ellison. 2007. "Social Network Sites: Definition, History, and Scholarship," *Journal of Computer-Mediated Communication* 13, no. 1 (October): 210–30.

Boykan, Martin. 2004. *Silence and Slow Time: Studies in Musical Narrative*. Lanham, MD: Scarecrow Press.

Bradley, Adam, and Andrew DuBois, eds. 2010. *The Anthology of Rap*. New Haven: Yale University Press.

Bradley, Regina N. 2017a. *Boondock Kollage: Stories from the Hip Hop South*. New York: Peter Lang.

Bradley, Regina N. 2017b. "Close-Up: Hip-Hop Cinema Introduction: Hip-Hop Cinema as a Lens of Contemporary Black Realities." *Black Camera: An International Film Journal* 8, no. 2 (Spring): 141–45.

Bradley, Regina N. 2021. *Chronicling Stankonia: The Rise of the Hip-Hop South.* Chapel Hill: University of North Carolina Press.

Brainer, Amy. 2019. *Queer Kinship and Family Change in Taiwan.* New Brunswick, NJ: Rutgers University Press.

Brooks, Daphne. 2008. "'All That You Can't Leave Behind': Black Female Soul Singing and the Politics of Surrogation in the Age of Catastrophe." *Meridians: feminism, race, transnationalism* 8, no. 1: 180–204.

Brown, Melissa. 2004. *Is Taiwan Chinese?: The Impact of Culture, Power, and Migration on Changing Identities.* Berkeley: University of California Press.

Bureau of East Asian and Pacific Affairs. 2018. "U.S. Relations with Taiwan." US Department of State. https://www.state.gov/u-s-relations-with-taiwan/.

Butler, Judith. 2009. *Frames of War: When Is Life Grievable?* London: Verso.

Cai, Wenshan 蔡文山. 2004. "Cong jiaoyu jihui jundengde guandian xing si Taiwan yuanzhumin xueshengde jiaoyu xiankuang yu zhanwang" 從教育機會均等的觀點省思台灣原住民學生的教育現況與展望 [Reflections on the current condition and prospects of the education of Aboriginal students in Taiwan from the perspective of equality of educational opportunity]. *Jiaoyu yu shehui yanjiu* 教育與社會研究 [Education and social research] 6 (January): 109–44.

Caldwell, Ernest. 2018. "Transitional Justice Legislation in Taiwan Before and During the Tsai Administration." *Washington International Law Journal* 27, no. 2: 449–84.

Cha-Jua, Sundiata Keita. 2008. "Black Audiences, Blaxploitation and Kung Fu Films, and Challenges to White Celluloid Masculinity." In *China Forever: The Shaw Brothers and Diasporic Cinema*, edited by Poshek Fu, 199–223. Urbana: University of Illinois Press.

Chang, Chao-wei 張釗維. 2003. *Shei zai nabian chang zijide ge: Taiwan xiandai minge yundong shi* 誰在那邊唱自己的歌 ：台灣現代民歌運動史 [Who there sings their own songs? History of the Taiwan modern folksong movement]. Taipei: Shibao wenhua chuban qiye gufen youxian gongsi.

Chang, Doris T. 2009. *Women's Movements in Twentieth-Century Taiwan.* Urbana: University of Illinois Press.

Chang, Doris T. 2018. "Studies of Taiwan's Feminist Discourses and Women's Movements." *International Journal of Taiwan Studies* 1, no. 1: 90–114.

Chang, Ivy I-Chu. 2018. "Encountering the Alienated Self: Hip-Hop *Jingju* Chasing Chinese Wind in Contemporary Legend Theatre's *108 Heroes*." In *Transnational Performance, Identity and Mobility in Asia*, edited by Iris H. Tuan and Ivy I-Chu Chang, 1–18. Singapore: Palgrave Pivot.

Chang, Jeff. 2005. *Can't Stop, Won't Stop: A History of the Hip Hop Generation.* New York: St. Martin's Press.

Chang, Jui-chuan 張睿銓. 2010. "My Language." Personal essay.

Chang, Sung-sheng Yvonne. 1993. *Modernism and the Nativist Resistance.* Durham: Duke University Press.

Chang, Sung-sheng Yvonne. 2004. *Literary Culture in Taiwan: Martial Law to Market Law.* New York: Columbia University Press.

Chao, Antonia. 2000. "Global Metaphors and Local Strategies in the Construction of Taiwan's Lesbian Identities." *Culture, Health & Sexuality* 2, no. 4: 377–90.

Chao, Yuen Ren. 1956. "Tone, Intonation, Singsong, Chanting, Recitative, Tonal Composition, and Atonal Composition in Chinese." In *For Roman Jakobson: Essays on the Occasion of His Sixtieth Birthday*, edited by M. Halle et al., 52–59. The Hague: Mouton.

Charry, Eric. 2012. "A Capsule History of African Rap." In *Hip Hop Africa: New African Music in a Globalizing World*, edited by Eric Charry, 1–26. Bloomington: Indiana University Press.

Chatman, Seymour. 1978. *Story and Discourse: Narrative Structure in Fiction and Film*. Ithaca: Cornell University Press.

Chen, Chun-bin. 2012. "The Unwritten and the Recorded: Tradition and Transfiguration in Taiwanese Aboriginal Music." *Asian Musicology* 19: 79–96.

Chen, Peichen 陳培真. 1998. "Waixianshi goutongzhong shuozhe yu tingzhe zhijiande guanxi: yi Zhutoupide raoshe ge weili" 外顯式溝通中說者與聽者之間的關係 ： 以豬頭皮的饒舌歌為例 [The speaker-audience relationship in ostensive communication: Jutoupi's rap songs]. Master's thesis, National Taiwan Normal University.

Chen, Szu-wei. 2005. "The Rise and Generic Features of Shanghai Popular Songs in the 1930s and 1940s." *Popular Music* 24, no. 1 (January): 107–25.

Chen, Szu-wei. 2020. "Producing Mandopop in 1960s Taiwan: When a Prolific Composer Met a Pioneering Entrepreneur." In *Made in Taiwan: Studies in Popular Music*, edited by Eva Tsai, Tung-hung Ho, and Miaoju Jian, 43–54. New York: Routledge.

Chen, Yufu. 2020. "Schools to Include Lessons on State-Inflicted Violence." *Taipei Times*, May 2020. https://www.taipeitimes.com/News/taiwan/archives/2020/05/22/2003736853.

Chen, Yuxiu 陳郁秀, ed. 2008. *Taiwan yinyue baike cishu* 台灣音樂百科辭書 [Encyclopedia of Taiwan music]. Taipei: Yuan-Liou Publishing.

Cheng, Dai-Lin 鄭黛林. 2011. "Taiwan shehui zhongde nanzi yigai renzhi" 台灣社會中的男子一概認知 [The perception of masculinity in Taiwan]. Master's thesis, Shih Hsin University.

Chiang, Tien-Hui 姜添輝. 2015. "Taiwan gaodeng jiaoyu zhengce yixun xin ziyou zhuyi de xianxiang yu queshi" 台灣高等教育政策依循新自由主義的現象與缺失 [Why do higher-education policies in Taiwan incline toward neoliberalism? A critique on this approach]. *Taiwan jiaoyu shehuixue yanjiu* 台灣教育社會學研究 [Taiwan journal of sociology of education] 15, no. 2: 131–65.

China Post. 2007. "Worker Anti-Discrimination Bill Passes," May 5. http://www.chinapost.com.tw/news/archives/taiwan/200755/108825.htm.

Ching, Leo T. S. 2001. *Becoming "Japanese": Colonial Taiwan and the Politics of Identity Formation*. Berkeley: University of California Press.

Chiung, Wi-vun Taiffalo 蔣為文. 2005. *Gí-giân, gín-tông kap kh-sit-bîn* 語言，認同與去殖民 [Language, identity, and decolonization]. Tainan: National Cheng Kung University.

Chou, Chien, and Meng-Jung Tsai. 2007. "Gender Differences in Taiwan High School Students' Computer Game Playing." *Computers in Human Behavior* 23: 812–24.

Chou, Chuing Prudence. 2008. "The Impact of Neo-Liberalism on Taiwanese Higher Education." *International Perspectives on Education and Society* 9: 297–311.

Chow, Yiu Fai, and Jeroen de Kloet. 2013. *Sonic Multiplicities: Hong Kong Pop and the Global Circulation of Sound and Image.* Bristol, UK: Intellect Ltd.

Chuang, Tzu-i. 2005. "The Power of Cuteness: Female Infantilization in Urban Taiwan." *Greater China* (Summer): 21–28.

Chuang, Ya-Chung. 2013. *Democracy on Trial: Social Movements and Cultural Politics in Post-Authoritarian Taiwan.* Hong Kong: Chinese University of Hong Kong Press.

Chun, Allen. 2011. "Nomadic Ethnoscapes in the Changing Global-Local Pop Music Industry: ICRT as IC." In *Popular Culture in Taiwan: Charismatic Modernity,* edited by Marc L. Moskowitz, 86–104. New York: Routledge.

Chun, Allen. 2017. *Forget Chineseness: On the Geopolitics of Cultural Identification.* Albany: State University of New York Press.

Clark, Cal, and Alexander C. Tan. 2012. *Taiwan's Political Economy: Meeting Challenges, Pursuing Progress.* Boulder, CO: Lynne Rienner.

Clark, Msia Kibona. 2014. "The Role of New and Social Media in Tanzanian Hip-Hop Production." *Cahiers d'Études Africaines* 54, no. 216: 1115–36.

Cliff, Michelle. 1988. "A Journey into Speech." In *The Graywolf Annual Five: Multi-Cultural Literacy,* edited by Rick Simonson and Scott Walker, 57–62. Saint Paul: Graywolf Press.

Community Service. n.d. "About." Facebook. Accessed February 14, 2020. https://www.facebook.com/CommunityService/.

Condry, Ian. 2006. *Hip-Hop Japan: Rap and the Paths of Cultural Globalization.* Durham: Duke University Press.

Connell, R. W. 2005. *Masculinities.* 2nd ed. Cambridge: Polity Press.

Corcuff, Stéphane. 2005. "History Textbooks, Identity Politics, and Ethnic Introspection in Taiwan: The June 1997 *Knowing Taiwan* Textbooks Controversy and the Questions It Raised on the Various Approaches to 'Han' Identity." In *History Education and National Identity in Asia,* edited by Edward Vickers and Alisa Jones, 133–69. New York: Routledge.

Creery, Jennifer. 2018. "Aristophanes: The Taiwanese Rapper Making Mandarin Waves in Global Hip-Hop." *The News Lens,* January 24. https://international.thenewslens.com/article/88319.

Crenshaw, Kimberlé. 1989. "Demarginalizing the Intersection of Race and Sex: A Black Feminist Critique of Antidiscrimination Doctrine, Feminist Theory and Antiracist Politics." *University of Chicago Legal Forum,* no. 1: 139–67.

Daughtry, J. Martin. 2015. *Listening to War: Sound, Music, Trauma, and Survival in Wartime Iraq.* Oxford: Oxford University Press.

De Certeau, Michel. 1984. *The Practice of Everyday Life.* Translated by Steven F. Rendall. Berkeley: University of California Press.

Dielh, Randy L., and Patrick C. M. Wong. 2002. "How Can the Lyrics of a Song in a Tone Language Be Understood?" *Psychology of Music* 30, no. 2: 202–9.

Ding, Yuh-Chyurn. 2007. "The Chi-Chi (Taiwan) Earthquake: Experiences on Post-Disaster Reconstruction for the 921 Earthquake." Paper presented at the Second International Conference on Urban Disaster Reduction, Taipei, Taiwan.

Disch, Lisa T. 1993. "More Truth than Fact: Storytelling as Critical Understanding in the Writings of Hannah Arendt." *Political Theory* 21, no. 4 (November): 665–94.

Drews Lucas, Sarah. 2017. "The Primacy of Narrative Agency: Re-reading Seyla Benhabib on Narrativity." *Feminist Theory* 19, no. 2: 123–43.

Drucker, Peter. 1959. *Landmarks of Tomorrow*. New York: Harper.

Dunbar, Eve. 2013. "Hip Hop (Feat. Women Writers): Reimagining Black Women and Agency through Hip Hop Fiction." In *Contemporary African American Literature: The Living Canon*, edited by Lovalerie King and Shirley Moody-Turner, 91–112. Bloomington: Indiana University Press.

Edkins, Jenny. 2003. *Trauma and the Memory of Politics.* Cambridge: Cambridge University Press.

Edmondson, Robert. 2002. "The February 28 Incident and National Identity." In *Memories of the Future: National Identity Issues and the Search for a New Taiwan*, edited by Stéphane Corcuff, 25–46. Armonk, NY: M. E. Sharpe.

Eidsheim, Nina Sun. 2019. *The Race of Sound: Listening, Timbre, and Vocality in African American Music.* Durham: Duke University Press.

Fei, Xiaotong 費孝通. 1947. *Xiangtu zhongguo* 鄉土中國 [From the soil]. Hong Kong: Xianggang zhonghe chuban, 2017.

Feld, Steven. 1990. "Wept Thoughts: The Voicing of Kaluli Memories." *Oral Tradition* 5, nos. 2–3: 241–66.

Fell, Dafydd. 2018. *Government and Politics in Taiwan.* 2nd ed. New York: Routledge.

Fetzer, Joel, and J. Christopher Soper. 2013. *Confucianism, Democratization, and Human Rights in Taiwan.* Lanham, MD: Lexington Books.

Fish, Isaac Stone. 2016. "Stop Calling Taiwan a 'Renegade Province.'" *Foreign Policy*, January 15. https://foreignpolicy.com/2016/01/15/stop-calling-taiwan-a-renegade-province/.

Fish, Stanley E. 1976. "Interpreting the *Variorum.*" *Critical Inquiry* 2 (Spring): 465–85.

Floyd, Samuel. 1995. *The Power of Black Music: Interpreting Its History from Africa to the United States.* New York: Oxford University Press.

Folami, Akilah N. 2007. "From Habermas to 'Get Rich or Die Tryin': Hip Hop, the Telecommunications Act of 1996, and the Black Public Sphere." *Michigan Journal of Race and Law* 12: 235–304.

Forman, Murray. 2002. *The 'Hood Comes First: Race, Space, and Place in Rap and Hip-Hop.* Middletown, CT: Wesleyan University Press.

Fox, Aaron. 2004. *Real Country: Music and Language in Working-Class Culture.* Durham: Duke University Press.

Freedman, R., et al. 1994. "The Fertility Transition in Taiwan." In *Social Change and the Family in Taiwan*, edited by Arland Thornton and Hui-Sheng Lin, 264–304. Chicago: University of Chicago Press.

Friedman, P. Kerim. 2018. "The Hegemony of the Local: Taiwanese Multicultural-ism and Indigenous Identity Politics." *boundary 2* 45, no. 3 (August): 79–105.

Frisbie, Charlotte J. 1980. "Vocables in Navajo Ceremonial Music." *Ethnomusicology* 24, no. 3 (September): 347–92.

Gao, Pat. 2007. "Music, Interrupted." *Taiwan Review* 57, no. 11. https://freemuse.org/news/ china-history-of-holo-pop-songs-censorship/.

Gao, Pat. 2010. "Toward a New Female Future." *Taiwan Review* 60, no. 6. https://taiwantoday.tw/news.php?post=22456&unit=12,29,33,45.

Gates, Henry Louis. 1998. *The Signifying Monkey: A Theory of Afro-American Liter-ary Criticism.* New York: Oxford University Press.

Gates, Henry Louis. 2010. Foreword to *The Anthology of Rap*, edited by Adam Brad-ley and Andrew DuBois, xxii–xxviii. New Haven: Yale University Press.

Gee, James Paul. 2004. *Situated Language and Learning: A Critique of Traditional Schooling.* New York: Routledge.

Geertz, Clifford. 2000. "Deep Hanging Out." In *Available Light: Anthropological Re-flections on Philosophical Topics,* 107–17. Princeton: Princeton University Press.

Genette, Gérard. 1980. *Narrative Discourse: An Essay in Method.* Translated by Jane E. Lewin. Ithaca: Cornell University Press.

George, Nelson. 2005. *Hip Hop America.* 2nd ed. New York: Penguin.

Gilman, Lisa, and John Fenn. 2006. "Dance, Gender, and Popular Music in Malawi: The Case of Rap and Ragga." *Popular Music* 25, no. 3: 369–81.

Golding, Shenequa. 2016. "Afrika Bambaataa Accused of Sex Abuse by Three More Men." *Vibe*, April 17. https://www.vibe.com/music/music-news/afrika-bambaataa-sexual-abuse-three-men-416693/.

Gosa, Travis L. 2015. "The Fifth Element: Knowledge." In *The Cambridge Companion to Hip-Hop*, edited by J. Williams, 56–70. Cambridge: Cambridge University Press.

Gray, Peter, and Kendrick Oliver, eds. 2004. *The Memory of Catastrophe.* Manches-ter, UK: Manchester University Press.

Gu, Ming Dong. 2006. *Chinese Theories of Fiction: A Non-Western Narrative System.* Albany: State University of Albany Press.

Guo, Lijuan 郭麗娟. 2011. "Jitazhongde rensheng gushi: Chen Mingzhang qingchun zaixian" 吉他中的人生故事 ： 陳明章青春再現 [Human stories in the guitar: Chen Ming-chang rediscovers his youth]. *Taiwan guanghua zazhi* 台灣光華雜誌 [Taiwan panorama]. August. https://www.taiwan-panorama.com/Articles /Details?Guid=ab555bfe-ab73-41fd-897a-f79015818b8d.

Guy, Nancy. 2001. "Syncretic Traditions and Western Idioms: Popular Music (Tai-wan)." In *The Garland Encyclopedia of World Music Online.* http://glnd.alexan derstreet.com.

Guy, Nancy. 2002. "'Republic of China National Anthem' on Taiwan: One Anthem, One Performance, Multiple Realities." *Ethnomusicology* 46, no. 1 (Winter): 96–119.

Guy, Nancy. 2005. *Peking Opera and Politics in Taiwan.* Urbana: University of Il-linois Press.

Guy, Nancy. 2008. "Feeling a Shared History through Song: 'A Flower in the Rainy Night' as a Key Cultural Symbol in Taiwan." *TDR: The Drama Review* 52, no. 4 (Winter): 64–81.

Guy, Nancy. 2011. Review of *Cries of Joy, Songs of Sorrow: Chinese Pop Music and Its Cultural Connotations*, by Marc L. Moskowitz. *Perfect Beat* 12, no. 2: 191–93.

Guy, Nancy. 2018. "Popular Music as a Barometer of Political Change." In *The Oxford Handbook of Music Censorship*, edited by Patricia Ann Hall, 275–303. New York: Oxford University Press.

Han, Sen 韓森. 2019. *Lai Han laoshi zheli xue raoshe: youle zhe yiben, rang ni raoshe bu zou yuanwang lu* 來韓老師這裡學饒舌 ：有了這一本 ，讓你饒舌不走冤枉路 ！ [Study rap with Professor H: with this book, your rap won't go astray]. Taipei: Shibao wenhua chuban qiye gufen youxian gongsi.

Hanafi, Sari. 2018. "Postcolonialism's After-Life in the Arab World: Toward a Post-Authoritarian Approach." In *Routledge Handbook of South-South Relations*, edited by Elena Fiddian-Qasmiyeh and Patricia Daley, 76–85. Abingdon, UK: Routledge.

Harrell, Stevan. 1996. Introduction to *Negotiating Ethnicities in China and Taiwan*, edited by Melissa J. Brown, 1–18. Berkeley: Institute of East Asian Studies, University of California.

Hatfield, D. J. n.d. "Invisible Hopes: Houses and Expansive Indigeneity in the Greater 'Amis World." Unpublished manuscript.

Hatfield, D. J. 2002. "How to Spell Global, or Transliteration Debates and Narratives of Globalization in Taipei/Taibei/Taipak/…for Example." *Proceedings of Knowledge and Discourse: Speculating on Disciplinary Futures, 2nd International Conference*, Hong Kong, June 25–29.

Hatfield, D. J. 2010. *Taiwanese Pilgrimage to China: Ritual, Complicity, Community*. New York: Palgrave Macmillan.

Hatfield, D. J. 2015. "Performed but Not Spoken (1)." *Life in Text and Stereo Sound* (blog). August 20. http://djhatfield.com/blog/2015/08/20/performed-but-not-spoken-1/.

Helbig, Adriana. 2011. *Hip Hop Ukraine: Music, Race, and African Migration*. Bloomington: Indiana University Press.

Her, Kelly. 2000. "Songs from the Heart." *Taipei Review* 50, no. 4. https://taiwantoday.tw/list_tt.php?unit=20&unitname=Culture-Taiwan-Review.

Herzog, Annabel. 2000. "Illuminating Inheritance: Benjamin's Influence on Arendt's Political Storytelling." *Philosophy Social Criticism* 26, no. 5 (September): 1–27.

Hioe, Brian. 2017. "Island's Sunrise." *Daybreak*, July 20. https://daybreak.newbloommag.net/2017/07/20/islands-sunrise/.

Hioe, Brian, and Wen Liu. 2014. "Chen Wei-Ting's Scandal and Taiwanese Civic Nationalism." *New Bloom*, December 30. https://newbloommag.net/2014/12/30/a-sexualized-movement-without-sexual-rights/.

Hirano, Katsuya, Lorenzo Veracini, and Toulouse-Antonin Roy. 2018. "Vanishing Natives and Taiwan's Settler-Colonial Unconsciousness." *Critical Asian Studies* 50, no. 2: 196–218.

Hisama, Ellie M. 2005. "'We're All Asian Really': Hip-Hop's Afro-Asian Cross-ings." In *Critical Minded: New Approaches to Hip Hop Studies*, edited by Ellie M. Hisama and Evan Rappaport, 1–21. Brooklyn: Institute for Studies in American Music.

Ho, Tung-Hung. 2009. "Taike Rock and Its Discontent." *Inter-Asia Cultural Studies* 10, no. 4: 565–84.

Ho, Tung-Hung. 2020. "Profiling a Postwar Trajectory of Taiwanese Popular Music: Nativism in Metamorphosis and Its Alternatives." In *Made in Taiwan: Studies in Popular Music*, edited by Eva Tsai, Tung-hung Ho, and Miaoju Jian, 23–42. New York: Routledge.

Ho, Wai-Chung. 2016. "National Identity in the Taiwanese System of Music Edu-cation." In *Patriotism and Nationalism in Music Education*, edited by David G. Herbert and Alexandra Kertz-Welzel, 59–76. Aldershot, UK: Ashgate.

hooks, bell. 1994. "Gangsta Culture—Sexism, Misogyny: Who Will Take the Rap?" In *Outlaw Culture: Resisting Representation*, 115–23. New York: Routledge.

Hsiao, Yuan. 2017. "Virtual Ecologies, Mobilization, and Democratic Groups with-out Leaders: Impacts of Internet Media on the Wild Strawberry Movement." In *Taiwan's Social Movements under Ma Ying-jeou*, edited by Dafydd Fell, 34–53. London: Routledge.

Hsiau, A-chin. 1997. "Language Ideology in Taiwan: The KMT's Language Policy, the Tai-yü Language Movement, and Ethnic Politics." *Journal of Multilingual and Multicultural Development*, 18, no. 4: 302–15.

Hsiau, A-chin. 2005. "The Indigenization of Taiwanese Literature: Historical Narra-tive, Strategic Essentialism, and State Violence." In *Cultural, Ethnic, and Political Nationalism in Contemporary Taiwan: Bentuhua*, edited by John Makeham and A-chin Hsiau, 125–55. New York: Palgrave Macmillan.

Hsu, Jinn-yuh. 2009. "The Spatial Encounter between Neoliberalism and Populism in Taiwan: Regional Restructuring under the DPP Regime in the New Millen-nium." *Political Geography* 28, no. 5: 296–308.

Huang, Shih-Ting. 2006. "Fulao Popular Songs during the Japanese Colonization of Taiwan." Master's thesis, University of Houston.

Huang, Ching-Lung. 2009. "The Changing Roles of the Media in Taiwan's Democ-ratization Process." Working Paper, Brookings Institution: Center for North-east Asian Policy Studies, Washington, DC. https://www.brookings.edu/wp-content/uploads/2016/ 06/07_taiwan_huang.pdf.

Hwang, Yih-Jye. 2014. "The 2004 Hand-in-Hand Rally in Taiwan: 'Traumatic' Memory, Commemoration, and Identity Formation." *Nationalism and Ethnic Politics* 20, no. 3: 287–308.

Jackson, Michael D. 1998. *Minima Ethnographica: Intersubjectivity and the Anthro-pological Project*. Chicago: University of Chicago Press.

Jackson, Michael D. 2002. *The Politics of Storytelling: Violence, Transgression and Intersubjectivity*. Copenhagen: Museum Tusculanum Press.

Jacobs, Andrew. 2009. "Taiwan's Leader Faces Anger Over Storm Response." *New York Times*, August 23.

Jan, Jie-Sheng, Ping-Yin Kuan, and Arlett Lomelí. 2016. "Social Context, Parental Exogamy and Hakka Language Retention in Taiwan." *Journal of Multilingual and Multicultural Development* 37, no. 8: 794–804.

Jay-Z. 2010. *Decoded.* New York: Spiegel and Grau.

Jeffries, Michael P. 2010. *Thug Life: Race, Gender, and the Meaning of Hip-Hop.* Chicago: University of Chicago Press.

Jian, Miaoju, Tung-hung Ho, and Eva Tsai. 2020. "Orbiting and Down-to-Earth: A Conversation with Lim Giong about His Music, Art, and Mind." In *Made in Taiwan: Studies in Popular Music*, edited by Eva Tsai, Tung-hung Ho, and Miaoju Jian, 231–47. New York: Routledge.

Jones, Alisa. 2013. "Triangulating Identity: Japan's Place in Taiwan's Textbooks." In *Imagining Japan in Post-War East Asia: Identity Politics, Schooling and Popular Culture*, edited by Paul Morris, Naoko Shimazu, and Edward Vickers, 170–89. New York: Routledge.

Jones, Andrew F. 2001. *Yellow Music: Media Culture and Colonial Modernity in the Chinese Jazz Age.* Durham: Duke University Press.

Jones, Andrew F. 2005. "Blacklist Studio." In *The Encyclopedia of Contemporary Chinese Culture*, edited by Edward Lawrence Davis. New York: Routledge.

Jones, Andrew F. 2016. "Circuit Listening: Grace Chang and the Dawn of the Chinese 1960s." In *Audible Empire: Music, Global Politics, Critique*, edited by Ronald Radano and Tejumola Olaniyan, 66–92. Durham: Duke University Press.

Kao, Ying-Chao, and Herng-Dar Bih. 2014. "Masculinity in Ambiguity: Constructing Taiwanese Masculine Identities between Great Powers." In *Masculinities in a Global Era*, edited by Joseph Gelfer, 175–91. New York: Springer Science+Business Media.

KAO!INC. 2018. *Xihazai: Taiwan Raoshe Gushi* 嘻哈囝 : 台灣饒舌故事 [Taiwan hip-hop kids]. Taipei: Bifenggang wenhua youxian gongsi.

Keyes, Cheryl L. 2002. *Rap Music and Street Consciousness.* Urbana: University of Illinois Press.

Knapp, Ronald. 2007. "The Shaping of Taiwan's Landscapes." In *Taiwan: A New History*, edited by Murray A. Rubinstein, 3–26. Armonk, NY: M. E. Sharpe.

Koh, Jocelle. 2017. "Interview with DJ Didilong A.K.A. YingHung 李英宏—The Enigma Pioneering New-Gen Taiwanese Language Hip-Hop." *Asian Pop Weekly*, November 12. https://asianpopweekly.com/features/interviews/interview-with -dj-didilong-a-k-a-yinghung-%e6%9d%8e%e8%8b%b1%e5%ae%8f-the-enigma -pioneering-new-gen-taiwanese-language-hip-hop/.

Komagome, Takeshi. 2006. "Colonial Modernity for an Elite Taiwanese, Lim Boseng: The Labyrinth of Cosmopolitanism." In *Taiwan under Japanese Colonial Rule, 1895–1945: History, Culture, Memory*, edited by Liao Ping-hui and David Der-wei Wang, 141–59. New York: Columbia University Press.

Kondo, Dorinne. 1997. *About Face: Performing Race in Fashion and Theater.* New York: Routledge.

Kou, Mei-Lin Lai. 2001. "Development of Music Education in Taiwan (1895–1995)." *Journal of Historical Research in Music Education* 22, no. 2: 177–90.

Kreiswirth, Martin. 2000. "Merely Telling Stories? Narrative and Knowledge in the Human Sciences." *Poetics Today* 21, no. 2: 293–318.

Kreuzer, Leonhard. 2009. "'Aiming at a Mirror': Towards a Critique of Gangsta Masculinity." In *Dichotonies: Gender and Music*, edited by Beate Neumeier, 197–215. Heidelberg: Universitätsverlag Winter.

Krims, Adam. 2000. *Rap Music and the Poetics of Identity*. New York: Cambridge University Press.

Kunshan Television 崑山電視台. 2009. "Taiwan liām-kua chuanren" 台灣唸歌傳人 [Heirs of Taiwan liām-kua]. Gudu wenyi 古都文藝 [Ancient capital of the arts]. February 3. https://www.youtube.com/watch?v=j3FP88xDbD0.

Kuo, Grace. 2011. "Capitalizing on Taiwan's Cultural Soft Power." *Taiwan Today*, October 9. https://taiwantoday.tw/news.php?unit=18,23,45,18&post=24476.

Kyodo. 2015. "Taiwanese Textbook Rules Student Protestor Commits Suicide." *South China Morning Post*, July 30. https://www.scmp.com/news/china/policies -politics/article/1845154/taiwanese-student-protesting-textbook-guidelines -kills.

Lai, Ming-yan. 2008. *Nativism and Modernity: Cultural Contestations in China and Taiwan under Global Capitalism*. Albany: State University of New York Press.

Lamley, Harry J. 1981. "Subethnic Rivalry in the Ch'ing Period." In *The Anthropology of Taiwanese Society*, edited by Emily Martin Ahern and Hill Gates, 282–318. Stanford: Stanford University Press.

Lawson, Francesca R. Sborgi. 2011. *The Narrative Arts of Tianjin: Between Music and Language*. Farnham, UK: Ashgate.

Lee, Ann. 2019. "Taiwanese Rapper Aristophanes Wants to Empower Women." *Culture Trip*, January 8. https://theculturetrip.com/asia/taiwan/articles/taiwanese -rapper-aristophanes-wants-to-empower-women/.

Lee, Kuan-Chen, Wei-feng Tzeng, Karl Ho, Harold Clarke. 2018. "Against Everything Involving China? Two Types of Sinophobia in Taiwan." *Journal of Asian and African Studies* 53, no. 6: 830–51.

Lee, Teng-hui. 1999. "Understanding Taiwan: Bridging the Perception Gap." *Foreign Affairs* 78, no. 6 (November–December): 9–14.

Li, Jing-Yi 李靜怡. 2007. "Taiwan qingshaonian xiha wenhuade rentong yu shijian" 台灣青少年嘻哈文化的認同與實踐 [Taiwanese youth hip-hop culture, identity, and practice]. Master's thesis, National Cheng Kung University.

Li, Shao Liang, Yi-Ren Lin, and Arthur Hou-ming Huang. 2017. "A Brief History of the Taiwanese Internet: The BBS Culture." In *The Routledge Companion to Global Internet Histories*, edited by Gerard Goggin and Mark McLelland, 182–96. London: Routledge.

Liao, Ping-hui. 1997. "Postmodern Literary Discourse and Contemporary Public Culture in Taiwan." *boundary 2* 24, no. 3 (Autumn): 41–63.

Lin, Ching-yi 林靜怡. 2010. "Guozhi shiqi chajin gequ falü guanzhi tixi zhi tantao" 國治時期查禁歌曲法律管制體系之探討 [The lawful restrictions for the forbidden songs under the KMT domination]. Master's thesis, National Taiwan University.

Lin, Guosian 林果顯. 2005. *Zhonghua wenhua fuxing yundong tuixing weiyuanhui zhi yanjiu (1966–1975): tongzhi zhengdangxingde jianli yu zhuanbian* 中華文化復興運動推行委員會之研究 (1966–1975)：統治正當性的建立與轉變 [Research on the implementation of the Chinese Cultural Renaissance Movement committee (1966–1975): the establishment and transformation of legitimate rule]. Taipei: Daw Shiang.

Lin, Hao-li. 2020. "Muscular Vernaculars: Braggadocio, 'Academic Rappers,' and Alternative Hip-Hop Masculinity in Taiwan." In *Made in Taiwan: Studies in Popular Music*, edited by Eva Tsai, Tung-hung Ho, and Miaoju Jian, 157–68. New York: Routledge.

Lin, Rachel, Hsiao-kuan Shih, and Jake Chung. 2018. "History Curriculum Review Starts Today." *Taipei Times*, August 11. https://www.taipeitimes.com/News/taiwan/archives/2018/08/11/2003698324.

Lin, Ro-Ting, Lung-Chang Chien, and Ichiro Kawachi. 2018. "Nonlinear Associations between Working Hours and Overwork-Related Cerebrovascular Diseases (CCVD)." *Scientific Reports* 8, Article 9694.

Lin, Sylvia Li-chun. 2003. "Toward a New Identity: Nativism and Popular Music in Taiwan." *China Information* 17, no. 2: 83–107.

Lin, Sylvia Li-chun. 2007. *Representing Atrocity in Taiwan: The 2/28 Incident and White Terror in Fiction and Film.* New York: Columbia University Press.

Lin, Teacher 林老師, Ill Mo 老莫, and Shortee 小個. 2008. *Sanpide raoshe da jihua* 參劈的饒舌大計劃 [Da project]. Taipei: Linking Books.

Lin, Tung-fa 林桶法. 2009. *1949 Dachetui* 1949 大撤退 [The great retreat of 1949]. Taipei: Linking Books.

Lin, Zonghong 林宗弘. 2009. "Zhuakuang ge" 抓狂歌 [Songs of madness]. In *Taiwan liuxing yinyue: zui jia zhuanji* 台灣流行音樂：200最佳專輯 [Taiwan popular music: 200 best albums], edited by Tao Xiaoqing 陶曉清, Ma Shih-fang 馬世芳, and Ye Yunping 葉雲平. Taipei: Shibao wenhua chuban qiye youxian gongsi.

List, George. 1963. "The Boundaries of Speech and Song." *Ethnomusicology* 7, no. 1 (January): 1–16.

Liu, Ching-chih. 2010. *A Critical History of New Music in China.* Translated by Caroline Mason. Hong Kong: Chinese University Press.

Loa, Iok-sin 賴有心. 2014. "228—67 Years On: Teachers Forgo Food in Protest Over Curriculum." *Taipei Times*, March 1. http://www.taipeitimes.com/News/taiwan/archives/2014/03/01/2003584621.

Louie, Kam. 2002. *Theorising Chinese Masculinity: Society and Gender in China.* Cambridge: Cambridge University Press.

Louie, Kam. 2015. *Chinese Masculinities in a Globalising World.* New York: Routledge.

Louie, Kam, and Louise Edwards. 1994. "Chinese Masculinity: Theorizing Wen and Wu." *East Asian History*, no. 8 (December): 135–48.

Lü, Yuxiu 呂鈺秀. 2003. *Taiwan yinyue shi* 台灣音樂史 [Taiwan music history]. Taipei: Wunan.

Luo, Zixin 羅子欣. 2018. "BCW houhui yin zang yuan min shenfen wang guang muyu pan zheyang zuo huikui buluo" BCW後悔隱藏原民身分忘光母語

盼這樣做回饋部落 [BCW regrets concealing Indigenous identity, hopes to give back to tribe]. *Liberty Times*, November 8. https://ent.ltn.com.tw/news/breakingnews/2605654.

Mack, Adrian. 2014. "Taiwan's Fire EX Is Proudly Rebellious after Igniting Sunflower Movement with 'Island's Sunrise.'" *The Georgia Straight*, August 27. https://www.straight.com/music/716261/taiwans-fire-ex-proudly-rebellious-after-igniting-sunflower-movement-islands-sunrise.

McKercher, Catherine, and Vincent Mosco. 2007. *Knowledge Workers in the Information Society*. Lanham, MD: Lexington Books.

McLuhan, Marshall. 1995. *Essential McLuhan*. Edited by Eric McLuhan and Frank Zingrone. New York: Basic Books.

Meintjes, Louise. 2004. "Shoot the Sergeant, Shatter the Mountain: The Production of Masculinity in Zulu Ngoma Song and Dance in Post-Apartheid South Africa." *Ethnomusicology Forum* 13, no. 2 (November): 173–201.

Meizel, Katherine. 2020. *Multivocality: Singing on the Borders of Identity*. New York: Oxford University Press.

Micic, Peter. 2008. "Funky Chinatown and the Asian Riff." Danwei.org. http://laodanwei.org/wp/guest-contributor/funky_chinatown_and_the_asian.php.

Ministry of Foreign Affairs. 2010. "Compulsory Military Service." http://www.taiwan.gov.tw/ct.asp?xItem=27218&ctNode=1967&mp=1001.

Mitchell, Tony. 2001a. "Introduction: Another Root—Hip-Hop Outside the USA." In *Global Noise: Rap and Hip-Hop Outside the USA*, edited by Tony Mitchell. Middletown, CT: Wesleyan University Press.

Mitchell, Tony. 2001b. "Kia Kaha! (Be Strong!): Maori and Pacific Islander Hip-Hop in Aoteatoa-New Zealand." In *Global Noise: Rap and Hip-Hop Outside the USA*, edited by Tony Mitchell, 280–306. Middletown, CT: Wesleyan University Press.

Mitchell, Tony, and Alastair Pennycook. 2009. "Hip Hop as Dusty Foot Philosophy: Engaging Locality." In *Global Linguistic Flows: Hip Hop Cultures, Youth Identities, and the Politics of Language*, edited by H. Samy Alim, Award Ibrahim, and Alastair Pennycook, 25–42. New York: Routledge.

Morgan, Marcyliena. 2009. *The Real Hiphop: Battling for Knowledge, Power, and Respect in the LA Underground*. Durham: Duke University Press.

Moskowitz, Marc L. 2010. *Cries of Joy, Songs of Sorrow: Chinese Pop Music and Its Cultural Connotations*. Honolulu: University of Hawai'i Press.

Mullen, Bill V. 2004. *Afro-Orientalism*. Minneapolis: University of Minnesota Press.

Neal, Jocelyn R. 2007. "Narrative Paradigms, Musical Signifiers, and Form as Function in Country Music." *Music Theory Spectrum* 29, no. 1 (Spring): 41–72.

Negus, Keith. 2012. "Narrative, Interpretation, and the Popular Song." *Musical Quarterly* 95, nos. 2–3 (Summer–Fall): 368–95.

Nicholls, David. 2007. "Narrative Theory as an Analytical Tool in the Study of Popular Music Texts." *Music & Letters* 88, no. 2: 297–315.

Nilsson, Martin. n.d. "The Musical Cliché Figure Signifying the Far East: Whence, Wherefore, Whither?" http://chinoiserie.atspace.com/index.html.

Ongiri, Amy Abugo. 2002. "'He Wanted to Be Just Like Bruce Lee': African Americans, Kung Fu Theater and Cultural Exchange at the Margins." *Journal of Asian American Studies* 5, no. 1: 31–40.

Osumare, Halifu. 2001. "Beat Streets in the Global Hood: Connective Marginalities of the Hip Hop Globe." *Journal of American Comparative Cultures* 24, nos. 1–2: 171–81.

Osumare, Halifu. 2007. *The Africanist Aesthetic in Global Hip-Hop: Power Moves.* New York: Palgrave Macmillan.

Pai, Iris Erh-Ya. 2017. *Sexual Identity and Lesbian Family Life: Lesbianism, Patriarchalism, and the Asian Family in Taiwan.* New York: Palgrave Macmillan.

Pan, Jason. 2017. "Sunflower Activists Cleared of Charges." *Taipei Times*, April 1. https://www.taipeitimes.com/News/front/archives/2017/04/01/2003667850.

Pennycook, Alastair. 2007. "Language, Localization, and the Real: Hip-Hop and the Global Spread of Authenticity." *Journal of Language Identity and Education* 6, no. 2 (June): 101–15.

Perkins, William Eric. 1996. "The Rap Attack: An Introduction." In *Droppin' Science: Critical Essays on Rap Music and Hip Hop Culture*, edited by William Eric Perkins, 1–45. Philadelphia: Temple University Press.

Perrin, Andrew. 2004. "What Taiwan Wants." *Time Magazine*, March 15.

Perry, Imani. 2004. *Prophets of the Hood: Politics and Poetics in Hip Hop.* Durham: Duke University Press.

Peterson, Marina. 2013. "Sound Work: Law, Labor, and Capital in the 1940s Recording Bans of the American Federation of Musicians." *Anthropological Quarterly* 86, no. 3: 791–824.

Phillipson, Robert. 1992. *Linguistic Imperialism.* Oxford: Oxford University Press.

Prescod-Weinstein, Chanda. 2016. "Black Lives Matter, Taiwan's '228 Incident,' and the Transnational Struggle for Liberation." *Black Youth Project*, December 20. http://blackyouthproject.com/black-lives-matter-taiwans-228-incident-and-the-transnational-struggle-for-liberation/.

Pun, Ngai, Yuan Shen, Yuhua Guo, Huilin Lu, and Jenny Chan. 2016. "Apple, Foxconn, and Chinese Workers' Struggles from a Global Labor Perspective." *Inter-Asia Cultural Studies* 17, no. 2: 166–85.

Quartly, Jules. 2006. "Taike Sells Out." *Taipei Times*, March 31. http://www.taipeitimes.com/News/feat/archives/2006/03/31/2003300209.

Rabaka, Reiland. 2012. *Hip Hop's Amnesia: From Blues and the Black Women's Club Movement to Rap and the Hip Hop Movement.* Lanham, MD: Rowman & Littlefield.

Ramzy, Austin. 2014. "Concession Offered, Taiwan Group to End Protest of China Trade Pact." *New York Times*, April 7. https://www.nytimes.com/2014/04/08/world/asia/concession-offered-taiwan-group-to-end-protest-of-china-trade-pact.html.

Richardson, Elaine, and Sean Lewis. 1999. "'Flippin' the Script'/'Blowin' Up the Spot': Puttin' Hip-Hop Online in (African) America and South Africa." In *Global*

Literacies and the World-Wide Web, edited by Gail E. Hawisher and Cynthia L. Selfe, 251–76. London: Routledge.

Ricoeur, Paul. 1990. *Time and Narrative*. Translated by Kathleen McLaughlin and David Pellauer. Chicago: University of Chicago Press.

Rigger, Shelley. 2011. "Strawberry Jam: National Identity, Cross-Strait Relations, and Taiwan's Youth." In *The Changing Dynamics of the Relations among China, Taiwan, and the United States*, edited by Cal Clark, 78–95. Newcastle-upon-Tyne, UK: Cambridge Scholars.

Rimmon-Kenan, Shlomith. 2006. "Concepts of Narrative." In *The Travelling Concept of Narrative*, edited by Mari Hatavara, Lars-Christer Hydén, and Matti Hyvärinen, 10–19. Helsinki: Helsinki Collegium for Advanced Studies, University of Helsinki.

Roach, Joseph. 1996. *Cities of the Dead: Circum-Atlantic Performance*. New York: Columbia University Press.

Rollefson, J. Griffith. 2018. "Hip Hop as Martial Art: A Political Economy of Violence in Rap Music." In *The Oxford Handbook of Hip Hop Music*, edited by Justin D. Burton and Jason Lee Oakes. Oxford: Oxford University Press.

Rose, Tricia. 1994. *Black Noise: Rap Music and Black Culture in Contemporary America*. Middletown, CT: Wesleyan University Press.

Rosenlee, Li-Hsiang Lisa. 2004. "*Neiwai*, Civility, and Gender Distinction." *Asian Philosophy* 14, no. 1: 41–58.

Rowen, Ian. 2015. "Inside Taiwan's Sunflower Movement: Twenty-Four Days in a Student-Occupied Parliament, and the Future of the Region." *Journal of Asian Studies* 74, no. 1 (February): 5–21.

Rubinstein, Murray A. 2004. "Lu Hsiu-lien and the Origins of Taiwanese Feminism, 1944–1977." In *Women in the New Taiwan: Gender Roles and Gender Consciousness in a Changing Society*, edited by Catherine S. P. Farris, Anru Lee, and Murray Rubinstein, 244–77. Armonk, NY: M. E. Sharpe.

Sandel, Todd L. 2003. "Linguistic Capital in Taiwan: The KMT's Mandarin Language Policy and Its Perceived Impact on Language Practices of Bilingual Mandarin and Tai-gi Speakers." *Language in Society* 32, no. 4 (September): 523–51.

Schloss, Joseph G. 2004. *Making Beats: The Art of Sample-Based Hip-Hop*. Middletown, CT: Wesleyan University Press.

Schneider, Claudia. 2008. "'National History' in Mainland Chinese and Taiwanese History Education: Its Current Role, Existing Challenges and Alternative Frameworks." *European Studies* 7: 163–77.

Schweig, Meredith. 2013. "The Song Readers: Rap Music and the Politics of Storytelling in Taiwan." PhD diss., Harvard University.

Schweig, Meredith. 2014. "Hoklo Hip-Hop: Re-signifying Rap as Local Narrative Tradition in Taiwan." *CHINOPERL: Journal of Chinese Oral and Performing Literature* 33, no. 1 (July): 37–59.

Schweig, Meredith. 2016. "'Young Soldiers, One Day We Will Change Taiwan': Masculinity Politics in the Taiwan Rap Scene." *Ethnomusicology* 60, no. 3 (Fall): 383–410.

Schweig, Meredith. 2019. "Like an *Erhu* Player on the Roof: Music as Multilayered Diasporic Negotiation at a Taiwanese and Jewish-American Wedding." In *Music in the American Diasporic Wedding*, edited by Inna Naroditskaya, 103–26. Bloomington: Indiana University Press.

Scott, Mandy, and Hak-Khiam Tiun. 2007. "Mandarin-Only to Mandarin-Plus: Taiwan." *Language Policy* 6, no. 1 (March): 53–72.

Seeger, Anthony. 1986. "Oratory Is Spoken, Myth Is Told, and Song Is Sung, but They Are All Music to My Ears." In *Native South American Discourse*, edited by Joel Sherzer and Greg Urban, 59–82. Berlin: Mouton de Gruyter.

Shelemay, Kay Kaufman. 2009. "The Power of Silent Voices: Women in the Syrian Jewish Musical Tradition." In *Music and the Play of Power in the Middle East, North Africa and Central Asia*, edited by Laudan Nooshin, 269–88. Burlington, VT: Ashgate.

Shih, Shu-Mei. 2003. "Globalisation and the (In)significance of Taiwan." *Postcolonial Studies* 6, no. 2: 143–53.

Silvio, Teri. 1998. "Drag Melodrama/Feminine Public Sphere/Folk Television: 'Local Opera' and Identity on Taiwan." PhD diss., University of Chicago.

Slobin, Mark. 1993. *Subcultural Sounds: Micromusics of the West*. Middletown, CT: Wesleyan University Press.

Smith, Craig A. 2012. "Aboriginal Autonomy and Its Place in Taiwan's National Trauma Narrative." *Modern Chinese Literature and Culture* 24, no. 2 (Fall): 209–40.

Solomon, Thomas. 2014. "Music and Race in American Cartoons: Multimedia, Subject Position, and the Racial Imagination." In *Music and Minorities from Around the World: Research, Documentation, and Interdisciplinary Study*, edited by Ursula Hemetek, Essica Marks, and Adelaida Reyes, 142–66. Newcastle, UK: Cambridge Scholars.

Spence, Lester K. 2011. *Stare in the Darkness: The Limits of Hip-Hop and Black Politics*. Minneapolis: University of Minnesota Press.

Stolojan, Vladimir. 2017. "Curriculum Reform and the Teaching of History in High Schools during the Ma Ying-jeou Presidency." *Journal of Current Chinese Affairs* 46, no. 1: 101–30.

Tan, Shzr Ee. 2008. "Returning to and from 'Innocence': Taiwan Aboriginal Recordings." *Journal of American Folklore* 121, no. 480 (Spring): 222–35.

Tang, Patricia. 2012. "The Rapper as Modern Griot: Reclaiming African Traditions." In *Hip Hop Africa: New African Music in a Globalizing World*, edited by Eric Charry, 79–91. Bloomington: Indiana University Press.

Tang, Wen-hui Anna, and Emma J. Teng. 2016. "Looking Again at Taiwan's Lü Hsiu-lien: A Female Vice President or a Feminist Vice President?" *Women's Studies International Forum* 56 (May–June): 92–102.

Tausig, Benjamin. 2019. "Women's March Colloquy—Introduction: At Risk of Repetition." *Music and Politics* 13, no. 1 (Winter). https://doi.org/10.3998/mp.9460447.0013.101.

Teng, Emma Jinhua. 2004. *Taiwan's Imagined Geography: Chinese Colonial Travel Writing and Pictures, 1683–1895*. Cambridge, MA: Harvard University Press.

Teng, Emma Jinhua. 2001. Introduction to *"A Brief Record of the Eastern Ocean* by Ding Shaoyi (fl. 1847)." In *Under Confucian Eyes: Writings on Gender in Chinese History*, edited by Susan Mann and Yu-yin Cheng, 253–62. Berkeley: University of California Press.

Thiong'o, Ngũgĩ wa. 1986. *Decolonising the Mind: The Politics of Language in African Literature*. London: James Currey; Nairobi: Heinemann Kenya; Portsmouth, NH: Heinemann; Harare: Zimbabwe Publishing House.

Thornton, Arland, and Hui-Sheng Lin. 1994. *Social Change and the Family in Taiwan*. Chicago: University of Chicago Press.

Trouillot, Michel-Rolph. (1995) 2015. *Silencing the Past: Power and the Production of History*. Boston: Beacon Press.

Tsai, Ming-Chang. 2001. "Dependency, the State and Class in the Neoliberal Transition of Taiwan." *Third World Quarterly* 22, no. 3 (June): 359–79.

Tsoi, Grace. 2015. "Taiwan Has Its Own Textbook Controversy Brewing." *Foreign Policy*, July 21. https://foreignpolicy.com/2015/07/21/taiwan-textbook -controversy-china-independence-history/.

Tsurumi, E. Patricia. 1979. "Education and Assimilation in Taiwan under Japanese Rule, 1895–1945." *Modern Asian Studies* 13, no. 4: 617–41.

Tubilewicz, Czeslaw, and Alain Guilloux. 2011. "Does Size Matter? Foreign Aid in Taiwan's Diplomatic Strategy, 2000–8." *Australian Journal of International Affairs* 65, no. 3: 322–39.

Turino, Thomas. 1999. "Signs of Imagination, Identity, and Experience: A Peircian Semiotic Theory for Music." *Ethnomusicology* 43, no. 2 (Spring–Summer): 221–55.

Urla, Jacqueline L. 2001. "'We Are All Malcolm X!': Negu Gorriak, Hip Hop, and the Basque Political Imaginary." In *Global Noise: Rap and Hip-Hop Outside the USA*, edited by Tony Mitchell, 171–93. Middletown, CT: Wesleyan University Press.

Valdés, Vanessa K. 2016. "Spaces of Sounds: The Peoples of the African Diaspora and Protest in the United States." *Sounding Out!*, December 12. https://sounds tudiesblog.com/2016/12/12/spaces-of-sounds-protest-in-the-united-states-and -the-peoples-of-the-african-diaspora/.

Von Dirke, Sabine. 2004. "Hip-Hop Made in Germany: From Old School to the Kanaksta Movement." In *German Pop Culture: How "American" Is It?*, edited by Agnes C. Mueller, 96–112. Ann Arbor: University of Michigan Press.

Walser, Robert. 1995. "Rhythm, Rhyme, and Rhetoric in the Music of Public Enemy." *Ethnomusicology* 39, no. 2 (Spring–Summer): 193–217.

Wang, Changmin 王昶閔. 2010. "Danshen yi de jingshenbing Yang Zhiliang kuai-zui you chuanghuo" 單身易得精神病 楊志良快嘴又闖禍 [Singles more likely to become mentally ill, Yaung Chih-liang blunders again]. *Ziyou dianzibao* 自由電子報 [Liberty Times Online], April 8. https://news.ltn.com.tw/news/life /paper/385987.

Wang, Chih-ming. 2017. "'The Future That Belongs to Us': Affective Politics, Neoliberalism and the Sunflower Movement." *International Journal of Cultural Studies* 20, no. 2: 177–92.

Wang, Grace. 2015. *Soundtracks of Asian America: Navigating Race through Musical Performance.* Durham: Duke University Press.

Wang, Hong-zen. 2001. "Ethnicized Social Mobility in Taiwan: Mobility Patterns among Owners of Small- and Medium-Scale Businesses." *Modern China* 27, no. 3 (July): 352–82.

Wang, Leehom 王力宏. 2004. Liner notes for *Xinzhongde riyue* 心中的日月 [Shangri-la]. Sony BMG, compact disc.

Wang, Ru-jer. 2003. "From Elitism to Mass Higher Education in Taiwan: The Problems Faced." *Higher Education* 46, no. 3 (October): 261–87.

Wang, Shunren 王順仁. 2016. "Yuanlai ba ma yong de lishi keben, shi zheyang tan 228 de a..." 原來爸媽用的歷史課本 ，是這漾談228的啊 [So this is how dad and mom's history textbooks talked about 228...]. *ETtoday*, March 1. https://forum .ettoday.net/news/655397.

Wang, Xiaoqing 王曉晴. 2008. "Cong youxuan lilun fenxi xiandai minnan yu gequ zhong yinyue yu yuyan zhi hudong" 從優選理論分析現代閩南語歌曲中音樂 與語言之互動 [Interaction between music and language in modern songs of Taiwan Southern Min: an optimality theory analysis]. Master's thesis, National Chengchi University.

Waswo, Richard. 1988. "The History That Literature Makes." *New Literary History* 19, no. 3 (Spring): 541–64.

Waterman, Christopher A. 1991. "*Jùjú* History: Toward a Theory of Sociomusical Practice." In *Ethnomusicology and Modern Music History*, edited by Stephen Blum, Philip Vilas Bohlman, and Daniel M. Neuman, 49–67. Urbana: University of Illinois Press.

Watkins, S. Craig. 1998. *Representing: Hip Hop Culture and the Production of Black Cinema.* Chicago: University of Chicago Press.

Wei, Jennifer M. 2006. "Language Choice and Ideology in Multicultural Taiwan." *Language and Linguistics* 7, no. 1: 87–107.

Weller, Robert P. 1999. *Alternate Civilities: Democracy and Culture in China and Taiwan.* New York: Routledge.

Whaley, Deborah Elizabeth. 2006. "Black Bodies/Yellow Masks: The Orientalist Aesthetic in Hip-Hop and Black Visual Culture." In *AfroAsian Encounters: Culture, History, Politics*, edited by Heike Raphael-Hernandez and Shannon Steen, 188–203. New York: New York University Press.

"What Is PTT?" n.d. https://www.ptt.cc/index.html (accessed October 17, 2021).

White, Miles. 2011. *From Jim Crow to Jay-Z: Race, Rap, and the Performance of Masculinity.* Urbana: University of Illinois Press.

Wilkins, Fanon Che. 2008. "Shaw Brothers Cinema and the Hip-Hop Imagination." In *China Forever: The Shaw Brothers and Diasporic Cinema*, edited by Poshek Fu, 224–45. Urbana: University of Illinois Press, 2008.

Williams, Jack F. 1994. "Vulnerability and Change in Chinese Agriculture." In *The Other Taiwan*, edited by Murray A. Rubinstein, 215–33. Armonk, NY: M. E. Sharpe.

Wong, Cynthia P. 2011. "A Dream Return to Tang Dynasty: Masculinity, Male Camaraderie, and Chinese Heavy Metal in the 1990s." In *Metal Rules the Globe:*

Heavy Metal Music Around the World, edited by Jeremy Wallach, Harris Berger, and Paul D. Greene, 63–85. Durham: Duke University Press.

Wong, Kee Chee 黃奇智. 2001. *Shidaiqu de liuguang suiyue (1930–1970)* 時代曲的流光歲月 (1930–1970) [The age of Shanghainese pops]. Hong Kong: Joint Publishing.

Wu, Chia-Fang, et al. 2010. "Second-Hand Smoke and Chronic Bronchitis in Taiwanese Women: A Health-Care Based Study." *BMC Public Health* 10. http://www.biomedcentral.com/1471-2458/10/44.

Wynter, Sylvia, and Katherine McKittrick. 2015. "Unparalleled Catastrophe for Our Species? Or, to Give Humanness a Different Future: Conversations." In *Sylvia Wynter: On Being Human as Praxis*, edited by Katherine McKittrick, 9–89. Durham: Duke University Press.

Xiao, Xinyan 蕭歆顏. 2019. "Ta cong honghai tai gan bian shen raoshe geshou! Chule Taiwan di yi ben raoshe jiaokeshu" 他從鴻海台幹變身饒舌歌手！ 出了台灣第一本饒舌教科書 [He went from Foxconn Taiwanese employee to rap singer! Published the first rap textbook in Taiwan]. *Yuanjian zazhi* 遠見雜誌 [Vision magazine], May 15. https://www.gvm.com.tw/article/60935.

Xu, Yue 許悅, Li, Yihui 李奕慧, and Ouyang, Yue 歐陽玥. 2020. "Zhuanfang 'Hua kang shaonü tinei fenzi' Yang Shuya" 專訪《華康少女體內份子》楊舒雅 [Interview with Yang Shuya of "Who is in my body?"]. *Taida yishi* 台大意識報 [National Taiwan University consciousness paper]. June 19. http://cpaper-blog.blogspot.com/2020/06/blog-post_30.html.

Yano, Christine R. 2003. *Tears of Longing: Nostalgia and the Nation in Japanese Popular Song.* Cambridge, MA: Harvard University Press.

Yano, Christine R. 2013. *Pink Globalization: Hello Kitty's Trek Across the Pacific.* Durham: Duke University Press.

Yasser, Mattar. 2003. "Virtual Communities and Hip-Hop Music Consumers in Singapore: Interplaying Global, Local and Subcultural Identities." *Leisure Studies* 22, no. 4 (October): 283–300.

Yeh, Shu-Ling. 2013. "The Process of Kinship in the Paternal/Fraternal House of the Austronesian-Speaking Amis of Taiwan." *Oceania* 82, no. 2: 186–204.

Yip, June. 2004. *Envisioning Taiwan: Fiction, Cinema, and the Nation in the Cultural Imaginary.* Durham: Duke University Press.

Yu, Harlem 庾澄慶. 1987. "Yinyan" 引言 [Introduction], Liner notes for *Baogao banzhang* 報告班長 [Yes, sir!]. Linfair Records, cassette tape.

Yu, Harlem 庾澄慶. 2002. *Ha Century Live Show.* Sony Music Taiwan, VCD.Yueh, Hsin-I. 2017. *Identity Politics and Popular Culture in Taiwan: A Sajiao Generation.* London: Lexington Books.

Yung, Bell. 1975. "The Role of Speech Tones in the Creative Process of Cantonese Opera." *CHINOPERL Papers*, no. 5: 157–67.

Yung, Bell. 1983. "Creative Process in Cantonese Opera I: The Role of Linguistic Tones." *Ethnomusicology* 27, no. 1 (January): 29–47.

Yung, Bell. 1989. "Linguistic Tones." In *Cantonese Opera: Performance as Creative Process*, 82–91. Cambridge: Cambridge University Press.

Yung, Bell. 1991. "The Relationship of Text and Tune in Chinese Opera." In *Music, Language, Speech and Brain*, edited by J. Sundberg, L. Nord, and R. Carlson, 408–18. London: Macmillan Press.

Zeitoun, Elizabeth, Ching-hua Yu, and Cui-xia Weng. 2003. "The Formosan Language Archive: Development of a Multimedia Tool to Salvage the Languages and Traditions of the Indigenous Tribes of Taiwan." *Oceanic Linguistics* 42, no. 1 (June): 218–32.

Zhang, Jinhua 張錦華. 1997. "Duoyuan wenhua zhuyi yu woguo guangbo zhengce: Yi Taiwan yuanzhumin yu kejiazuqun wei li" 多元文化主義與我國廣播政策—以台灣原住民與客家族群為例 [Multiculturalism and Taiwan's broadcasting policies: the cases of Indigenous peoples and Hakka], *Guangbo yu dianshi* 廣播與電視, no. 9: 1–23.

Zhou, Qinghua 周慶華. 1996. *Taiwan dangdai wenxue lilun* [Contemporary Taiwanese literary theory]. Taipei: Yangzhi wenhua shiye gufen youxian gongsi.

Zhuang, Yongming 莊永明. 1994. *Taiwan geyao zuixiangqu* 台灣歌謠追想曲 [Remembrance of Taiwanese songs]. Taipei: Qianwei.

Zhuang, Yongming 莊永明. 2009. *1930 Niandai jueban taiyu liuxing* ge 1930 年代絕版臺語流行歌 [Out-of-print Hoklo popular songs of the 1930s]. Taipei: Taibeishi zhengfu wenhua ju.

INDEX

"History of Taipei City, The" (Kou Chou Ching), 171

Ho, Wai-Chung, 204n6

Hoklo language, 147, 149, 152, 174, 192n20, 195n28; musical quality of, 150–51

Hoklo people, xviii–xxii, 6–7, 86, 145, 152, 162, 168, 189n11, 189n18; culture, 50; music of, 50; patrifocality of, 69; public humiliation, 147; social shaming and financial precarity, 147. See also *benshengren*; Native Taiwanese

Hoklo popular songs, 41–43, 48–49, 52–53, 87–88, 151; *enka*, imprint of, 44

Hoklo rap, 40–41, 46, 81, 146, 149, 152–53, 161; as resistance vernacular, 148

"Homesickness" (Soft Lipa), 88–90

homo narrans, 4

homophobia, 81, 198–99n25

homosocial relations, 66, 97

Hong, Qingqi, 117–18

Hong Kong (SAR of the PRC), 42, 83–84, 193n8, 206n1

H.O.T., 81

Hou, Dejian: "Descendants of the Dragon," 47, 194n20

Hou, Patty, 85

Houston, Texas, 200n1

Hsiao, Jam, 79–80

Hsiau, A-chin, 204–5n7

Hsu, Tsang-houei, 50–51

Hsu, Yuki 81

Huang, Feihong, 77

Huang, Jeff, 25, 37

Huang, Stanley, 25

"Hunting Song" (Kao), 170

Hurt, Mississippi John, 51, 54

"I Am Insane" (RPG), 125, 127–32, 203n33; accompaniment of, 133–34; flow style, 133; narrative function of, 134

"I Am Not Jay Chou" (Totem), 47

Ice Cube, xx

I Ching, 99

"I'll Be Around" (Spinners), 87

Illmatic (Nas), 29

Ill Mo, 24, 36, 38, 104, 105, 111–14, 119–21, 135, 141, 178, 201n11, 201n13, 207n8; academic rappers, 202n16; "1947 Overture," 96; "Not Afraid," 179

"I Love Taiwan Girls" (Hotdog and Chang), 83–87, 90, 134

"Imperial Taipei" (Blacklist Workshop), 45

"Improvisation on the Burning of a Fishnet-Drying Hut" (Uncle Qilin), 57, 59, 139

Indigenous communities, xix, xxiii, 5, 7, 67, 69, 105–6, 141, 168, 171, 187n4, 189n11, 189n18, 192–93n2, 206n28; 'Amis, 47, 86, 144, 152, 169, 188n6, 192n16, 196–97n8, 205n15; Atayal, 152, 188n6, 205n15; Bunun, 28, 169, 188n6; deer trade, 170, 206n30; Paiwan, 169, 176, 188n6; Puyuma, 169, 188n6; rappers, 151–52, 202n18, 205n15; recording industry, 42; Sediq, 188n6, 205n15; slow erasure of, 169; subsistence hunting, 170; Taivoan, xv; Tao, 150, 169, 188n6

International Community Radio Taipei (ICRT), 43

intersubjectivity, 125

Iron Bamboo, 36, 201n11

Irvine, California, 25–26

"Island's Sunrise" (Yang), 174, 177–78, 207n2

"It's Just Begun" (Jimmy Castor Bunch), 24

"I Want to Talk to You" (Nas), 133

Jackson, Michael, 22, 111

Jackson, Michael D., 4, 125

Japan, 5, 25, 37–38, 50, 70, 99; *kawaii* (cute) culture, 197n13; language,

Teacher Lin (Lin Hao-li), 14, 23–24, 30, 35, 82, 88, 100, 105–6, 108–10, 113–14, 116, 120, 127, 135, 198–99n25, 202n21, 205n15
Telus TaiwanFest, 12
Teng, Emma Jinhua, 196–97n8
Teng, Teresa, 43, 73–74
Texas, 10
Tha Dogg Pound, 82
Thiong'o, Ngũgĩ wa, 144
T-ho Brothers, 142; "Conquer," 169; "Formosa 2003," 169; Kao, Yi-sheng, presence in, 170; "KMT 1947," 168–69; "Orchid Island Protest," 169; "Taiwan Ti-ho," 170; *T-ho Brothers*, 170
T-ho Brothers (T-ho Brothers), 170
"Tiu Tiu Thinking Of" (Kou Chou Ching), 57
T.K. Rock Festival, 86
toasting, 2
Tokyo (Japan), 21, 25, 41–42
Too $hort, 86–87
Totem, 47
Tower Records, 30
Transitional Justice Commission, 167
trauma, xv, xviii–xix, 88, 144, 171
"Treasure Island New Taiwan" (song), 194n22
Treaty of Shimonoseki, 5
Tribal (streetwear label), xvi–xvii
Tribe Called Quest, A: *Midnight Marauders*, 29
Tripoets, 23–24, 30, 36, 100, 105–6, 119–20, 152–53
Trouillot, Michel-Rolph, 154–55
True Color (record label), 37, 103–4, 120
Tsai, Ing-wen, 71, 158, 167, 206n27
tsa̍p-liām-á, 53
Tseng, Kuan Jung, 31. *See also* Dwagie
T.T.M. (Top Trouble Makers), 35
Tu, Cheng-sheng, 155–56; concentric circles, 205–6n19
turntablism, 21–22, 24

2-28 Incident, 6, 13, 96, 157, 165, 170, 206n26; civilian deaths, 188–89n9
Typhoon Fanapi, 100
Typhoon Morakot, xviii, xx, xxii–xxiii, 16; casualties of, xv; government response to, xv–xvi; 921 Earthquake, linked to, xvi; outrage at disaster response, xv

Umbrella Revolution, 206n1
Uncle Qilin: "Improvisation on the Burning of a Fishnet-Drying Hut," 57, 59, 139
underground rap, 30, 35–36
"Unforgettable Pain" (Dwagie and J-Wu), xxi
United Nations (UN), 11, 189n17, 190n26
United States, 2–3, 7, 11–13, 19–21, 23, 25–27, 29, 37–38, 42, 43, 51, 82, 102, 104, 106, 110, 120, 135, 146, 153, 167, 189n16, 190n1, 193n9; Black communities, state violence inflicted on, xix; as imperialist power, 148; oriental riff, 81; rap, as indigenous to, 48
United States Taiwan Defense Command (USTDC), 193n9
Universal Music Group, 74
Universal Music Taiwan, 37
Universal Zulu Nation, 9, 23, 102, 189–90n22

Vancouver (British Columbia), 12
Vanilla Ice, 26
Vietnam, 37–38
Vietnam War, 196n7
Viva network, 22
vocality, 71; of women, 72

wai (outside), 67–69, 78, 92
wai-ness, 95
waishengren (people from outside the province), 6–7, 152, 170, 189n18. *See also* Mainlanders